Louis L'Amour's Wild West

LOUIS L'AMOUR'S WILD WEST

AN ILLUSTRATED CELEBRATION OF AMERICA'S FAVORITE WRITER OF WESTERNS

BRUCE WEXLER

Skyhorse Publishing

First published in the United States in 2013 by Skyhorse Publishing, Inc.

Skyhorse Publishing books may be purchased in bulk at special discounts for sales promotion, corporate gifts, fund-raising, or educational purposes. Special editions can also be created to specifications. For details, contact the Special Sales Department, Skyhorse Publishing, 307 West 36th Street, 11th Floor, New York, NY 10018 or info@skyhorsepublishing.com.

www.skyhorsepublishing.com

10 9 8 7 6 5 4 3 2

Library of Congress Cataloging-in-Publication Data is available on file.

ISBN: 978-1-62087-653-4

Printed in China

CONTENTS

THE LAUREATE OF THE LARIAT

A BIOGRAPHY OF LOUIS L'AMOUR

Louis L'Amour, the man destined to become an American national treasure in his own lifetime, was born on March 22, 1908, just as the final days of the American frontier were playing themselves out. Louis Dearborn LaMoore was the youngest of seven children born to Dr. Louis Charles LaMoore and Emily Dearborn LaMoore in Jamestown, North Dakota. His family were of French-Irish stock, and he claimed himself as a descendant of Francois Rene, Vicompte de Chateaubriand, writer, statesman, and well-known epicure.

Louis L'Amour in later life. Still a cowboy.

Jamestown was a substantial farming community, and Louis's father was a large animal veterinary surgeon. He had come to the territory in 1882. He later went on to sell farm machinery and manage harvesting crews. But Jamestown was also a hub on the Northern Pacific Railroad and the LaMoore brothers often encountered cowboys on their way back West, travelling to their ranches in western North Dakota, or on their way East to cattle markets with full stockcars. Dr. LaMoore became very involved in this traffic as a state Livestock Inspector, certifying the health of the cattle in transit.

But Louis's closest contact with the Old West and his frontiersman heritage was through his maternal grandfather, Abraham Truman Dearborn, who lived in a little house at the back of the LaMoore property. He had fought in both the Civil and Indian Wars, and two of his sons had worked on cattle ranches. Besides this, Abraham was also in contact with many Indians who came to visit, drinking copious cups of tea and coffee with him. This is rather ironic, in view of the fact that Louis's great grandfather met his end by being scalped by a Sioux Indian in North Dakota. Louis later credited his grandfather and his old-timer friends with bringing him up in an atmosphere rich with tales and stories of life on the American Frontier. After his grandfather died, the Indians melted away.

> *'Louis L'Amour was the kind heart of America. The walking, talking, smiling and story-telling best of what we like to think we really are.'*
>
> HARLAN ELLISON

Education was highly valued in the LaMoore household (Louis's mother had been trained as a teacher), and the entire family was intelligent and well read. Emily was well known locally as an avid reader, storyteller, and amateur poet. The infant Louis was taught to read by his beloved sister Emmy Lou, who died young in the Spanish flu epidemic of 1918. The family culture certainly rubbed off onto the embryonic storyteller. Dr. LaMoore loved horses and dogs, and taught his youngest son the ways of the animal kingdom. He was also a personal inspiration to his son, instilling him with a deep belief in hard work and self-reliance. Dr. LaMoore also taught all of his sons to box, something that both shaped Louis's early life, and turns up in several of his characters, while he was also a spiritual man that taught Sunday school. Louis's siblings also exerted their influence on the youngest member of the family. His elder brother Parker was a newspaperman, and a reportage-like edge certainly found its way into Louis's writing, as did several honorable members of the press. As for Louis's other siblings, his brother Yale managed a grocery store, where Louis and his adopted brother John often earned a little pocket money. Twin sisters Clara and Clarice had died in infancy, while elder sister Edna worked as a librarian at the Alfred Dickey Free Library, later moving away from the family home to pursue a career as a schoolteacher.

This supportive and dynamic family encouraged the young Louis to become a voracious reader and enabled him to become a largely self-educated man. He supplemented the three hundred book home library (that contained works by Whittier, Lowell, Longfellow, Poe, and the five-volume 'Collier's History of the World') with copious volumes from the Alfred Dickey Free Library, and read broadly. Louis was mostly attracted by books on history and the natural sciences, the informative Little Blue Books of E. Haldeman-Julius, but was also captivated by the fictional works of Robert Louis Stevenson, Jack London, Charles Dickens, and Edgar Rice Burroughs. These were books just like his own later works, filled with tales of adventure, hardship, and epic survival, but also infused with humanity and deep emotion. By the end of his life, L'Amour was to have a collection of more than 10,000 volumes, mostly books on history and archaeology, to which he referred constantly in the course of his writing. Louis expressed his all-consuming belief in the importance of books passionately: 'Books are the building blocks of civilization, for without the written word, a man knows nothing beyond what occurs during his own brief years and, perhaps, in a few tales his parents tell him.'

But the subliminal effect of his family background was just as fundamental to Louis, instilling deep and irrevocable feelings of family loyalty, duty, and a clear sense of right and wrong. These are not only characteristics that clung to the man himself throughout his life, but shine through in many of his heroes, who are often either deeply aware of their own roots, or yearning for a family to belong to. He also grew to epitomize the adage that education is the key to success

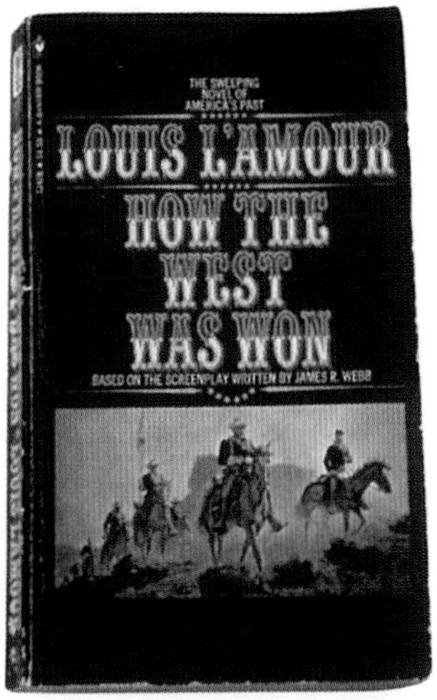

An edition of *How the West Was Won* from the early '70s, the author's own well-thumbed copy.

and a good life—though he was also living proof that this didn't necessarily need to be of the formal academic kind, having more the 'Education of a Wandering Man.'

But, as for so many American families, things got really tough for the LaMoore family in the 1920s, and they moved on to Oklahoma, looking for better prospects. It was at this point that the fifteen-year-old Louis decided to leave home, not wishing to be a burden on his parents. He also decided to revert to the original family name of L'Amour, which his father had anglicized. For a man who grew up to be a professional writer, honored by President Reagan with a Congressional Gold Medal and the Presidential Medal of Freedom, and to be awarded an honorary doctorate in literature by Jamestown College, he hadn't even made it through to the end of tenth grade. His education now became less formal, but more character forming. His stated main aim was to 'see the country,' and he set off on a twenty-year adventure that was to become a fund of stories that he would develop into his published work. As he said, 'My stories have come from incidents in my own life, anecdotes I've heard, stories repeated by miners, cowhands, Indians, and others whom I've known.'

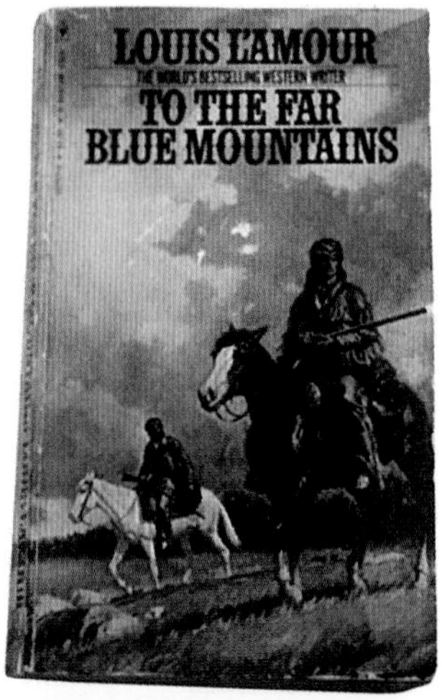

The author's copy of *To the Far Blue Mountains.* An edition from the '70s.

Essentially, during this period, he lived the life of one of his own Louis L'Amour heroes. A big powerful man, already over six-foot tall in his teens, he took any number of back breaking and dangerous jobs. Longshoreman, ranch hand, lumberjack, circus elephant handler, fruit picker, hay shocker, flume builder, railroad worker (for the Southern Pacific Railroad), and gold prospector. He hopped freight trains with men who had been riding the tracks for over half a century, packing his clothes with newspaper to keep warm. L'Amour also travelled from town to town fighting professionally as a bare-knuckle boxer. He won all but five of his fifty-nine professional bouts, forty-five of them with knockouts, claiming that he 'never lost a fight when I was eating regularly.' He won the biggest purse of his career, $1,800, in Singapore, winning by a knockout after seven rounds. He later characterized these times as 'rough years; often I was hungry, out of work and facing situations such as I have written about.' In writing his autobiography, his son Beau describes how he searched out the 'homes, hotel rooms, boarding houses, auto courts, lumber piles, and hobo jungles where Louis slept as a youth.' But as well as a wealth of experience from which he could draw, these chequered experiences were also the crucible in which the man, Louis L'Amour, was formed. The same man that illuminates his books; warm, modest, and straight.

He traveled extensively during this time: biking across India along the route followed by Rudyard Kipling's character, Kim; traveling throughout Europe; sailing around the Far East as a merchant seaman; circumnavigating the world on a freighter; sailing a dhow on the Red Sea, visiting Egypt; being shipwrecked in the West Indies; and being stranded for twenty-two desperate days in the blazing Mojave Desert. All kinds of stories emanate from this colorful period of his life, including a well-circulated tale that he used the proceeds of a Macaoan treasure trove to fund a trip to Paris and the great cultural cities of Europe.

But he also often returned home to America and traveled all over the dirt roads of the West working as a miner, lumberjack, and ranch hand, saying 'I was all over the West that way.' He described the most difficult time of this period of his life as the three months when he was on shore in San Pedro, between ships, and completely broke. He was forced to sleep in boxcars and under piles of lumber and to go without eating for days at a time. Stories from these days turned up later in his book *Yondering*—'I didn't beg or steal, just went without.... I have a penchant for stories about survival, lessons in survival. I've been a survivor for most of my life.'

These years of peripatetic freedom gave depth and complexity to both the man and his writing, together with a feeling of conflict often manifested by many L'Amour heroes when it comes time to settle down. Linus Rawlings epitomizes this in *How the West Was Won*. Even though deep love draws him into domestic life, he can't forget the call of the woods and wild places.

Louis L'Amour was a practitioner of 'The kind of storytelling that makes the wolves come out of the woods to listen.'

PEOPLE MAGAZINE

In the late 1930s and now approaching his thirties, Louis finally returned to the family home in Choctaw, Oklahoma, deciding to follow the family tradition of settling down to become a writer. Louis reckoned that he had 'wanted to write from the time I could walk' and claimed that since 1816, thirty-three members of his family had been writers of one kind or another. His family background and personal experience of wanderlust all seemed to culminate in his desire to write stories. Louis had sold his first short story 'Anything for a Pal' in 1935, and sold several other articles during his wandering years, including the 1937 story 'Gloves for a Tiger' to *Thrilling Adventures Magazine*, and 'The Admiral' to *Story*. He gradually became a regular contributor to Western 'pulp' magazines, using the name 'Jim Mayo.'

Publishing short stories in magazines was a direct response to the difficult economic conditions of the time. There was a huge demand for this kind of escapist literature in the '30s, and a huge range of magazines was offered for sale. Louis deliberately chose to submit his work to the popular 'pulps' because highbrow literary magazines didn't pay their contributors at all, and although the middle market 'slicks' (magazines printed on shiny coated paper) paid better rates, they only remitted the money to the author on publication, and often required extensive rewrites.

On the other hand, the rates paid by the 'pulps' (named for their rough, 'pulp' paper) were lower, but they paid their contributors promptly (within fourteen days of submission) and usually required the author to prepare a single draft. To a man like Louis L'Amour, living on the bread line, this prompt payment and quick turnaround was critical.

The volume of stories required by this market also meant that writers had to come up with a large number of ideas quickly, an inventive skill that Louis was to retain throughout his career. Several of L'Amour's 'pulp' short stories were later extended into complete novels. Beau L'Amour recounts how the short story 'The Gift of the Cochise' was later developed into *Hondo*, Louis L'Amour's first really successful Western novel. *Hondo* was published in 1953 and was made into a film starring John Wayne, who described the book as the 'Best western novel I have read.' By 1983, the book had sold 2,300,000 copies.

Beau also describes how his father occasionally risked his working time and money, writing stories specifically for the 'slicks,' balancing the cost of the postage against the better rates paid by these classier publications. But he generally found that writing in the tried and tested action formulae required by the pulps was far less risky.

But back in 1939, Louis's first officially published book, *Smoke from This Altar*, was something completely different, a book of poems inspired by his global tour. But despite its rather surprising format, the book can most accurately be described as 'vintage L'Amour storytelling—in verse—about nature, the land, and the people who loved and braved it.' The book was originally available only in Oklahoma bookstores. Although not a commercial success, it attracted good reviews, and he was commended for his 'love for words, industry and something to say' by the Daily Oklahoma reviewer.

But after just a couple of years, L'Amour's nascent writing career was interrupted by the outbreak of WWII.

He joined the army in 1942 and following two years stationed in the States, served overseas as (amongst other things) a Lieutenant in the 3622 Quartermaster Truck Company, posted as part of a tank destroyer unit on front line positions in France and Germany. These were also formative experiences for Louis that turned up in *Yondering*.

Like so many men of his generation, L'Amour had to start his life again on his return from active duty. In 1946, he settled in Los Angeles, now almost forty. He immediately began to submit detective stories, tales of adventure, Western yarns, and sports anecdotes to various magazines in the hope of publication. Short stories formed the backbone of his work in the years 1946-50, but this genre gradually fell victim to the upsurge in TV ownership and pressure from radio drama and paperback books, so Louis was obliged to change his métier. He first graduated to novel writing by producing four Hopalong Cassidy novels using the pseudonym Tex Burns. These books were based on the 'Hopalong' character that had originally been created by Clarence Mulford (who wrote 28 'Hopalong' books between 1907 and 1941). Louis refused to acknowledge these books for several years, because the original idea had not been his own. But this slightly embarrassing episode was crucial in pointing the way to Louis's true genre—that of the Western novel, and indeed the four 'Hopalong' titles were re-published in the early 1990s and remain available.

'My books are for the people who do the work of the world, who struggle to make ends meet, who build, the people who do!'

LOUIS L'AMOUR

This 'westerly' creative direction was reinforced by the advice of an editor L'Amour met a New York cocktail party, who advised Louis to concentrate on writing down the frontier tales with which he had enthralled him. Initially, L'Amour had his reservations about pursuing this style of writing—he knew that the critics never took Western literature seriously, but ultimately decided to 'take the ball and run with it' and make sure that his books became the best of their kind, and bestsellers. 'No one ever went into writing with a more calculated career attitude than I did' he said, recalling how he determined to keep his name in front of the public by keeping a constant stream of new novels on offer. Fortuitously, the '50s were the heyday of the paperback Western, and Louis determined to be the next great exponent of the genre.

L'Amour's first Western novel, *Westward the Tide* was published in England in 1950. But his real breakthrough came when he encountered Saul David, the editorial director of Bantam Books. David recalls how they met for the first time in the Beverly Hills Hotel, Louis bringing a selection of writing from *Hondo* to show him. David says the material 'knocked me out. I signed him to a long-term contract on the spot.' *Hondo* was published in 1953. According to David, the only problem was Louis's name, his superiors in New York thought L'Amour much too fluffy for a hard Western writer, like a 'Western written in lipstick,' and his next two books *Showdown at Yellow Butte* (1953) and *Utah Blaine* (1954) were published under the pseudonym of Jim Mayo. But this was soon abandoned in favor of 'Louis L'Amour,' and no soft editor from New York was unwise enough to mention 'lipstick' to the bare-knuckle prizefighter from North Dakota.

From the start, Louis was acutely aware that novel writing is an extremely competitive field, with authors fighting for the attention of the public. Plus, book publishing itself has to struggle for a share of the entertainment market. To this end, he made a conscious decision that he would grab the reader from the very first sentence of every book, and ensure that his stories were 'unputdownable' right to the end. A key element to this was complete transparency of style. 'If you can read something and it's so simple and clear that you think you could write it better, you can bet you can't.'

This consciousness of the audience meant that from his first book, Louis aimed to forge a deep bond with his reader, by telling his stories simply, in a staccato style bereft of long internal monologues and descriptive passages, relying instead on pace and plot to enthrall. He also deliberately refrained from offending with gratuitous sex, profanity, and violence. Just as Louis had anticipated, his style was dismissed by the literary establishment of the time. But L'Amour had effectively circumvented critical acclaim to make a solemn contract with his readership, which was by far and away the most important thing to him as a writer.

Louis L'Amour is 'the only movable piece of Mount Rushmore.'

SAUL DAVID

This mutual loyalty persists to this day. All of his 101 books remain in print, over thirty of his novels have been made into movies (between 1953 and 1971), and an estimated 225 million copies of his titles are in print. From the beginning, his creative pace never abated. From the publication of his first novel, L'Amour averaged three or four books a year, and never retired, dying during the composition of *Borden Chantry II* (the sequel to his classic earlier novel). Several L'Amour novels and other works, including *The Sackett Companion* were published posthumously, and collections of his works are compiled and released to this day.

Louis's son Beau very interestingly describes his father's day-to-day creative process. Louis would begin a novel with just a scene, or the beginning of a story, genuinely not knowing where this would take him. If the first chapter kept his interest as he knocked it out, he assumed that the reader would feel the same, and he kept going with it. If not, he would discard the idea to a slush pile, and turn his attention to another project. Fragments of stories rattled around for literally decades before he got around to writing these fully. Beau also describes how, upon Louis's death, he came upon hundreds of incomplete stories, fragments of discarded plots and themes that had never been developed. This is a real reflection of just how prolific Louis L'Amour was throughout his long career. He was at his typewriter by seven every day of his life including weekends and holidays, writing five to ten pages each day. Nor was he precious about his writing environment, claiming that he 'could sit in the middle of Sunset Boulevard and write with my typewriter on my knees; temperamental I am not.' To some extent, his ferocious work rate was necessitated by financial imperatives. It wasn't until the '70s that L'Amour was earning what Beau describes as a 'good living,' although, by this time, he had published some of his most popular and archetypal novels. These included a good part of the fantastically successful Sackett saga and the seminal works *Shalako*, *Catlow*, *Chancy*, and *The Empty Land*. It wasn't until 1973 that the family were able to move house to a more up-market Los Angeles neighborhood, by which time Louis was 65. He finally felt independent and financially secure for the first time in his life, and in the literary market place, he was outselling even popular authors like James Michener. Around this time, Louis signed a thirty-book contract with Bantam to keep himself in employment, and working to a series of deadlines.

L'Amour himself believed that the crux of his popularity was his extreme attention to authenticity. 'The West was wilder than any man can write it, but my facts, my terrain, my guns, my Indians are real. I've ridden and hunted the country. When I write about a spring, that spring is there, and the water is good to drink.' He always researched every book, wherever it was set, and the Western novels were often based in the minutiae of contemporary diaries and newspapers and the stories of 'old timers' for absolute veracity. 'His readers felt that he had walked the land the characters did' said Stuart Applebaum, Louis's Bantam editor at the time of his death. But it wasn't

'Writing is sharing. I'm working for the reader.'

LOUIS L'AMOUR

only the terrain that Louis wanted to bring to life as accurately as possible. He actively sought out old gunfighters and outlaws, eventually knowing thirty or thirty-five of them personally, and interviewed every kind of frontier character. It was his proud claim that 'I am probably the last writer who will ever have known the people who lived the frontier life.... They'd be standoffish at first, but I'd keep talking and they'd warm up and tell me wonderful stories. I heard that when Zane Grey travelled the West he always 'made his own campfire,' and kept his distance. I wasn't like that. I was one of them.' Saul David accurately described his style as though he was writing for 'people just beyond the campfire of his typewriter.'

'Louis L'Amour has become part of our cultural consciousness.'

DONALD DALE JACKSON

In his trawl for authentic Western characters, Louis met five people who had met Billy The Kid, including the woman who prepared his body for the grave. He also talked with Emmett Dalton of the Dalton Gang, Tom Pickett (whose claim to fame was that he had had his thumb shot off in the Lincoln County War), Elgagio Baca, a New Mexican lawyer who had fought a famous gunfight with over eighty of Tom Slaughter's cowboys, and Jeff Milton of the Arizona Border Patrol who had been a Texas Ranger, together with Jim Roberts the last survivor of the Tonto Basin War, who later became the Marshal of Jerome, Arizona. He also developed a huge regard for the original cowboys, believing that they were far from the illiterate men on horseback of popular folklore, but rather men who were drawn West (from Europe or the Eastern US) by a romantic ideal, only to experience a brutally hard life of grindingly hard work.

Personally, L'Amour's life revolved around the same loadstars as those of his heroes—home and family. He waited until he had a little more financial stability before marrying his wife, aspiring actress Katherine Elizabeth Adams in 1956, who had appeared in several plays and TV's *Gunsmoke* and *Death Valley Days*. Kathy was the daughter of a resort developer and silent movie star and had grown up roving the deserts and mountains of Southern California. They set up home in a relatively modest house in Los Angeles, on the proceeds from the successful Sackett series. Kathy willingly gave up her own career to travel with Louis and serve as his personal assistant, and he gave her a good deal of credit for helping him with the research by which he held such store. She said 'I feel that the most rewarding, the most adventurous, the most exciting, the most fun thing I ever did was to marry Louis.' Theirs was a lifelong partnership. Kathy acted as her husband's literary agent for the final thirty years of his life, and became President of Louis L'Amour Enterprises after his death. The couple had two children, Beau Dearborn (in 1961) and Angelique Gabrielle (in 1964).

'Our professor emeritus of how the West was won.'

MORLEY SAFER

By 1981, Louis was one of the five best-selling authors still working, in a select coterie including Harold Robbins, Barbara Cartland, Irving Wallace, and Janet Dailey, outselling any other Western writer. He is now reckoned to be the third top-selling author in the world, translated into dozens of languages. He never stopped developing his craft, believing that he was only achieving 'full command' of his powers as he reached his seventies. Even then, he was described as being 'still ruggedly handsome... with eyebrows that peak in gray-brown arrowheads. He wears Western shirts and string ties and cowboy boots and speaks in a measured, confident baritone.' Although Louis ultimately had all the trappings of success, and received massive adulation from his huge fan base, he never received critical acclaim in his lifetime. Just like Dickens and Shakespeare, his work was dismissed as lowbrow, and the fact that, like them, he wrote with a financial imperative snapping at his heels until relatively late in his writing career, seemed to result in his work not being taken seriously in a critical sense. In many ways, Dickens and L'Amour have a great deal in common. Both wrote episodically for the 'pulps' of their day and were hard working professionals, with no hint of dilettantism. Both were hounded by the need to earn a living for their families, and took this responsibility very seriously. Their own lives were very much reflected in what they wrote, and their fictional heroes often seem to achieve resolution to difficulties experienced in their own lives.

Despite the admiration of several Presidents, including Dwight D. Eisenhower, Johnson, Gerald Ford, Jimmy Carter, and Ronald Reagan, this lack of critical respect seems to have been the source of some irritation to Louis. He was determined that his work was indeed 'literature,' and said 'I don't give a damn what anyone else thinks,' he said 'I know it's literature and I know will be read 100 years from now.'

Although he lived and worked in Los Angeles until the end of his life, Louis's later financial success enabled him to buy a tract of land in the West of his imagination. He purchased Maggie Rock in 1983, together with the surrounding 1,800 acres.

Although *Louis L'Amour's Wild West* concentrates on the themes and ideas developed in his Western novels, which form the hub of his output, several of his later works inhabited different worlds altogether. Medieval Europe is the backdrop for *The Walking Drum* (1984), the supernatural thriller *Haunted Mesa* (1988) is set in the contemporary Southwest, and the *Last of the Breed* (1986) evokes the Siberian landscape of Lake Baikal. But L'Amour's attention to detail and authenticity remains a paramount consideration throughout his work. 'If my book is set in 1600, I write so that someone who lived then would recognize the road I'm describing.' This is literally true. The sixteenth-century London evoked in *To the Far Blue Mountains* (1977) is completely historically accurate—the Prospect of Whitby pub was there then, and you can take a drink in this Thames-side hostelry to this very day.

Louis died in June 1988, tragically falling victim to lung cancer, though a lifelong non-smoker. His doctors attributed the disease to harmful dust to which he had been exposed during his time as a miner. He continued to write throughout his illness, starting work on *Education of a Wandering Man* only after being diagnosed as terminally ill. The only concession he made to his failing health was to move work from his office to a desk in an upstairs bedroom, and finally into the master bedroom. He was editing *Wandering Man* only hours before he died, a few days after being told that his sales had topped the two hundred million mark, outselling John Steinbeck 5:1. His death has done nothing to stem his popularity. 'Louis L'Amour' is now an international brand, with its own credit card and merchandising empire.

The author's copy of *The Man Called Noon*, with a typical cover from the early '80s.

Louis enjoyed eighty years of a 'one-of-a-kind life lived to the fullest,' and his life 'inspired the books that will forever enable us to relive our glorious frontier heritage.' Latterly, he had also enjoyed fame, fortune, and recognition of his extraordinary creative stature. But, like one of his own heroes, L'Amour had retained a modest demeanor, shunning the Tinsel Town lifestyle in favor of the clean stillness of the mountains.

By the end of his life, Louis L'Amour the man and Louis L'Amour the author were almost completely interchangeable. His daughter, Angelique, said that, 'By reading his words, each reader has met a part of my father. Each hero has a bit of Dad's experience that makes him who he is.'

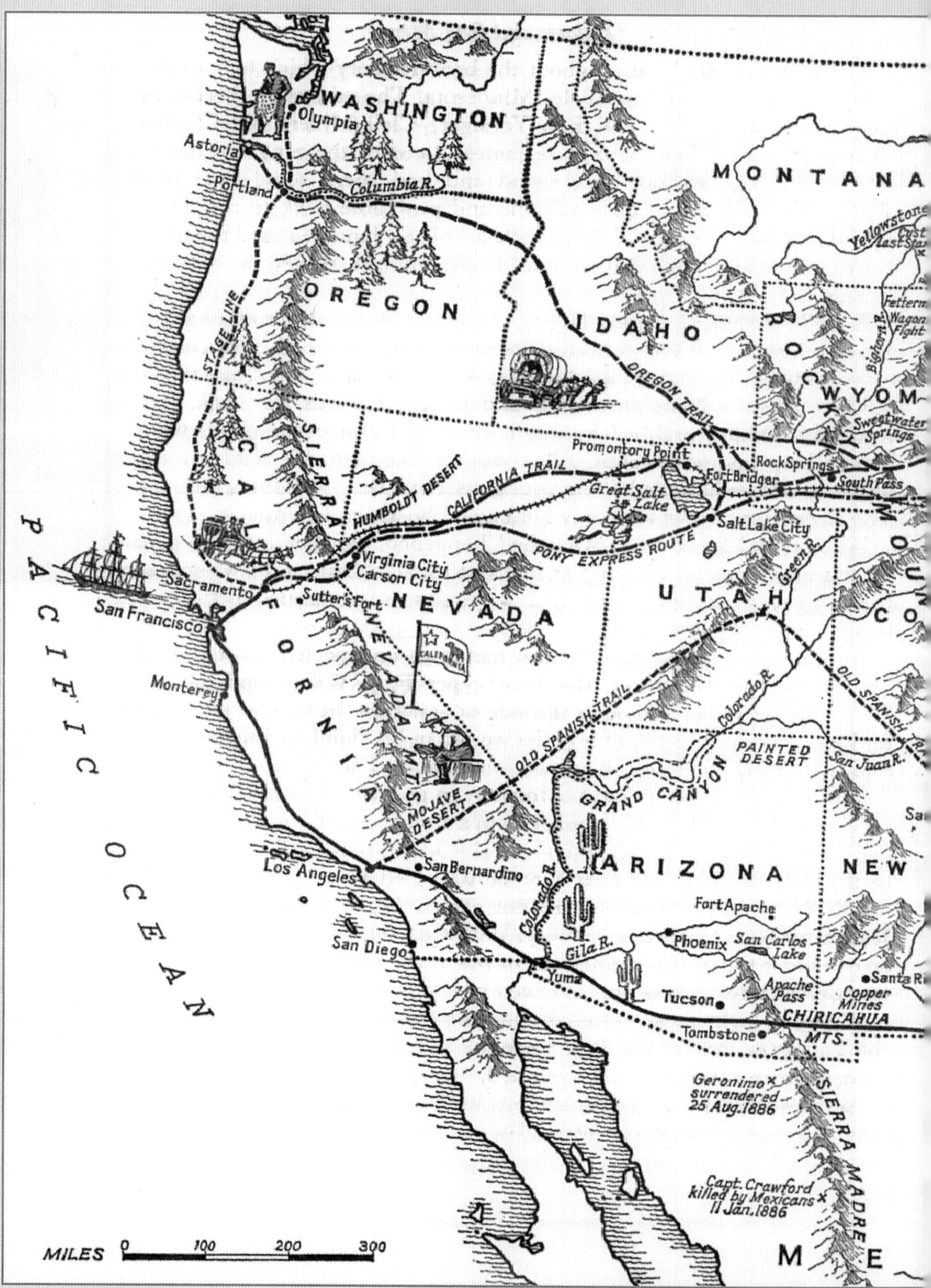
WASHINGTON
Olympia
Astoria
Portland
Columbia R.
MONTANA
Yellowstone
OREGON
STAGE LINE
IDAHO
OREGON TRAIL
ROCKY
WYOM
Fetterman Wagon Fight
Bighorn R.
Sweetwater Springs
Promontory Point
Rock Springs
Fort Bridger
South Pass
CALIFORNIA TRAIL
Great Salt Lake
Salt Lake City
HUMBOLDT DESERT
SIERRA
PONY EXPRESS ROUTE
Virginia City
Carson City
Sacramento
Sutter's Fort
NEVADA
UTAH
Green R.
San Francisco
PACIFIC OCEAN
CALIFORNIA
NEVADA MTS.
Monterey
OLD SPANISH TRAIL
Colorado R.
PAINTED DESERT
San Juan R.
GRAND CANYON
MOJAVE DESERT
Los Angeles
San Bernardino
ARIZONA
NEW
Colorado R.
Fort Apache
Phoenix
San Carlos Lake
Gila R.
San Diego
Yuma
Tucson
Apache Pass
Copper Mines
Santa Ri
CHIRICAHUA MTS.
Tombstone
Geronimo surrendered 25 Aug. 1886
SIERRA MADRE
Capt. Crawford killed by Mexicans 11 Jan. 1886
MILES 0 100 200 300
ME

ORTH DAKOTA
Fargo
Sitting Bull killed here
MINNESOTA
LAKE SUPERIOR
LAKE HURON
LAKE MICHIGAN
WISCONSIN
MICHIGAN
SOUTH DAKOTA
BAD LANDS
BLACK HILLS
Wounded Knee
Pine Ridge Agency
Northfield
Bank robbery by Jesse James
Mississippi R.
Missouri R.
IOWA
Des Moines
OREGON TRAIL AND CALIFORNIA TRAIL
NEBRASKA
UNION PACIFIC RAILWAY
Council Bluffs
Omaha
Platte R.
Ogalla
Julesburg
PONY EXPRESS ROUTE
St. Joseph
ILLINOIS
INDIANA
OHIO
Kansas City
Westport
St. Louis
Ohio R.
Abilene
KANSAS PACIFIC RAILWAY
Topeka
MISSOURI
KENTUCKY
KANSAS
SANTA FE TRAIL
Newton
Wichita
OZARKS
Arkansas R.
Dodge City
Medicine Lodge Creek
Cimarron R.
CHISHOLM CATTLE TRAIL
INDIAN TERRITORY
WESTERN CATTLE TRAIL
Arkansas R.
TENNESSEE
Adobe Walls
Canadian R.
OKLAHOMA
Fort Smith
ARKANSAS
Mississippi R.
Sumner
Red R.
MISSISSIPPI
ALABAMA
CATTLE TRAIL
Dallas
Fort Worth
TEXAS
OVERLAND MAIL
Fort Concho
Waco
Brazos R.
Colorado R.
LOUISIANA
Horsehead Crossing
Pecos R.
Austin
Langtry
The Alamo
San Antonio
Galveston
Nueces R.
Corpus Christi
GULF OF MEXICO
Laredo
CO

THE WAY WEST

The American West 'is a dream. It is what people who have come here from the beginning of time have dreamed...it is a landscape that has to be seen to be believed, and may have to be believed to be seen.'

N. SCOTT MOMADAY, KIOWA POET

Perhaps the single most important theme that drives Louis L'Amour's Western novels is the way west itself.

The first settlers from the Old World voyaged west across the ocean to the shores of America. They were almost always in search of a free life in the New World, and were often hounded by injustice and undeserved troubles. There is a clear sense in L'Amour's work that their first landfall in the East also became corrupted, necessitating a move further west across the face of America itself. A journey once more driven by the need for freedom, land, and opportunity; intertwined with a certain indefinable longing for a pure and simple life.

Written over seventeen novels and ten generations, the Sackett family saga is a fantastic evocation of both of these strands of westward emigration. In *To The Far Blue Mountains*, Barney Sackett follows the example of the Pilgrim Fathers by risking everything to reach 'Raleigh's Land,' to escape a corrupt and oppressive regime. Barney has been imprisoned, and threatened with torture to force a confession to crimes he hasn't committed. He is accused of the murder of the influential but villainous Genester (although this was actually the result of an honorable duel) and is also (wrongly) suspected of having stolen the lost royal treasure of the Wash. He is forced to realize that in a debased society, even a law-abiding man can't always look to the law of the land for protection. His travelling companion, Black Tom Watkins, faces the gallows for smuggling. This was a virtually universal 'crime' practiced by many wealthy people, churchmen and lawyers, but for which only the poor are punished. The upshot of this is, that for Tom and Barney, the 'forest' of the untamed new territory 'seems safer than the London streets' where

The hanging of a pirate at Wapping Dock in London. Black Tom Watkins flees England to avoid this fate.

The pure grandeur and beauty of America awaiting those brave enough to make the ocean crossing.

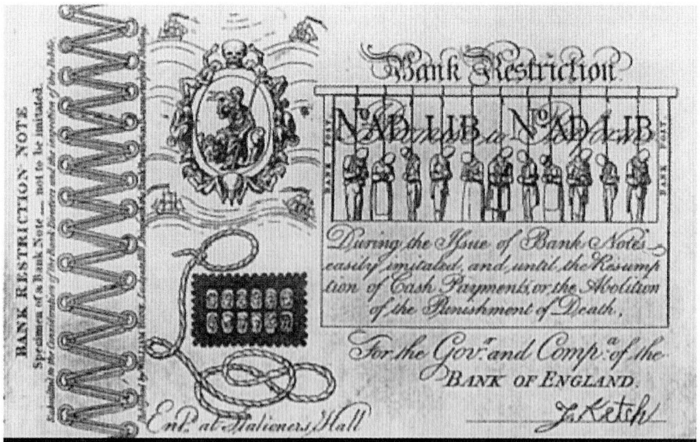

A fake bank note satirizing Britain's readiness to hang felons for even the smallest of crimes.

injustice and persecution lurk in the shadows.

Sackett's followers have less pressing, but equally heart felt reasons for their journeys. As John Quill says, the wide open spaces of America promise 'So much land, and so few people, when in our country people long for the land and have none, for it all belongs to the great lords. Even the wild game is theirs.' The practice of 'enclosing' land had indeed led to the dispossession of the English peasantry. It had begun in the Middle Ages, and led to the virtual enslavement of the vast majority of the population. Men were obliged to labour unpaid for the local landowners, in the very fields that had once been theirs. Poaching even wild animals for the pot was a capital crime, punishable by hanging.

Even by the late sixteenth century, when Barney decides to make his break for freedom, there were only very limited opportunities for personal improvement. People's destinies were almost entirely circumscribed by their birth and social position. Little wonder then that a resourceful, intelligent, and courageous man like Sackett yearns for the chance to lead a 'wild, free life,' unfettered by social convention.

Typically for a Louis L'Amour hero, the only element of 'civilization' that Barney considers important enough to carry to America is a selection of books, so that he will have 'a chance to listen to the words of other men who had lived their lives, to share with them trials and troubles.' These include the bible and his father's favorite, Plutarch. L'Amour strongly implies that men like Sackett who had 'some impulse…some selective device that chose (them)…to venture' effectively defined the character of the New World itself. For only men of his stamp, who were both intellectually and practically capable ('my hands are cunning with tools'), would be able to survive without the trappings of society. As Black Tom Watkins says, the 'entry into a new land is a hard, hard thing.' Strength of character is also a recurring theme in L'Amour's Western novels. Although the action of *Hanging Woman Creek* takes place a couple of centuries later, Irishman Philo Farley restates L'Amour's belief in personal merit over background and social status, 'Over there (in England), education and position seem the most important things, but out here…well, it's the way it should be everywhere—character comes first…stamina, courage, and a strong sense of justice.' Sadly, for Philo, the immigrant experience leads only to death, although his sister marries into the Western way of life.

Prospective settlers first had to brave the hardship of the voyage itself. Barney Sackett tries to keep this in perspective by recounting even more epic voyages

The rigors of the sea passage meant that new immigrants were ready to face almost anything.

undertaken in earlier times: 'men had sailed farther, long before. The Malays had sailed from the islands south of the Equator, from Java and Sumatra to Madagascar. And Cheng Ho, the eunuch from the court of Imperial China, had sailed five times to Africa before Columbus or Vasco Da Gama.' He is also an explorer, following in their footsteps. Like them, he steps out of the known world into only vaguely charted territory. The belief that the world was flat had only lately been abandoned, although Barney insists that this idea was not one that had had much credit

A group of immigrants photographed while waiting to board ship at Plymouth harbor, England. The first phase of their journey West.

with 'seafaring' men, 'It was a tale told to landsmen, or to merchants who might be inclined to compete for markets.'

But Barney seems unwilling to credit himself with an entirely conscious impetus to make for the new land. As he says, and this very much sounds like the conviction of L'Amour himself, 'Since the beginning of time men have moved across the face of the world, and we like to believe this is a result of our individual will, our choice, and it may be so, but might it not be that we are moved by tides buried in our natures? Tides we cannot resist?' It sounds entirely cogent that a man's subliminal nature may well be

the driving force that sets out to shape the new continent. This is also typical of the modesty of the classic L'Amour hero. Generally, only fools and criminals are arrogant and over-confident in his books.

But despite his flight from the stifling restraint of the Old World, Barney does not wish to break with his own past, or that of his family. For although he believes 'pride of title or family is an empty thing,' he retains a value in family tradition, 'for a child without tradition is a child crippled before the world.' This so truly reflects America's immigrant tradition, where incoming families have been forced to abandon everything but their customs and pride in their family origin.

Even having made it to the New World, the Sackett

contingent continue their way west, overtaking those who have already settled on the Eastern seaboard. He still doesn't feel safe from his past. Though he finally makes it to the Blue Mountains, this is only to die by Indian attack. But nevertheless, Barney has left a signpost for his descendants to follow.

Like so many other Americans, the Sackett clan continue their westward journey over the centuries. L'Amour characterizes the pull of the 'fair, wild land' as being that of freedom and self-respect, away from corruption and injustice. The same hunger for a clean life, and self-determination (particularly symbolized by land ownership) impelled so many families, of all kinds of different backgrounds, to keep trekking. 'There's a new land yonder where there are no lords or gamekeepers, and the air had the flavor of freedom in it.'

In the very first Sackett novel published, *The Daybreakers*, brothers Tyrell and Orrin continue the family trek westward after the Civil War, escaping from the poverty and blood feuds of the Tennessee Mountains. Ultimately, they bring law and order to a swathe of the new territory.

THESE PAGES: The immigrants to the 'fair, wild land' met with Native Americans from various tribes, who had been on the continent for thousands of years. Barney Sackett understands that the Indians can teach the new arrivals many things about the land.

A map of the Fur Country of the West, with an inset picture of Jim Bridger. Trappers helped to map the new territory.

Meriwether Lewis and William Clark were charged with discovering the Northwest Passage, but became the first Americans to cross the Rockies.

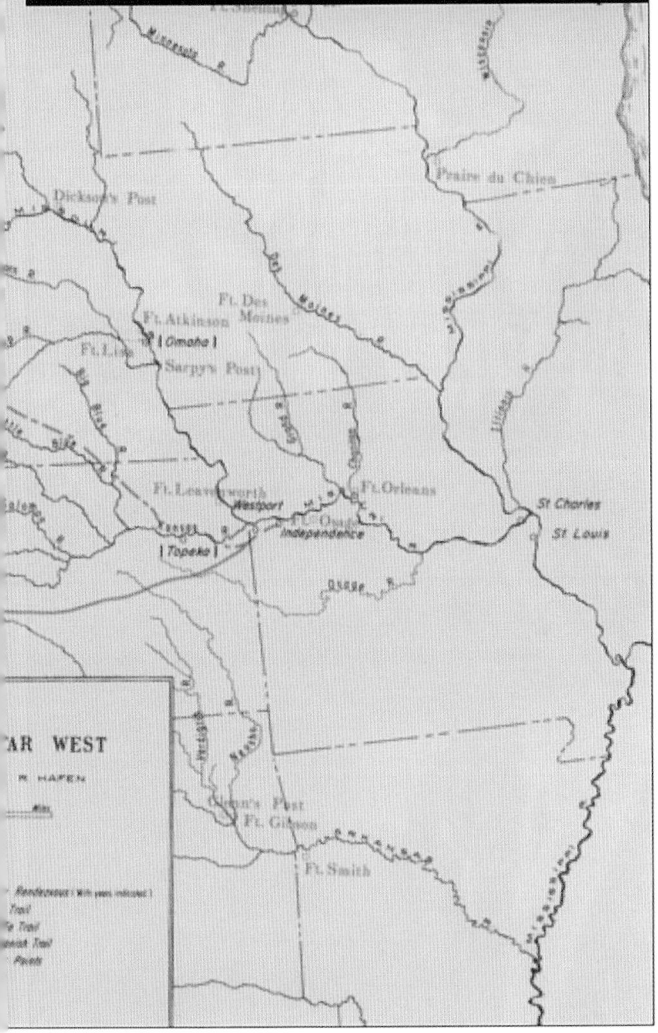

Kit Carson, another famous mountain man who helped open up the trails to the West.

The same hunger for freedom, land and opportunity that inspired the Sacketts infuses L'Amour's great tour de force *How the West Was Won*. By the nineteenth century, the East is almost as densely settled as Europe itself, and the rules of Society are almost as fixed and relentless. It's certainly no place for the rugged individualists that populate Louis L'Amour's imagination. But the historical tide of events turns in their favor.

L'Amour describes how the whole psychology of a

nation was reinvigorated by President Thomas Jefferson's Louisiana Purchase of 1803: 800,000 square miles of territory between the Mississippi and the Rockies bought for $15 million from Napoleon. Jefferson was fascinated by everything from dinosaurs to fine wine, but had been spellbound by tales of the West from his boyhood, and had amassed the largest collection of books about the region on earth. He now persuaded Congress to authorize $2,500, to finance the westward expedition of adventurers Meriwether Lewis (Jefferson's personal secretary, a skilled hunter and amateur scientist) and William Clark (Jefferson's old army commander and talented woodsman) across this newly acquired land. Jefferson told them that the chief object of their mission was to find the (non-existent) Northwest Passage, but they ended up being the first Americans to cross the Rockies, finding the overland way to the West. Their courage blazed a trail for

LEFT & ABOVE: **A well-equipped frontiersman stands proud in the unspoiled and virgin territory.**

Many Indian tribes were hugely helpful to the early western pioneers. Amongst other things, they taught them how to use canoes to get around the new land. Others were less well disposed to the white insurgents.

A wagon trail rolls westwards, but not all of the would-be settlers made it, and the trail was littered with sad memorials.

other men such as Kit Carson, Jim Bridger, Bill Williams, Joe Walker…and L'Amour's own heroes, of course.

These rugged, westward moving frontiersmen and women were cut from the very same cloth as L'Amour's own antecedents. He strongly maintained that 'there was no period in the world's history that is so fascinating as the era in which the American West was opening up.'

In *How The West Was Won*, there is a strong feeling that an entire continent is responding to some magnetic westward impulse. Hawkins, the Ohio River pirate, graphically describes the trek West as a 'colossal binge, a gigantic migration…. The world has never seen the like, folks from all the lands of creation, streamin' west, flowin' like a great tide, some of them walkin', some drivin' wagons, and some a-horseback…to populate a new land.' But there is an undercurrent of fear, for 'no new land is gained without blood and suffering…how many would die before the West was won?' The Prescott family, around whom the different sections of the book revolve, board a boat in Albany, setting off on their journey West. They are looking for more, fertile land to farm, taking everything they own on the immensely precarious trip. Their experience must reflect that of so many that started out on this perilous trek. They are afraid, but courageous, and excited by their new prospects.

But like so many other families that set off in the spirit of hopefulness, the Prescotts don't all make it West at this time, being obliged to settle where they are overtaken by hardship. In fact, it takes a couple of generations for the family to arrive in the Western lands.

For those that do make it West, L'Amour makes it clear that the same qualities and resilience demonstrated by the original settlers are needed to tame the new 'strange, lonely land.' The same mental readjustments are also required. Tracker and fur trader Linus Rawlings describes the negative reaction of many of the new settlers to the

A romantic view of wagons in a rather well manicured wilderness.

Western landscape, 'folks back east spent two hundred years learning how to pioneer in timber country, and when they first see the plains they call it a desert. It ain't nothing of the kind, just a different way of living, that's all.'

But despite the hardships, to many frontiers people, 'West was the magic word. It was the "Open Sesame" to fantastic futures.' Inevitably, not only the pure in heart were lured by the possibility of making their fortunes. Gamblers, cardsharps, land-grabbers, incorrigible villains, and women of uncertain virtue also followed the trail West. But just like the ocean voyages of the first white Americans, journeying to the West remained a metaphor for freedom and personal fulfilment. For others, it remained a flight from persecution. The Mormons, for example, to whom L'Amour refers on several occasions, make their pilgrimage to Utah in order to establish a settlement where they could practice their religious beliefs free from the discrimination they had met with in the East. The Mormon trek became legendary because so many of their number died en route, succumbing to the terrible conditions of their trek across the Rockies.

What the first people arriving in the West ultimately found was somewhat reminiscent of the East in the sixteenth century. Fluid communities sprang up and died down just as quickly, when overtaken by misfortune: disease, Indian attack, or natural disaster.

But the sheer obduracy of the still-virgin territory and the hardness of the life it offered bred a plethora of

The conditions of the trek varied from bitter cold to extreme heat, and the terrain itself was invariably hostile.

Snakes were just one of the many hazards faced by those trekking West.

fascinating characters for L'Amour to mine in his fiction. As he said 'You cannot invent people like the real-life Molly Brown or the silver-mining baron Spencer Penrose who built his house in Virginia City, Nevada, with solid silver doorknobs throughout. They are all bigger than life and they did fantastic things…(and) these old characters were tough. If you didn't shoot them they lived forever.' Their unforgettable alter egos flit through L'Amour's work, hundreds of different characters telling their fascinating stories and bringing an entire world back to life.

In their company, we can still make the journey West, in the footsteps of our guide and storyteller, Louis L'Amour.

RIGHT: This wagon is equipped with a barrel of precious water.

LEFT: A marker stone commemorates the Oregon Trail, one of the famous routes to the West.

The iconic wagon looks frail in the vast Western landscape.

BOWIE KNIFE

RIGHT: The Classic Bowie blade profile with the 'clip' point.

BELOW: Handmade Bowie knife with an 8 inch clip point blade and 'coffin-shaped' carved leather hilt with a brass pommel.

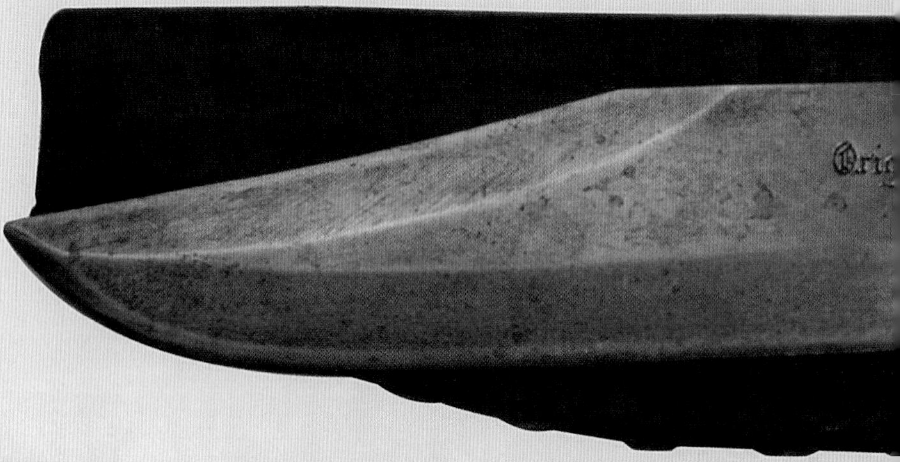

When times were tough and a man's gun and horse had been stolen or lost he always had his trusty Bowie knife to fall back on. Our introduction to Utah Blaine, after he has rescued Joe Neal from a lynch-mob, is as follows: Joe Neal says 'Where's your horse?'

Blaine replies, 'Don't have one.' The young man's possessions appeared to be nothing but the blankets and canteen. The flannel shirt he wore was ragged and sunfaded, the jeans did not fit him, and he had no hat. His only weapon was a Bowie knife with a bone handle.'

It is named for James Bowie, whose twin claims to fame were his death at the Alamo in 1836, and the imposing hunting and fighting knife that he carried.

Bowie was born in Kentucky in 1796, later moving to Louisiana where he engaged in the slave trade and land ventures. His reputation for fighting skills stemmed from a legendary brawl in 1827 known as the 'Sandbar Fight' in which he finished off his opponent with one thrust of 'a large butcher knife.' The fame of Bowie and his knife spread and soon men all over the expanding US territories were arming themselves in a similar manner.

Bowie has been the subject of many screen portrayals including being played by Richard Widmark in *The Alamo* [1960] and Scott Forbes in the TV series *The*

Adventures of Jim Bowie [1956-58]. The knife, too, was awarded star status when the Warner Bros. props department created their own rather flashy version with a gold plated back edge to the blade and Jim Bowie's name on a brass plate on the handle, which couldn't have made for a comfortable grip in a tight corner. This version was used in a number of movies including *The Alamo*, Disney's *Davy Crockett*, and the TV series.

Sadly, reality doesn't always live up to the legend, and when Jim Bowie died at the Alamo on the cold dawn of March 6th, 1836, he was suffering from typhoid fever and probably had little fight left in him as he raised himself from his sickbed to face the onrushing Mexican forces.

The legend has him dispatching a dozen enemy soldiers with his trusty blade.

Our example is a fairly workaday knife with a plain sewn leather scabbard such as L'Amour's characters would have carried. It has a 9 1/2 inch clip-point blade marked with an anvil and owners initials on the left side of the ricasso—the flat unbeveled part of the blade between the tang and the edged portion of the blade. It has a small extravagance—a silver cross guard and pommel. Silver decoration was popular in the West.

MOUNTAIN MEN

'Every man in his life deserved one good dog and one good woman'

JIM BRIDGER

Louis L'Amour mentions several of the most famous of the mountain men in his work, and models several characters after them.

The original Western mountain men were members of the Ashley-Henry expedition of 1822. This was organized by the Rocky Mountain Fur Company in an attempt to break the fur-trading monopoly of the Hudson Bay Company. They met Cheyenne and Crow on their way West, and wisely learned all they could from them about trapping and surviving in the inhospitable climate. Perhaps the most famous of their number was twenty-three-year-old Jedediah Strong Smith, a Methodist

Kit Carson and his fellow trappers gather around a roaring camp fire, to 'yarn' away the evening.

Mountain men curing beaver pelts.

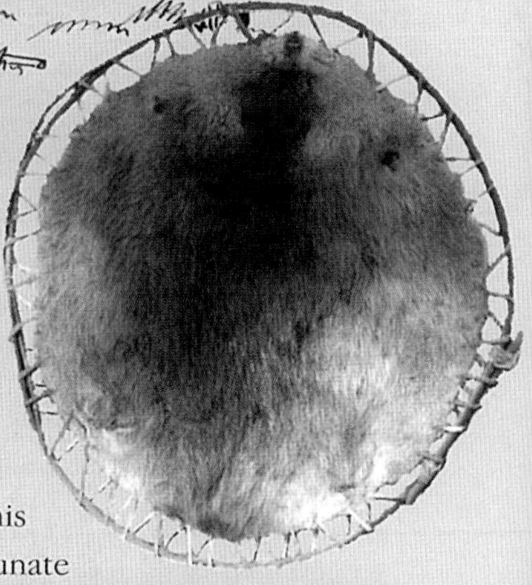

Jim Beckwourth was another of the most notable mountain men. He was half African American.

storekeeper's son from New York State. His companions were obliged to sew his ear back on after an encounter with an enraged grizzly. He wore his hair long after this unfortunate incident.

Initially, the company was hugely successful, and the fur trade dominated the Rockies. The Rocky Mountain Fur Company arranged a unique method of collecting furs, where trappers met annually at pre-arranged 'Rendezvous' sites. The first was held in 1825 at Burnt Fork on the Green River, Wyoming. The backbone of the industry was beaver pelts, as the felt hat industry demanded a huge number of these every year. The most famous of the mountain men also convened at these meetings, to trade furs and collect winter supplies, including Jim Bridger

THE ESSENTIALS OF A MOUNTAIN MAN'S LIFE.

A Buffalo hide covered water canteens with wooden stoppers
B Possibles bag in buffalo hide
C Handmade butcher knife, possibly Green River brand
D Felt hat with buffalo fur band
E Pipe
F Assortment of handmade horn tools
G Horn spoon
H Powder horn
I Buffalo fur gauntlets

(who Linus Rawlings had known) and Kit Carson. Like Louis L'Amour's characters Jethro Stuart and Osborne Russell, Carson had originally worked for the company, but left to become a free trapper, working for himself.

The typical mountain man that appeared at the Rendezvous often originated from the farms of the South or Midwest, and had become a trapper to share in this hugely profitable trade. Most wore felt hats, buckskin jackets, leggings, and moccasins, and carried a Green River Butcher Knife and Plains Rifle or Flintlock. Almost half of

them married Indian women, who helped them prepare the skins. Mountain men were also tremendously active in blazing trails across the West, and were responsible for discovering the South Pass, known as the 'Great Gap of the Rocky Mountains.'

But the life of a mountain man was hard and dangerous, and hugely destructive to the wildlife of the West. They fell victim to grizzly attack, froze to death retrieving their traps from icy streams, were killed by Blackfeet, and succumbed to starvation. Survival could be

Another convivial evening scene. Almost every man has a pipe to hand.

almost worse, taking into account the appalling experiences that both Hugh Glass and John Coulter underwent after being attacked by the Blackfeet. All of this made them very tough indeed. As Rowdy Jim Lowe says of mountain man Jethro Stuart, 'Talk soft around those old mountain men. You might kill one, but you'll have lead in you first. They die mighty hard—mighty hard indeed!'

By the time hat makers started to make silk top

A typical mountain man costume of buckskin shirt and leggings.

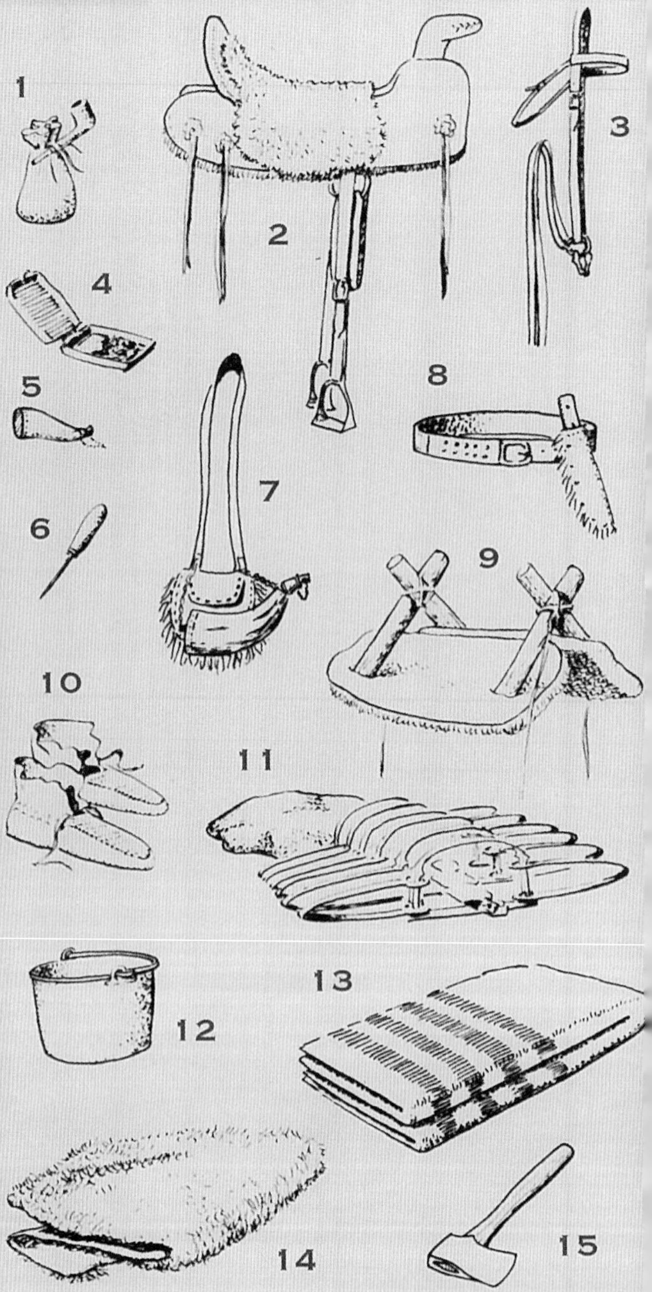

EQUIPMENT:

1 Tobacco sack and pipe
2 Riding saddle.
3 Bear trap
4 Flints in striker box
5 Powder horn
6 Awl
7 Possibles bag
8 Butcher knife in sheath on belt
9 Pack saddle
10 Moccasins
11 Beaver traps
12 Iron kettle
13 Indian blanket
14 Buffalo hide blanket
15 Tomahawk

hats that didn't require pelts, the fur-bearing animals of the frontier had been all but exterminated. The Rocky Mountain Fur Company collapsed in 1834, and most of the mountain men were obliged to take other forms of employment. By 1840, the year of the final Rendezvous, the fur trade was in terminal decline. Jim Bridger was obliged to hunt buffalo, and guide wagon trains through the vast territory that he and his ilk had helped to chart.

The very men who had found glory in the big sky of the West, and its shining mountains had denuded it of its wildlife, and went back to the life of ordinary white men once they had taken their spoils.

Mountain men needed speedy horses to outrun attacking Indians.

Indian attack was one of the most serious hazards that beset the lives of the mountain men.

REMINGTON ROLLING BLOCK RIFLE

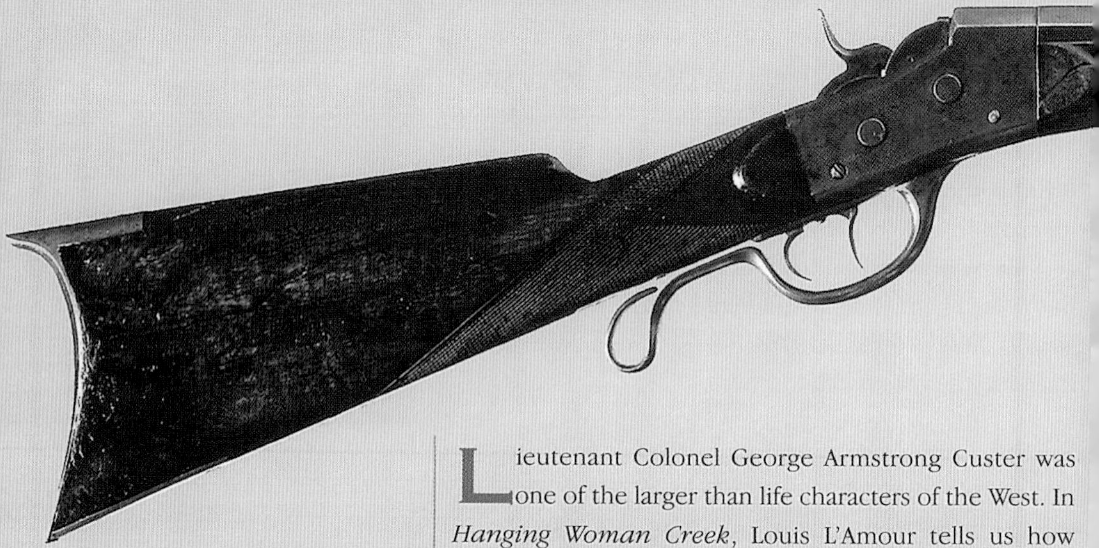

RIGHT: The distinctive design of the Remington rifle clearly distinguishes it from other western arms.

BELOW: A fine piece of gunsmithing from both Remington and Carlos Gove. Note the fancy touches like the silver fore end cap. Checkered stock and double set trigger show that this was a real shooter's gun.

Lieutenant Colonel George Armstrong Custer was one of the larger than life characters of the West. In *Hanging Woman Creek*, Louis L'Amour tells us how Custer's troops cleaned up towns like Fargo-in-the Timber, 'Destroying local villains like Jack O 'Neil.'

Custer's time on the frontier with the US Cavalry was not just spent quelling Indians. He also took time off to go hunting in the Yellowstone National Park, where he used his favorite weapon, a Remington Rolling Block Sporting rifle. In a letter written to the Remington

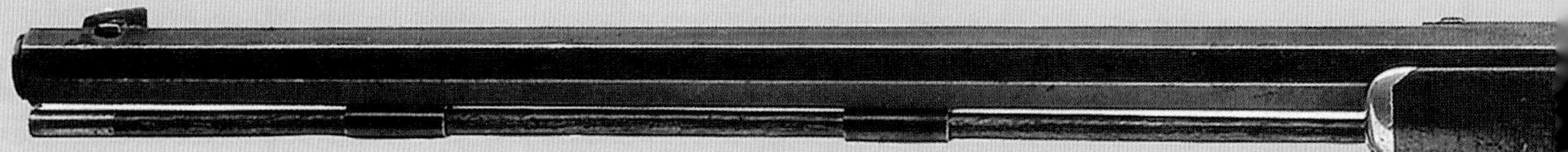

SPECIFICATIONS

CALIBER: 0.40–.70	ACTION: Single shot/breech loading
LENGTH OF BARREL: 30 inches	YEAR OF MANUFACTURE: 1874
BARREL SHAPE: Octagonal	MANUFACTURER:
FINISH: Blue casehardened	Remington/C. Gove & Co., Denver Armory, 340
STOCK: Walnut	Blake Street, Denver, Colorado

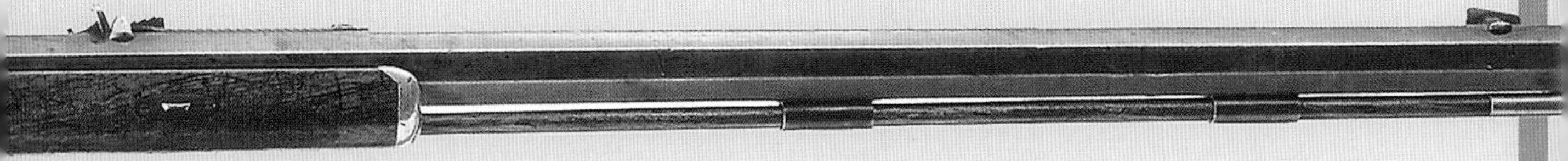

Company on October 5th, 1873 from his base at Fort Abraham Lincoln, Custer claimed that he killed far more game than all the other professional shots on the trip.

It is easy to think of rifles like the Winchester 1873 as the standard equipment for western shots but the Rolling Block rifle also made its mark. In the years following the Civil War, Remington was preoccupied with chasing lucrative military contracts, but many rifles were also sold to sportsmen and hunters. They were generally used for larger game, where a powerful, large caliber weapon was required. 'The Remington system' as it was correctly known, was developed by Joseph Rider as an improvement to his split breech concept, which was used on War models. The gun was a single-shot breech-loader that would take a heavy charge center-fire cartridge, based on the design of army sharpshooter Colonel Hiram Berdan. Ultimately, however, the US Army decided in favor of rifles with the Allin 'trap door' action. This was a cheaper option as Allin was a government employee and the government could avoid paying a royalty to use the system.

But the US Navy did order significant quantities of Rolling Block rifles and carbines, and this contributed greatly to Remington's success. The Company must have been particularly pleased when a famed western hero and serving soldier like Custer praised their products.

Our featured gun has been converted to under-lever action by Carlos Gove, the pioneer gunmaker of Denver, and has double set triggers. Carlos Gove rebuilt guns using this technique from 1873–77. The gun was handed down through a western family for several generations, having been given to Charlie Robbie, the original owner, for killing an Indian at the Sand Creek Massacre.

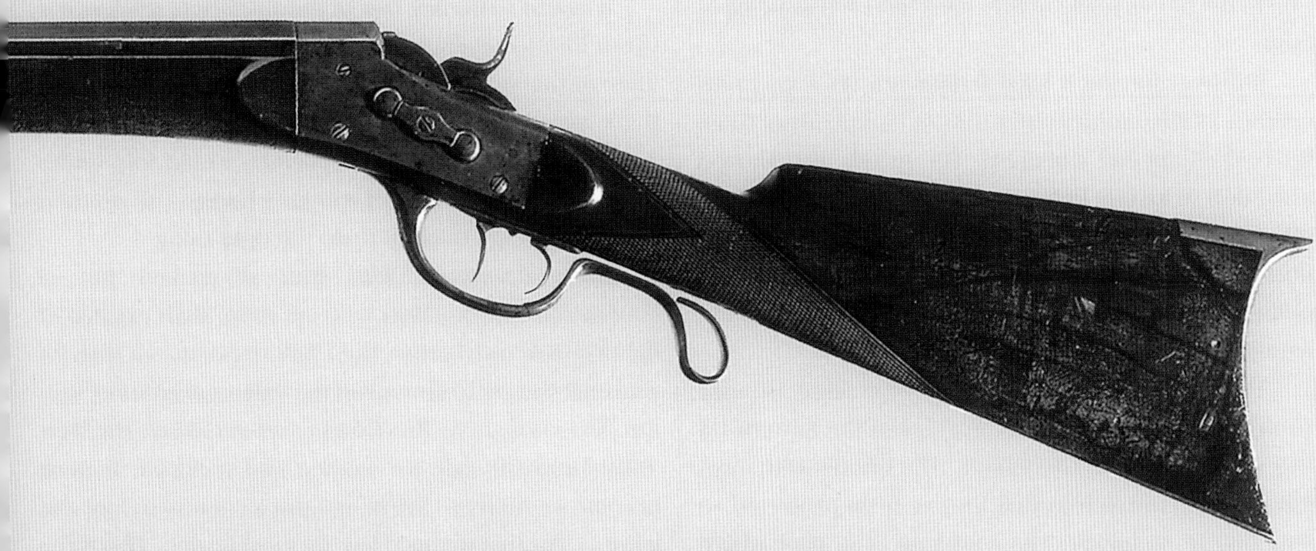

LAW AND ORDER IN THE WEST

OUTLAWS AND LAWMEN

Throughout his work, Louis L'Amour makes it crystal clear that he believes the rule of law is the crux of civilization, without which society just can't function. The establishment of law and order is a fundamental theme that appears time and time again in Western literature, history, and film. Good men try to uphold the law, to protect the good and drive out the bad. As L'Amour says, 'here in these western lands men were fighting the age-old struggle for freedom and for civilization'. It's interesting that L'Amour often twins these two abstracts, which others (including many of his characters) see as being at odds.

But in enforcing a legal framework on a raw, new country, he also demonstrates that there is plenty of room for backsliding and ambiguity. The novels also show a good deal of friction between the 'law,' and 'right,' which often don't amount to the same thing. L'Amour tellingly portrays how the quality of the law often depends on the caliber of the law enforcer, and how even good law in the wrong hands can make for bad justice.

The young civilization of the West is often strongly contrasted to that of the Old World, and the Eastern US that the settlers have left behind. 'The trouble with most folks coming out here is that they've been protected so long they're no longer even conscious of it. Back where they come from there are rules and laws, curbstones and sidewalks, and policemen to handle violence. The result is that violence is no longer real for them.' This naiveté leaves incomers pathetically vulnerable. As Barney Pike says of Ann Farley (in *Hanging Woman Creek*), she 'wasn't long from England, and over there they have respect for the law, and let the law take its course, as should be done everywhere.' A lawless vacuum, with nothing to check the power of unscrupulous and self-interested men, ends up costing her brother's life.

It's clear to Barney, that in the absence of the law, it is up to him to revenge Philo's murder and protect Ann: 'here in the West there sometimes wasn't much law, and there were some things the law and other folks preferred a man settle for himself.' Lesser men would fold under these dire pressures, but L'Amour's heroes call on their strength and self-reliance to do the right thing.

Louis L'Amour's Wild West is packed full of courageous individualists who are more than capable of fighting their own battles. But L'Amour points out that, for a normal society to emerge in the 'beautiful country,' this just isn't enough. As Ben Cowan says in *Catlow,* the West 'must be made safe for women and children. It must become a country to live in, not just a country to loot and leave.... For that we need law, we need justice.' Ben is the

ABOVE: An early advertisement for Colt, one of the archetypal guns of the West.

LEFT: A sheriff's star. Wearing one could seriously shorten your life expectancy.

voice of law in the book, which can be read as a brilliant allegory of the struggle between the law abiding, and the lawbreakers. But it also points out that neither side has the monopoly on either good or evil. Ben believes the 'law doesn't work against a man, it works for him. Without it, every house would have to be a fortress...'

Matt Coburn, the justice man at the center of *The Empty Land* develops this theme further, pointing out that there is also a strong element of personal responsibility in upholding the law. 'Law and order is a job for all of us. If we shirk it long enough we will have anarchy, and all we've built will be destroyed.... This is the old war, the war of civilization against the barbarian; of peacefulness, order, and hard work against the heedless, the cruel, the destructive.' Coburn is clearly one of L'Amour's most respected lawmen, and his dedication to *The Empty Land* is telling, 'To My Father...Who knew what it meant to wear the badge.' But for Matt, it comes at a bitter price. The fact that he has killed four men loses him his love, Laurie. He has been forced to descend to the same level of violence as the criminal element in order to clean up the town, and has become tainted in her eyes. He has also had to take a huge risk with his own life, to

Holster and belt set indentified as from the T Anchor ranch. The holster is a Lawrence 508/150Lmodel. The single belt is a combination cartridge and money belt.

The Town Marshal's office also often served as the local jail. It showed that there was a local commitment to the forces of law and order.

protect cowards, as well as the helpless. As Fife says, 'He's been doin' the job you hired him for.... The job none of us could do, so that men like Gage (the gutless store keeper) can stay after all and 'feel safer now'.'

L'Amour is also quick to point out that not everyone with the frontier mentality welcomes the introduction of a judicial society. The West's very lawlessness was attractive to some. As Charlie Gant says to Zeb Rawlings, 'I don't like what you and your kind have done to this country.... Used to be a man felt free around here, now a man can hardly breathe.' But L'Amour's portrayal of Gant as greedy and narrow-minded makes it pretty clear that his own sympathies lie with Zeb, who replies, 'I haven't noticed any honest men having trouble.' L'Amour also shows how the vacuum created by the lack of a justice system leads to strong individuals laying down a twisted 'law' of their own. The unscrupulous cattle baron, Ben Curry, lives likes a 'feudal lord and has no respect for any law he did not make himself.'

Zeb Rawlings also voices one of the other pillars of

Just as Wild Bill Hickok did in Abilene, and Rocky White did in Red Creek, this marshal has attempted to ban the carrying of guns within the town limits.

L'Amour's views on law enforcement, 'It will be necessary for the men of peace to have guns, as long as men of violence do. We can't put all the force in the hands of evil.' In fact, Louis L'Amour is pretty unambiguous that his heroes have the absolute right to bear arms, to defend themselves and others. The contemporary lawyer, William Blackstone, argued the legality of being able to 'repel force by force' in self-defense, and in the context of the time and place, it seems obvious to L'Amour that good people must be just as prepared to use force as wrongdoers are. As Eddie Holt tells his partner, Barney Pike, 'You're a kindly man, Pronto...but you can only be kindly up to a point, when you live in a world where evil men go armed.' In the real life West, there actually were a few pacifists, like Marshal 'Bear River' Tom Smith, who refused to use their guns. Smith was axed to death by an angry homesteader.

But the novels also carry a strong sense that L'Amour is well aware that strength and power also have the capacity to corrupt. That even justified killing has consequences. Several of his heroes worry that the violence they are forced to use may reduce them to soulless 'killers.' Matt Coburn (*The Empty Land*) has made 'a dozen towns decent to live in' (according to Matt Sturd). But he fears that he is losing his patience, and will end up a professional killer. L'Amour describes how this

'Autie' Custer and his men were responsible for cleaning up many Western towns, but also stirred up trouble from the dispossessed Indians (seen below plundering a hidden cache).

fate can also happen to professional lawmen. In *Catlow*, he tells of Lynch Manly, a 'noted man-hunter and a man-killer who had once been a Royal Northwest Mounted police officer.' L'Amour women seem to know instinctively that 'turnin' bad' is a real hazard of this tough way of life. Though women like Laurie turn to strong men for protection, they can't necessarily accept what this entails.

The first organized law enforcement in the West was undertaken by the US army. They decriminalized many Western towns, including Fargo-in-the-Timber. L'Amour tells how 'Custer's soldiers cleaned it out,' dispatching some of the local villains like Jack O'Neil. Unfortunately, 'Autie' was also responsible for stirring up attacks from burnt-out and dispossessed Indians, reduced to attacking settlers to survive. The Army was also employed by the railroad kings to protect their huge capital investment in schemes like the transcontinental rail route. This is how Zeb Rawlings enters the scene in *How The West Was Won* as an army Lieutenant, protecting railroad workers from Arapahoe attack.

The first variety of 'citizen's law' was an ugly and violent force, regulated by greed and self-interest rather than a desire to regulate frontier life. *Utah Blaine* opens with the attempted lynching of the elderly Joe Neal in a 'land grab' conspiracy, not by a 'committee of honest citizens but some dark and ugly bunch out to do business that demanded night and secrecy.' Utah Blaine himself is an example of just how easy it was to cross and recross the line of the law. He had been the Marshal of Alta, and had 'tamed' the town. He then became a mercenary

Vigilantes bring in an outlaw. There is probably a reward posted for him.L'Amour heroes are often ambiguous about this kind of 'man-hunting.'

fighter in the Mexican revolution, and ended up as a prisoner. Through hitching up with Joe Neal, he now becomes a man with a stake in society again, fighting the vigilante forces of the corrupt locals. He is a good example of a man with a reputation on both sides of the law.

Lynch law is a pretty common thread that runs through the novels. Nevers offers five hundred dollars for Utah Blaine, 'dead or alive.' Mercer threatens to take the law into his own hands, and hang Catlow as a cattle rustler. 'Hired guns' could be employed on either side of the criminal divide, depending on who hired them. Todd and Peebles are criminals and drunks, but other professional guns were more discriminating about their employers. Although Western men may be handy enough with a gun to solve their own difficulties, they are not necessarily interested in resolving other people's problems. As Barney Pike tells Granville Stuart, when the rancher tries to hire him to clean up a plague of cattle rustlers (in *Hanging Woman Creek*) 'When it comes to the law, I leave it to the law.... I'm not a man-hunter.'

The first sheriffs and marshals were often directly employed by the local townspeople and landowners to 'clean up' their towns and the surrounding lands, leaving them to live and do their business in peace. This brought a gradual drift towards professionalism, and the use of

Deputy sheriffs could be appointed ad hoc in times of crisis.

Cattle rustling and range wars were constant problems for cattle ranchers during this period. They often led to violence, but were often outside the scope of the local lawmen.

Wyeth's magnificent painting celebrates 'The Noble Outlaw.' But in reality, men of this type were often violent and depraved.

The legendary Judge Roy Bean dispensed justice from The Jersey Lilly in Langtry, Texas. There is a museum to commemorate his influence on the town.

more recognizable policing methods. For example, L'Amour describes how the violent and disruptive Range Wars finally drive the townspeople of Red Creek to get their own marshal, Rocky White. His job is to ensure that 'the violence stops, guns (are) checked upon entry of the town limits…' and that there is 'protection for citizens.' This system was obviously open to abuse, and the hard nature of the work meant that the men employed to do it were often distasteful to their employers. A well-known real life example of this is that of Wild Bill Hickok, who brought law, order, and gun control to Abilene, only to be sacked by the town council for his unsavory and violent methods.

In *The Empty Land*, Matt Coburn suggests that Confusion should employ a rough and ready brand of law enforcement, effectively vigilantism; a citizens committee enforcing the law with Winchesters; and the motto 'uplift society…use a rope to do the lifting.' But his employer, Felton, says that the town wants to see an end to violence, and that there 'just has to be another way.' The relationship between the townspeople and their 'hired law' was often full of irony. Felton considers Coburn to be little better than a gunfighter, but Coburn insists that he has 'never hired my gun to anybody but the law.' In fact, he had once dreamt of becoming a lawyer, and bought a copy of 'Blackstone,' the famous legal textbook. He finally accepts the job as Sheriff of Confusion after the first man to be offered the position (McGuiness) is shot dead, and the second, 'thief and highbinder' Hick Sutton is ridden out of town. L'Amour describes Coburn's increasing weariness at the task. He had initially found rough new towns like Confusion interesting—a challenge. 'He had come to them to bring law and order…but all too often he had discovered that even those who hired him became his enemies' and he goes on to describe how 'a man in my line of work doesn't have too many friends.' Despite the huge risks he and his kind take to 'clean up,' and enforce justice, they receive very little gratitude and are often lonely and isolated.

Two town marshals who L'Amour created and admired, Borden Chantry and Tyrel Sackett, appear in *Son of A Wanted Man* (Tyrel also appears in several Sackett saga novels). They both espouse the aspirations of real life lawman Dave Cook, who brought a new level of professionalism to the role. They follow his precept of cooperation between lawmen, in tracking criminals down and bringing them to justice (as the Texas Rangers did). Cook believed that 'Any town marshal worth his salt could in a few minutes detect the presence of strangers, of lone riders, or drifters, even in a town that was strange to him.' Chantry very modestly describes himself as being 'no detective or even a marshal except by wish of these folks in town.' In fact, he is both the town marshal and county sheriff, drawing the salary for both jobs. He is a completely honest and incorruptible man, impervious to bribery, 'I'm not for sale. An officer who turns crooked is worse than any thief. A police officer takes an oath to support the law.' He feels satisfaction when he, Sackett, and Kim Baca have wiped out the outlaw band coming to rob the town bank, 'This was his town, and it was safe once more.' But this safety for the citizens was bought at a tremendously high price, and only because men of his stamp were willing to take such huge personal risks. Chantry, and men of his caliber, are truly 'mighty square.'Another man of this ilk is Zeb Rawlings. He resigns his army commission goes into civilian law enforcement and ultimately becomes a Deputy US Marshal. He is known 'as a man who was never anxious to shoot, which was rare in old-time marshals who had grown into their jobs at a time when it was often safer to shoot first and ask the questions afterwards.' He is brave and self-disciplined. Like Chantry and Sackett, Rawlings also believes that lawmen must cooperate to get better results, and use modern 'technology' to track down criminals. 'The law was organized now. Descriptions were mailed around from office to office, and conceit (on the part of the lawbreakers) led to carelessness…

'Mysterious' Dave Mather, a new breed of law officer who would go looking for trouble, and 'shot you where they found you.'

imprisonment or death.'

In *How The West Was Won*, Louis L'Amour very interestingly categorizes three types of frontier marshal. Courageous and restrained men like Zeb Rawlings, in the stamp of real life lawmen such as Bill Tilghman, Jim Gillette, and Jeff Milton; a second type as personified by Bill Hickok who 'gave you no second chance'; then a third kind of man, exemplified by Mysterious Dave Mather who proactively went looking for troublemakers. Men like this 'shot you where they found you'—if you were on the wrong side of the law, of course. Inevitably, this meant that the personality of the lawmen was reflected in the quality of the law dispensed in these towns, which must have been pretty variable.

But the law gradually became more codified, and law enforcement itself more uniform and professional. On the other hand, criminals seem to have become more hardened and depraved. Western society itself became far less tolerant of the blight of lawlessness. L'Amour describes how, in the past, an outlaw might have been seen as 'some wild youngster full of liquor,' but would now be considered 'a bad man, dangerous to the community.' L'Amour sums up the situation by saying 'To defend against the kind of outlaws I write about…as the towns of the western frontier began to develop…there was a great need for law enforcement officials to become more professional.' This professional approach, and the better results it produced, greatly reduced vigilantism. More criminals were sent to prison, rather than being summarily strung up, so a prison service was also established. Finn Cagle is described as having served a term in Yuma's Territorial Prison.

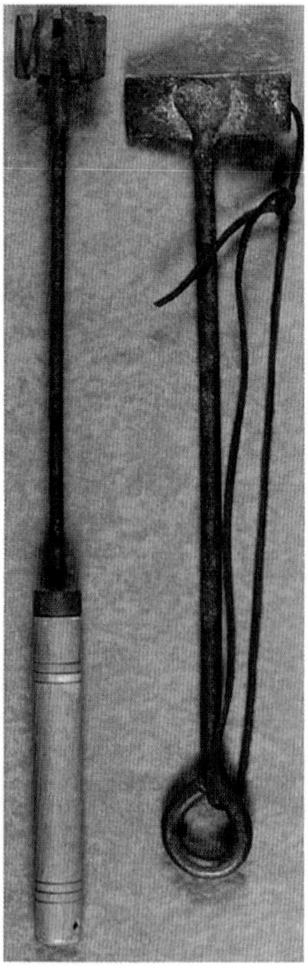

ABOVE AND LEFT: **Irons like these were used to brand and (feloniously) re-brand cattle. As this drawing shows, this was often done by night, and was highly angerous for the participants.**

While L'Amour's portrayal of Western lawmen is often admiring, he seems a good deal less impressed by lawyers (his evocations of them are far more variable) and members of the judiciary. Dean Cullane was a 'jackleg lawyer, and one who dealt with men on the wrong side of the law in ways not concerned with the legal profession.' But Judge Niland (*The Man Called Noon*) must be a candidate for the most corrupted man of law in the novels. He offers Ruble Noon the opportunity to rob Fan Davidge of her inheritance, and incites him to murder the (almost equally depraved) Peg Cullane.

Another interesting factor is that, in L'Amour, the divide between lawmen and criminals often seems quite fluid. Cowan and Catlow are two sides of the same coin, and were brought up together. 'By the time (they) were fifteen years old, each had saved the other's life no less than three times.'Both have a similar character and outlook. But they end up on opposing sides of the law, as 'There was a line beyond which a man might not go, even in the tolerant West.' By the age of twenty-three, Ben is a

Cowboys who had spent weeks or months herding cattle were thirsty when they finally made it into town, and their behavior was often rowdy and distressing to the townsfolk. Some towns, like Abilene, tried to discourage them from coming into town at all.

Deputy US Marshal whilst Catlow is 'a known cattle rustler, and an outlaw with three killings behind him.' Despite this, L'Amour makes it clear that he considers both to be men of honor, and that it is possible to be a good man, on either side of the law. Moreover, they have mutual regard and respect, epitomized by their naming their sons for each other. Ben Cowan refuses to honor false warrants served on Catlow and his men, and Catlow praises Cowan. 'For a sheriff, you're a pretty good sort.' It was also possible to pass the divide in reverse. Several of the most famous lawmen of the West were retired gunmen, including Wyatt Earp.

Fictional L'Amour heroes often cross and re-cross the 'line' of criminality. In *To The Blue Mountains*, Barney Sackett is wanted for crimes he hasn't committed, and is forced to become a pirate to escape injustice. He sums up the confusing nature of his position, 'Whether I was a good man, I did not know. I knew I was a man who wished to survive.'

The harsh nature of the West itself, with 'little law and much of that…enforced by men big enough to get away with it,' seems to engender criminality. Ben Curry says that when he first came out West 'it was dog eat dog and if you lived you had to have big teeth.' He had been run off his ranch and his mining operation before he decided to 'bite back.' In this way, an essentially good man was forced to turn to crime, and with no

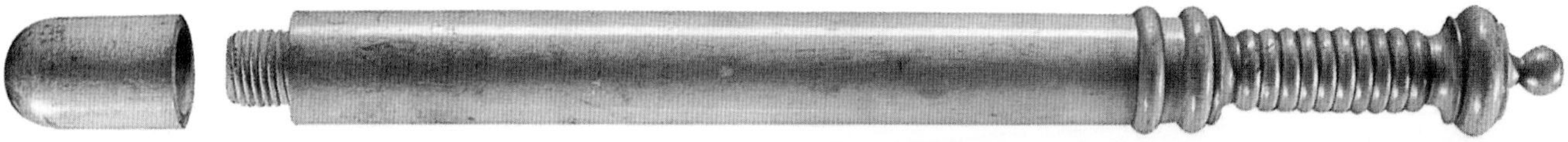

A law enforcer's baton with a hidden metal insert to increase the deadliness of its blow.

way back to his former life, was obliged to make it his way of life: 'I was an outlaw whether I liked it or not.'

But there is a category of men in the novels, the true villain with no pretensions to being any kind of honorable criminal, that L'Amour profiles at some length, creating many examples of the type. This class of desperado is often described as leading a vicious and pathetic existence. Unlike many of L'Amours positive role models, who are self-reliant and often ride alone, criminals seem to hang together. L'Amour views the criminal 'gang' as being proof of the fundamental weakness of these men, 'the world of most criminals is incredibly small.... Few can stand alone.... The gang is their protection and their strength.' Neither does he have a high regard for their intelligence. In *Hanging Woman Creek*, Barney Pike says 'No thief ever knows when he's well off, and every one of them thinks he is going to be the one who gets away with it. To be a thief at all, a man has to be either a damned fool

Abilene,Texas at the time of Wild Bill Hickok. It looks surprisingly like a flimsy set for a Western movie.

Even pillars of Western society like Wells Fargo offices were not immune to hold-ups.

or mighty egotistical, and it could amount to the same thing.... They always make light of honest men.' Zeb Rawlings says something similar, 'To be a criminal... required certain peculiar attitudes of mind.... One was contempt for people and the law; another was optimism.' Many L'Amour criminals mock the efficacy of the law, like Van Bokkelen, who says, 'I couldn't find a lawman I couldn't outfigure,' but their inevitably violent ends expose the folly of their thinking. Slightly less stupid villains, like Harry Meadows in *The Empty Land*, play the odds a little more cleverly, passing up a slim chance to steal the huge sum of $100,000 in order to stay out of jail.

L'Amour also explodes the romantic myths associated with criminal life, even that of the notorious villains. He vividly describes the miserable, paranoid existence of the James gang, 'In their sixteen years as outlaws, few of the James gang even made a decent living... most of that time they were on the dodge, hiding out in caves, barns and shacks, poorly fed, poorly clothed, suspicious of each other...(James) had already murdered two of his own gang and was planning to kill others.' James met a similar end, killed by one of his own men. Barney describes Van Bokkelen's life as equally futile, 'you'll have a fat roll of greenbacks from time to time, and years in prison to pay for it, and always the fear that the next step you make will be the wrong one.'

COLT 1851 NAVY REVOLVER

Not only Western men needed to be armed. In *Utah Blaine*, Russ Nevers and his gang besiege Angie Kinyon's lonely ranch. 'There was an old pistol, a Navy revolver her father had left behind him. It was on a shelf in a closed, wooden box, and fully loaded. Her awareness of the gun did a little to ease her fear.'

Many Western homes would have had such a gun on a shelf or in a drawer. The peopling of the West really took off after the Civil War and the Colt Navy Revolver had been a popular firearm in the conflict. Many such weapons were carried West by their owners.

But by the time Angie was reaching for her gun it was, to a large degree, an obsolete weapon. The gun was loaded with a swivel ramrod, which charged each of the chambers in the cylinder from the front. A percussion cap was then pressed onto each nipple at the rear of the cylinder. This was all quite a performance in an age when rim fire metal cartridges were becoming the norm and center-fire technology was just around the corner. Because of these limitations, the gun was only able to use relatively low black powder charges. Coupled with the small caliber of .36 inch meant that its stopping power was limited. But it did have the advantage of being a multi-shot weapon when many firearms were still single shot.

The gun had mainly been used for military purposes, not only in the US but also in India by the British. One story tells of an officer at the siege of Calcutta emptying his whole chamber into a hostile tribesman and failing to stop the man who, undeterred, drove his lance into the officer's chest, killing him outright. Little wonder then, that the Colt Navy was not a favorite of Western

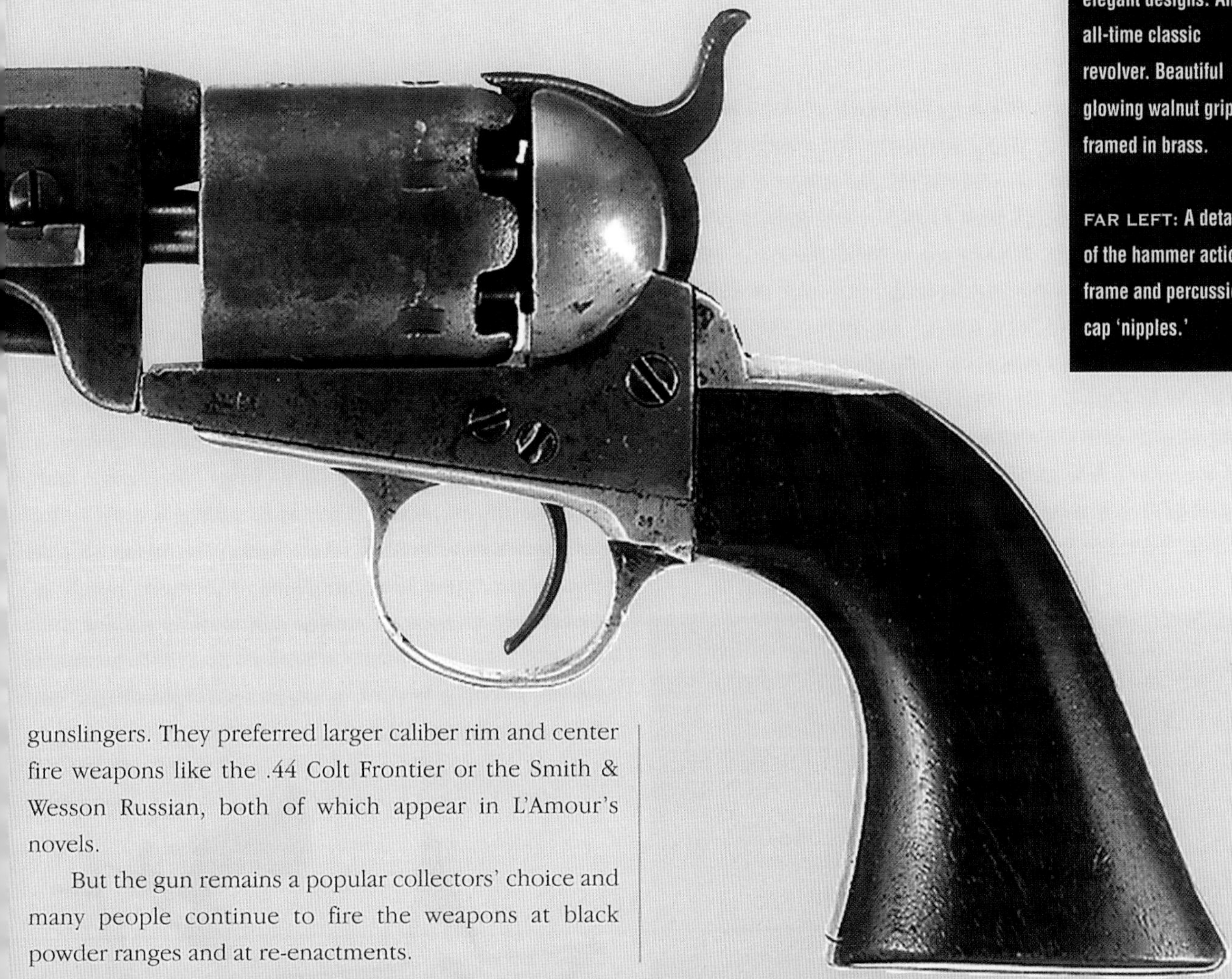

LEFT: One of Colt's cleanest and most elegant designs. An all-time classic revolver. Beautiful glowing walnut grip framed in brass.

FAR LEFT: A detail of the hammer action, frame and percussion cap 'nipples.'

gunslingers. They preferred larger caliber rim and center fire weapons like the .44 Colt Frontier or the Smith & Wesson Russian, both of which appear in L'Amour's novels.

But the gun remains a popular collectors' choice and many people continue to fire the weapons at black powder ranges and at re-enactments.

SPECIFICATIONS	
CALIBER: 0.36	GRIPS: Walnut
LENGTH OF BARREL: 7 inches	ACTION: Six shot single action repeater
BARREL SHAPE: Octagonal	YEAR OF MANUFACTURE: 1851
FINISH: Blue steel, brass back strap and trigger guard	MANUFACTURER: Samuel Colt, New York City

THE AGE OF THE GUNFIGHTER

The gunfighter fills a special place in the folklore of the American West, alongside the cowboy, Indian, mountain man, scout, and sheriff. His image is still fresh in the mind, although over a century has passed since he squeezed a trigger. But like many Western characters, his figure evokes conflicting feelings, for men of this type ranged all the way from being 'man-killers' to 'civilizers.' Louis L'Amour had met many men of the class, and he was clearly fascinated by them, having written profiles of thousands more. He attempts to explain their position to the reader, 'Few gunfighters were actually outlaws.... A gunfighter, or gunman, was actually no more than a man who, because of some unusual gift of dexterity, coordination, and nerve, became better with a gun than others.' But evidently, he himself had ambiguous feelings about men of this stamp. Some of his gunmen are cold, contract killers, others are depraved and vicious, 'thoroughly bad men,' while others are more 'gentlemen thieves,' like the 'Admirable Outlaw' in N.C. Wyeth's painting. Often, they were law enforcers (like the real life Bat Masterson and Bill Tilghman, on whom Zeb Rawlings is based), and standing indomitably on the side of right. Yet another class of gunman, like the often-mentioned 'Wild' Bill Hickok and the Earp brothers, were economically motivated. They used their gun skills to find work between other jobs, often 'taking the badge' of a law officer. Other men, like Utah Blaine, were more 'unofficial' gunfighters, using their modus operandi to achieve their own ends. He is variously described as a 'hell-on-wheels gunman from the Neuces,' a 'ragged-tailed gunslinger' and 'damned driftin' outlaw.'

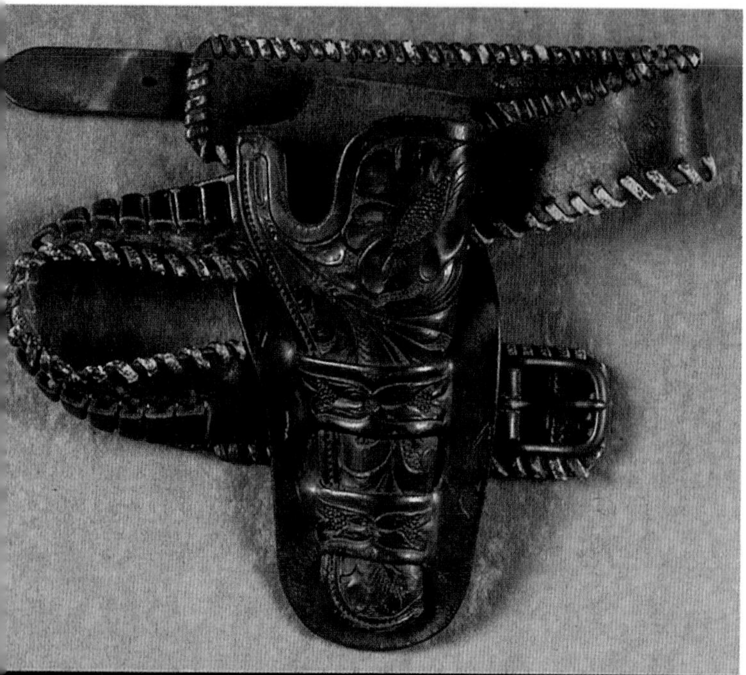

Western Heiser Holster with belt. The two loop holster is marked with the straight 'Heiser Denver' mark.

Professional gunfighters and law enforcers were often difficult to tell apart in the hurly burly of the wild, wild West. Speed of the draw was everything for both classes. Without it, a marshal's badge was no protection.

The saloon was the location for many a Western fracas.

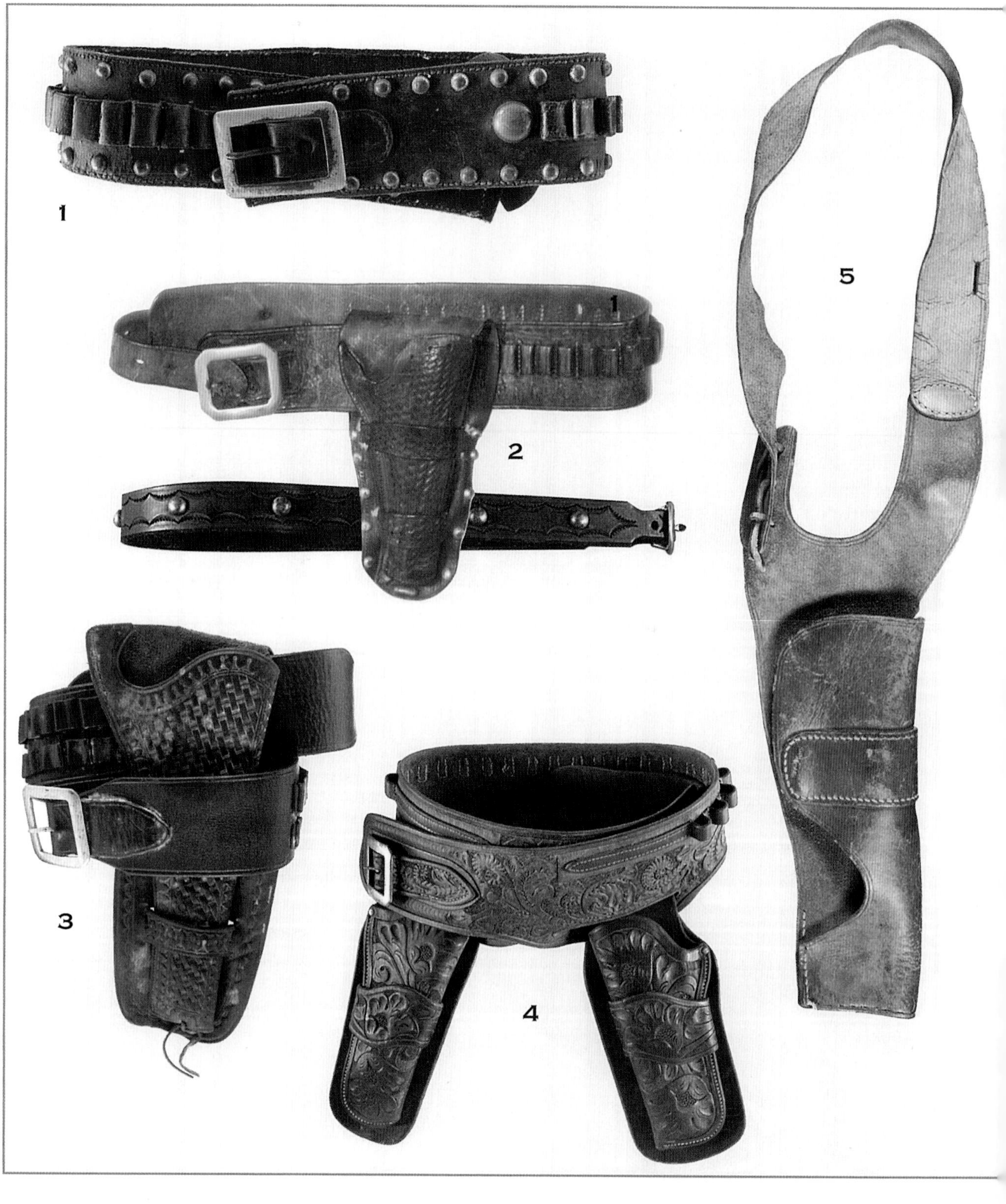
1
1
2
3
4
5

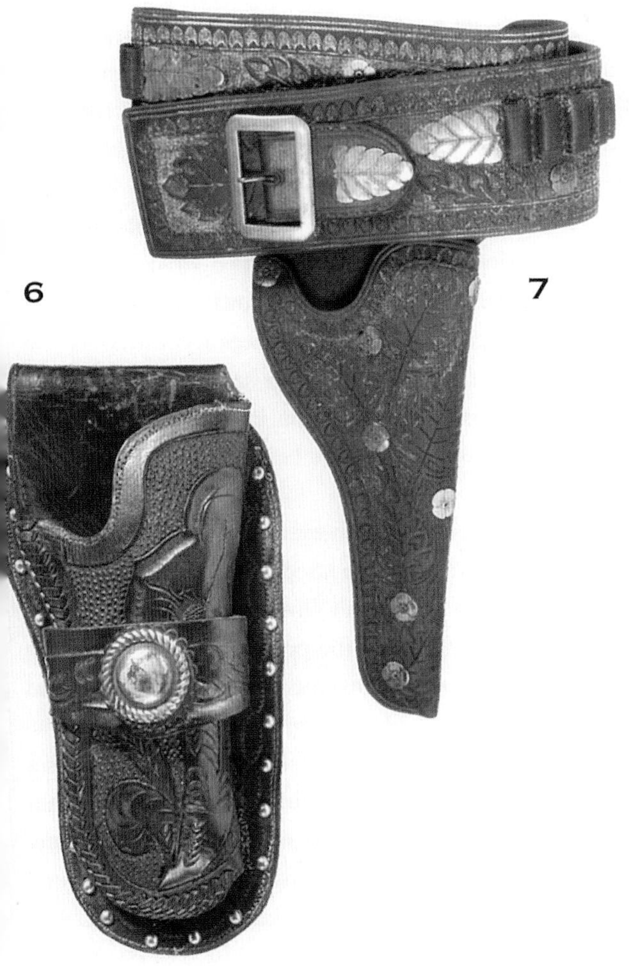

1 Combination cartridge and money belt with 35 large caliber, cartridge loops
2 Small Western belt with 3/8 inch plated brass tacks
3 Cartridge belt and holster for Colt Single Action
4 Buscadero fancy holster rig. Twin holsters in tooled leather for a pair of Colt Peacemakers
5 Gunfighter's Heiser shoulder holster marked H.H. Heiser/Maker/ Denver/Colo
6 Fine Texas holster stamped J.D.Banks/Amarillo/Texas
7 Fancy tooled leather holster and belt for a Colt Army Revolver

In *How the West Was Won*, L'Amour composes a fascinating profile of the hugely diverse backgrounds that these men came from: 'Most gunfighters had been officers of the law.... Hickok had been a stagedriver and scout for the army. Wyatt Earp, Bat Masterson, Billy Brooks, and many others had been buffalo hunters. Clay Allison, Pink Higgins, and John Slaughter had been ranchers, Ben Thompson a gambler, Doc Holliday a dentist, Temple Houston a lawyer. Billy the Kid had been a drifting cowhand and gambler, then a feudist in the Lincoln County War...Chris Madsen had been a soldier in several armies...Buckey O'Neill was a newspaper editor, probate judge, and a superintendent of schools, as well as a frontier sheriff; many gunfighters have been ex-soldiers.' Many other famous names also turn up in L'Amour's pages, including Frank and George Coe, Dick Brewer, Jesse Evans, and Wes Hardin. Ben Curry's 'bunch of outlaws' (in *Son of a Wanted Man*) recalls real life outfits like the Dalton Gang.

L'Amour's version very much reflects contemporary accounts of the gunman phenomenon. A sketch in a similar vein appeared in the Kansas City Journal in 1881, 'The gentleman who has 'killed his man' is by no means a rara avis.... He is met daily on Main street.... He may be seen on 'change, and in the congregations of the most aristocratic churches. He resides on 'Quality Hill,' or perhaps on the East Side.... He may be found behind the bar in a Main street saloon...or he may be behind the rosewood counters of a bank.' But men who lived and died by the gun as a profession were an exception to the rule, even in *Louis L'Amour's Wild West*.

In reality, the gunfighter emerged from the turbulent conditions prevalent in the frontier West, when little or no help could be expected from the law. Men like Matt Giles started out with respectable backgrounds but are sucked into the way of the gun by the forces of history, beginning 'his killing as mere boy in the Moderators and Regulators wars of northeast Texas, and had graduated to a sharpshooter in the Confederate Army.' He describes Pike Sides, the 'Cherry Creek Gunman' in *The Empty Land*, who came to killing via a similar route, having been involved in the Lincoln County War, and was subsequently hired to slaughter several men around the west. L'Amour obviously disapproves of this kind of 'cold' contract killing; he describes Pike as having 'curiously unalive (eyes), reminding Matt of a snake.' Pike's soul is dead.

'God created man, but Sam Colt made them equal!'

In the alternative moral order of the West, one of the lowest forms of 'gunman' that turns up in the novels is Eve Rawlings's sickly younger brother Zeke (now known as Ralls) in *How the West Was Won*. This is a case of a very bad apple coming from a good barrel, and L'Amour interestingly describes how a boy from a good, loving family (that has also turned out men of the stature of Zeb Rawlings), has turned into a 'particularly vicious killer.' Zeke is a thoroughly bad man who never did a day's work in his life. He doesn't even espouse the virtue of honor amongst thieves. He abandoned his own gang to be hung in Jack Slade's cleanup, when vigilantes accounted for the deaths of twenty-six outlaws who had been terrorizing their town—Virginia City, Montana. Even outlaws had their standards, the lowest of the low being referred to as 'scalp hunters' and 'back-shootin' killers.' Most would be appalled to learn of Zeke's intention to murder a relative, although he does attempt to justify this, by explaining that the elderly Jethro Stuart isn't blood kin.

One positive aspect of the prominence of gunmen in the Western environment was the tremendous affect it had on the manufacture of ever more sophisticated guns. Samuel Colt patented the revolver in 1835, which was a huge step forward in automatic firing. Some men said that 'God created man, but Sam Colt made them equal!' Many Louis L'Amour heroes and villains carry Colts of several different kinds, revolving shotguns, .45s and .44s. Winchesters are also rated, and appear just as often (Models 1866, 1873 etc.). In *The Man Called Noon*, Ruble Noon is trying to recover his memory and his identity, and discovers that he was the president and owner of an arms company,

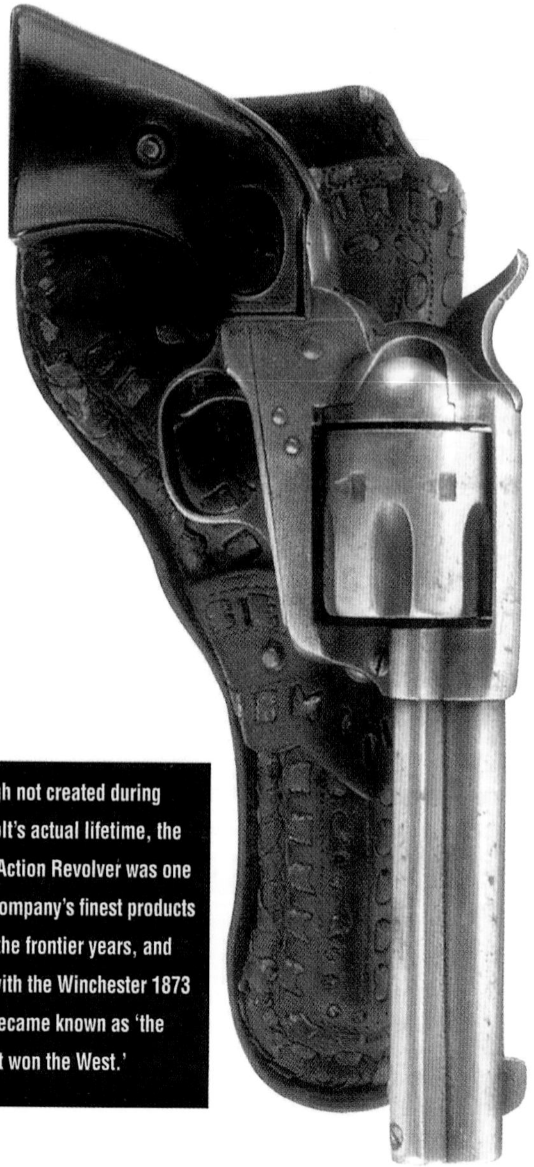

Although not created during Sam Colt's actual lifetime, the Single Action Revolver was one of the company's finest products during the frontier years, and along with the Winchester 1873 Rifle, became known as 'the gun that won the West.'

Sam Colt was a major firearms manufacturer, and became a huge asset to the Union cause in the Civil War, supplying them with many different models.

a famous marksman, and big game hunter. Interestingly, he carries a Winchester. The English Daily Telegraph remarked in 1869 that 'Duellists, travellers, and the rowdy bullies of the New World enjoy the doubtful honor of having brought the pistol to its present sanguinary perfection.

It is the weapon of the self-dependent man.' This weapon was indeed one of the factors that helped to 'win' the West for white men.

But in some L'Amour's novels, there is also a sense that the true day of the gunman is drawing to a close. Ben Curry articulates this feeling: 'All of us…Wyatt Earp, Billy the Kid, Bill Hickok, we've all lived out our time in a world we never made.' Progress, and the incoming force of law are sweeping these men aside, together with the wilderness itself.

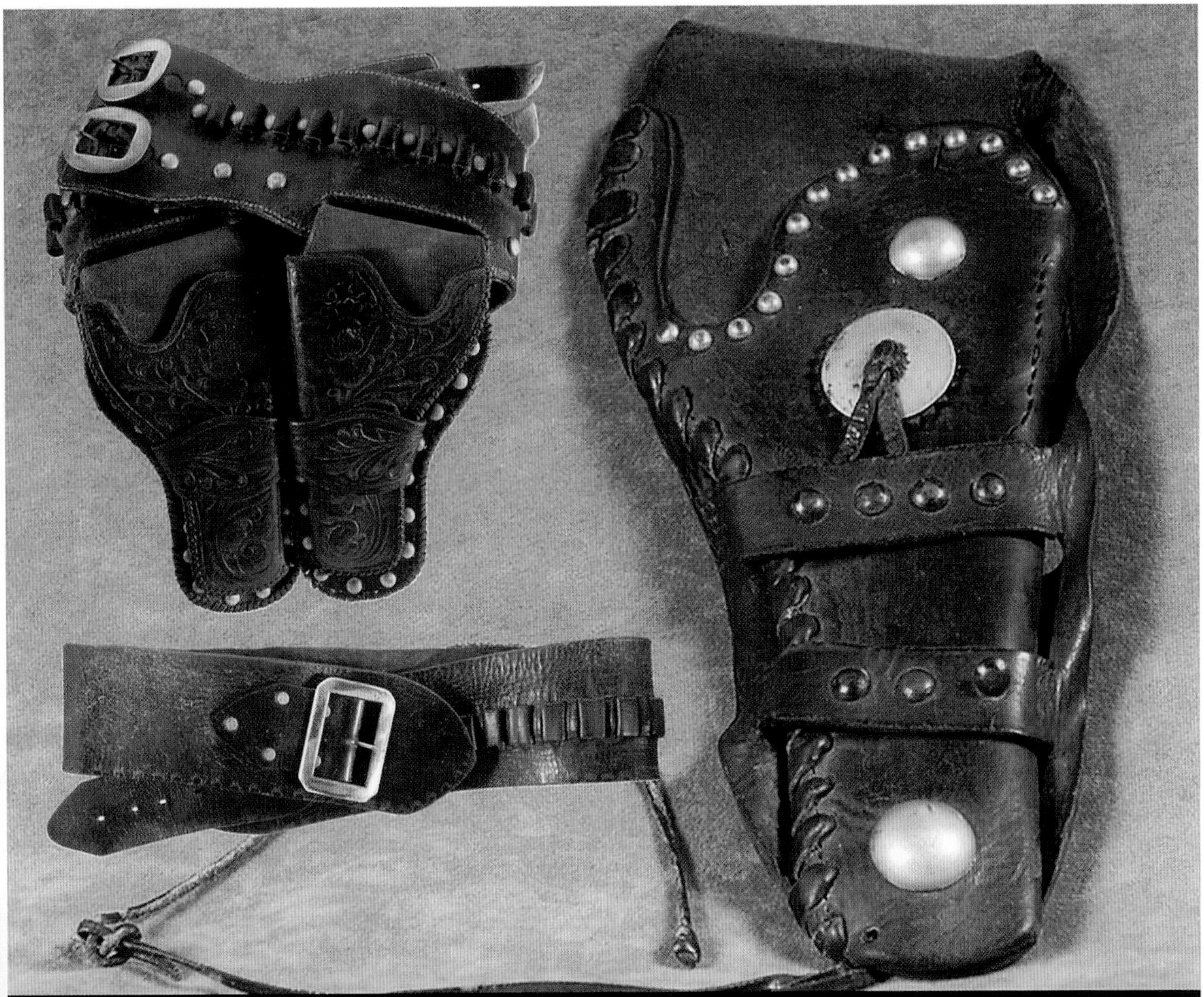

A Fancy Buscadero holster rig with double buckle belt decorated with brass tacks. A single cartridge belt. A single holster for a Colt Peacemaker with leather thong, which tied the assembly to the gunfighters leg for a faster draw.

COLT MODEL 1860 ARMY REVOLVER

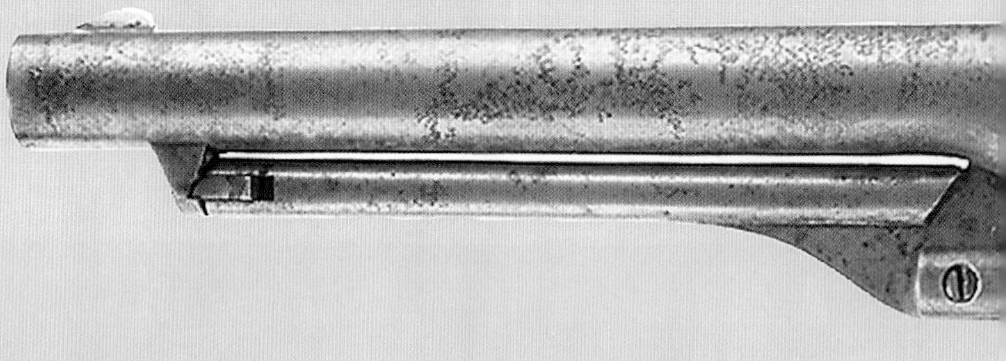

Detail of the cylinder and hammer. The frame screws have seen better days!

When the Civil War began, Samuel Colt was anxious to support the Union forces despite having made pre-war sales worth around $3 million to the South. His plans for his own special division, 'Colts Rifles' which would have operated outside state control were thwarted. But it was recognized that his ability to produce some of the finest firearms then available was a major asset to the Union cause. In replacing the Dragoon in 1860, he was determined to correct one of that model's major disadvantages – it's weight.

The earlier gun weighed a full four pounds, two ounces. But the later version weighed in at a more manageable two pounds, ten ounces. The new gun was produced between 1860 and 1873, when the Peacemaker finally replaced it. Over 200,000 examples were manufactured. The Union government purchased 120,000 of these to supply their Civil War troops. The result was that plenty of Colt Armys were in circulation on the Frontier during the 1870s. In fact, it is likely that Louis L'Amour's vaunted lawman Wyatt Earp carried one of these weapons, rather than the Buntline Special that legend has decreed.

The gun itself is probably one of the most familiar looking Colts ever made, and has rather elegant

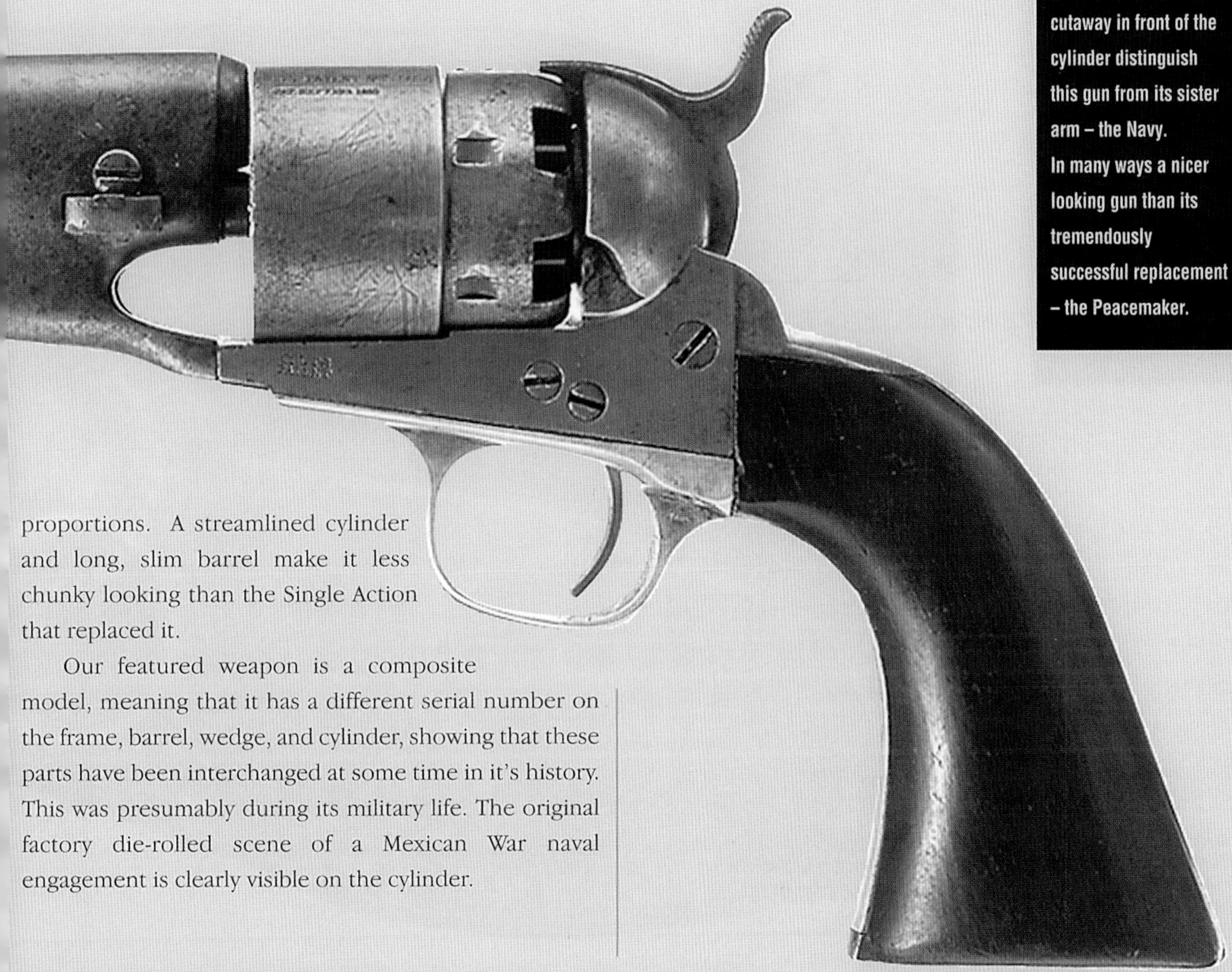

LEFT: The rounded barrel section and cutaway in front of the cylinder distinguish this gun from its sister arm – the Navy.
In many ways a nicer looking gun than its tremendously successful replacement – the Peacemaker.

proportions. A streamlined cylinder and long, slim barrel make it less chunky looking than the Single Action that replaced it.

Our featured weapon is a composite model, meaning that it has a different serial number on the frame, barrel, wedge, and cylinder, showing that these parts have been interchanged at some time in it's history. This was presumably during its military life. The original factory die-rolled scene of a Mexican War naval engagement is clearly visible on the cylinder.

SPECIFICATIONS

CALIBER: 0.44	**ACTION:** Single
LENGTH OF BARREL: 8 inches	**YEAR OF MANUFACTURE:** 1860
BARREL SHAPE: Round	**MANUFACTURER:** Samuel Colt, Hartford, Connecticut
FINISH: Gray patina	
GRIPS: Walnut	

COLT PEACEMAKER

RIGHT: The gun shown here was the property of the Sheriff of Magdalena, New Mexico. The gun is shown with what is believed to be its original leather tooled holster.

No weapons appraisal of the West of Louis L'Amour could be considered complete without the Peacemaker, or Single Action Army Revolver as it was more properly called. Along with the Winchester 73, the .45 Colt Peacemaker became famous as 'the gun that won the west.' The civilian Frontier version of the Colt Model 1873 and the Winchester were deliberately marketed to use the same ammunition, namely .44/40 caliber. This meant that it was only necessary to carry one type of shell, a self-contained center fire cartridge. The two guns presented the all round flexibility of a repeating rifle for long-range work, with the quick shot revolver for use at short range. Both had outstanding stopping power, provided by the large caliber ammunition.

In *Hanging Woman Creek*, 'Pronto' Pike is presented with both guns by his new employer, Bill Justin, as part of a wagon load of essential supplies: 'two brand-new Winchester 73s, and boxes with about 500 rounds of

ammunition. Alongside the rifles lay two .44 caliber Colts, both new.

This image of the cowboy carrying both weapons as part of his outfit was promoted by Hollywood. But the Colt was tremendously expensive at $17 (around $700 today). Back in 1874, this would have been around a month's wages for the average cowhand. The gun was probably not immediately in as wide as use as commonly believed.

But the Colt .45 Peacemaker was a familiar part of John Wayne's screen image, and when he starred in the screen version of *Hondo*, the image stuck. The gun became the model that all toy guns were based on - my own nickel-plated die cast version was a personal childhood favorite -as it was with countless millions of other kids that grew up in the golden age of Westerns.

Ironically, the gun was not the direct result of Samuel Colt's own design as he died in 1862. This was before the advent of the type of ammunition that made the 1873 revolver so effective. But it can certainly be argued that Colt's powerful vision for revolving firearms propelled the company forward for many years after his death. After all, as the popular saying went, 'God made man, but Colonel Colt made them equal.'

The featured example was the property of the Sheriff of Magdalena New Mexico. It has its original handmade single loop holster, decorated with brass tacks and braided rawhide edging. Many guns of this type have been handed down in families for generations.

SPECIFICATIONS

CALIBER: 0.45 and .44/40	**GRIPS:** Hard Rubber
LENGTH OF BARREL: various, this example 4 inches	**YEAR OF MANUFACTURE:** 1896
BARREL SHAPE: Round	**MANUFACTURER:** Colt's PT.F.A. MFG. CO., Hartford, Connecticut
FINISH: Smooth gray patina with traces of blue	

GAMBLING

Gambling was a major ingredient in the cocktail of Western life. 'A mania for gambling' was common to all the frontier regions, and it was the chief draw of saloon life. Most gamblers were parasitic. They migrated to wherever there was money, in the mining and cow towns, or the tent towns at the end of the railroad tracks. In these places, gambling and prostitution formed a corrosive mix that greatly increased the level of violence. Towns like Abilene tried to control the activities of the 'pasteboard pirates' with a stringent system of fines, but its own marshal, Bill Hickok, was a professional gambler who ran the town from a saloon table. Indeed, Bat Masterson wrote that 'gambling was not only the principle and best-paying industry of the town at the time, but it was also reckoned among its most respectable.' Gaming certainly attracted many professional players, including many of the West's most famous gunmen.

Top hat with cheaters mirror in the crown.

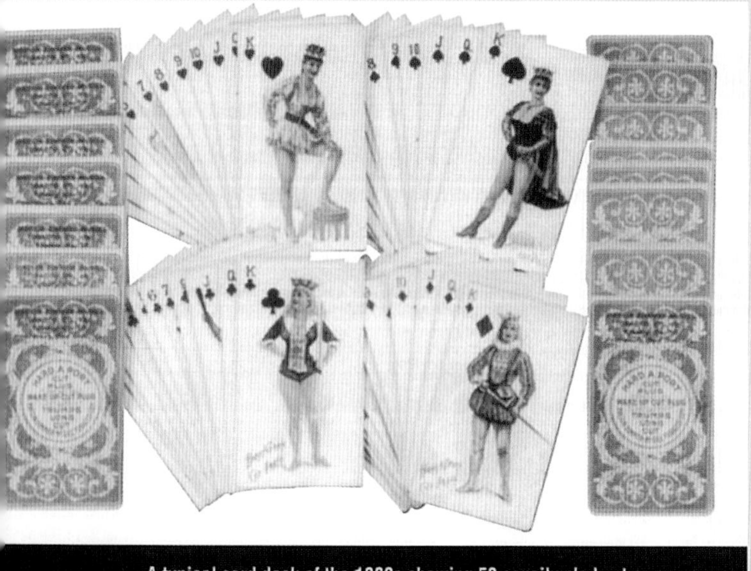
A typical card deck of the 1880s showing 53 saucily clad actresses.

Several of Louis L'Amour's most colorful characters are also gamblers. Not one is successful. As Lilith Van Valen says, 'A man's a fool to gamble, take that from me, who was married to a gambler. But you'd best know how, because there might come a time.' When she met him, her husband Cleve was a washed up riverboat gambler, whose luck had run out. And in any case, as Barney Pike says, 'Gamblin' money don't stick to a man.' He himself is penniless, despite winning $300 in a Chicago dice game.

Other characters, like Doc Sawyer, use gambling to

A tin type photograph of four men playing cards.

A fine riverboat which was actually a floating magnet to the gambling fraternity.

Gambling was one of the darker threads that ran through Western life. Gamblers dirk, which would have been clipped inside a waistband for cutting one's way out of a tight corner.

Highly ornate poker chips from the frontier days.

collect saloon intelligence. He later cheats, by card marking, in a game he plays with Ben Curry and Garlin. 'You shuffle them cards any more, Doc...and I'll get worried what you're doin' to that deck.' Cheats and 'short-card artists' were also instrumental in cranking up the level of gun fighting in Western towns. The Abilene Chronicle published a whole list of well-known card tricks and cheating methods for their more 'respectable' readers to watch out for.

Mike Bastian also pretends to have an (unlikely) interest in 'draw poker' to explain his appearance in the saloon to the sheriff of Weaver. At the other end of the moral spectrum, outlaw and thief Charlie Gant seems to indicate the depths of his debauchery by setting up a roulette wheel. Gunman Wyatt Earp made his fortune doing this very thing.

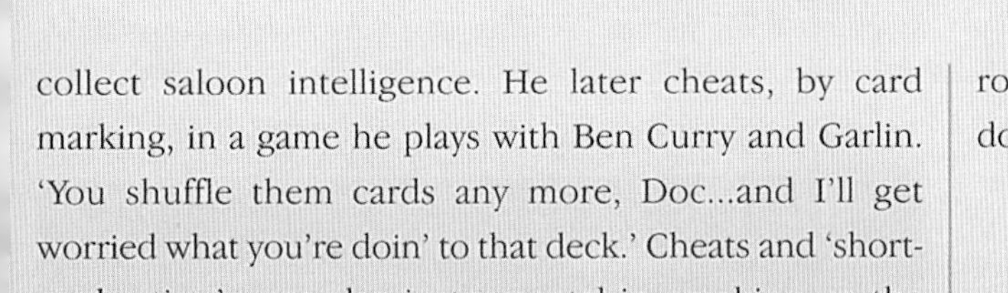

An ivory top of a gambler's cane contains three dice in a silver plated canister.

SMITH & WESSON MODEL NO. 3 ARMY REVOLVER

Utah Blaine is holed up at the hotel in Red Creek when he notices a man staring up at his window outside in the street. There is something sinister in his fixed scrutiny.

Blaine turns from the window and he opens a carpetbag and to take out a pair of holsters and a wide gun belt. 'He slung the belt around him and buckled it, then he took from the bag two beautifully matched pistols. They were .44 Russians. He checked their loads, then played with them briefly, spinning them, doing a couple of border shifts, and then dropping them into their holsters. Suddenly, his hands flashed and the guns were in his hands.'

The .44 Russians were in fact Smith & Wesson Model No. 3 Army revolvers. The guns got their nomenclature, as they were part of a massive order from the Russian authorities, which absorbed Smith & Wesson's entire manufacturing capacity for a full five years. The gun was manufactured around a special .44 inch cartridge specified by the Russian Army. This cartridge gave it excellent power and made the gun a serious rival to Colt's equivalent models of the 1870s. The design evolved into the double-

The actual guns manufactured for the Russian Army have a spur on the trigger guard. Most Frontier users considered them highly impractical and many were removed.

Unlike Colt, the whole barrel and chamber assembly folded down to load. Note the intricate pattern around the pivot pin.

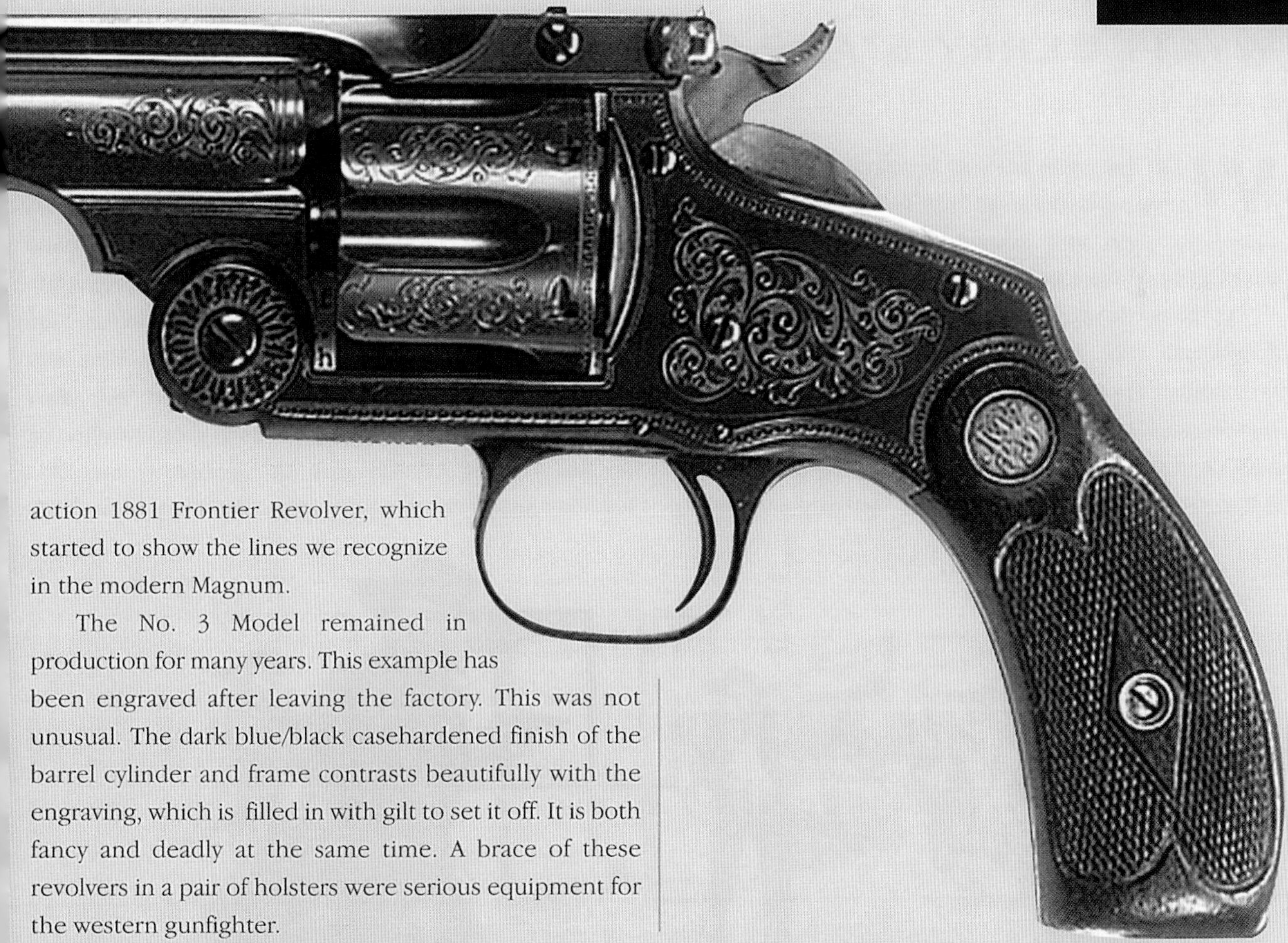

LEFT: **A Work of Art – the beautifully engineered .44 Russian revolver.**

action 1881 Frontier Revolver, which started to show the lines we recognize in the modern Magnum.

The No. 3 Model remained in production for many years. This example has been engraved after leaving the factory. This was not unusual. The dark blue/black casehardened finish of the barrel cylinder and frame contrasts beautifully with the engraving, which is filled in with gilt to set it off. It is both fancy and deadly at the same time. A brace of these revolvers in a pair of holsters were serious equipment for the western gunfighter.

SPECIFICATIONS	
CALIBER: 0.44	ACTION: Six shot repeater
LENGTH OF BARREL: 6 inches	YEAR OF MANUFACTURE: From 1875
BARREL SHAPE: Ribbed	MANUFACTURER:
FINISH: Blue/black steel with gilt inlay engraving	Smith & Wesson, Springfield, Massachusetts
GRIPS: Checkered walnut	

GUNFIGHTER PROFILES

WYATT BERRY STAPP EARP 1848-1929

Wyatt Earp was born in Monmouth, Illinois, and grew up on an Iowa farm. He became one of the most complex and interesting of the gunfighter frontiersmen of the West.

In 1864, Wyatt and his brothers moved to Colton, California, with their parents (which is near San Bernadino). He took various jobs, working as a shotgun messenger for Wells Fargo, a railway worker, and a buffalo hunter. Like Bill Hickok, he also worked in law enforcement to boost his career, serving as deputy marshal in Wichita, Kansas, and in Dodge City. He was reputed to have carried a Colt handgun, either an Army or a Peacemaker. Less reliably, legend has it that he used a Colt 'Buntline Special,' with a detachable carbine. But this particular weapon may have been presented to him in the 1920s, by an admiring fan. Personally, Earp was noted as a tough and decisive man, but was also considered by many to be a 'cold fish.' Despite this, he became lifelong friends with Bat Masterson and Doc Holliday during this Kansas period. Like many of his kind,

Wyatt Earp at the most famous shoot-out of all time, the O. K. Corral in Tombstone, where the three Earp brothers swapped lead with the Clanton-McLaury gang. They survived, but some of their opponents were not so lucky. Frank and Tom McLaury fell, as did Billy Clanton.

The Dodge City Peace Commission of 1883. Back (left to right): Harris, Short, Masterson, W.F. Petillon (added later to the genuine photograph). Front: C. E. Bassett, Wyatt Earp, M.F. Mclain, and Neil Brown. The 'Commission' assembled to support fellow gunslinger Luke Short.

he also gained a reputation as a professional gambler.

Earp had returned East and married in 1870, but his new wife died suddenly. He remarried, and left Dodge City in 1878, setting up home with his brothers and their wives in Tombstone, Arizona. In dress and manner, the Earp brothers exemplified the typical gunmen of the time, poised and stylish. Wyatt acquired the gambling concession in the Oriental Saloon, and his brother Virgil became town marshal. Brother Morgan worked for the local police department. Earp's second marriage failed, and he met his third wife, Josephine Marcus in Tombstone. But everything in Tombstone wasn't rosy. A feud developed between the Earps and Ike Clanton's gang that culminated in 1881 with the most famous gunfight of them all, outside the O.K. Corral, where the Earp brothers 'swapped lead' with the Clanton-McLaury gang. The three Earp bothers survived, but a fourth brother, Morgan, was gunned-down by an unknown assassin in the following year. The remaining brothers avenged his death, and Wyatt was obliged to skip town to Colorado to avoid being tried for these revenge killings.

But Earp remained a law enforcer, of sorts. In 1893,

Wyatt Earp's Oriental Saloon in Tombstone. This was one of his first investments in property and real estate.

he became of member of the so-called 'Dodge City Peace Commission' (together with men such as Bat Masterson and Charlie Bassett), which convened to support fellow gunslinger and saloon owner Luke Short. The city fathers of Dodge City wanted to clean up the town and make it more attractive to settlers, so they tried to evict undesirable elements like Short and his ilk. They soon backed down when Luke's friends turned up.

Wyatt and Josie spent the next few years tramping around the booming mining towns of the frontier, gambling and investing in real estate and saloons as they passed through. In 1897, they operated a saloon in Alaska at the peak of the gold rush there, and made a fortune estimated at $80,000. They then headed for Tonopah, Nevada, cashing in on that town's gold strike.

Earp ultimately took up prospecting seriously, and staked many claims in the Mojave Desert, including several just outside Death Valley. At one stage, he was reputed to have sold a worked-out silver mine for $30,000. He struck gold and copper in 1906 and spent the final winters of his life working these veins. He and Josie lived in Los Angeles in the summer, mixing with the Hollywood glitterati of the time.

Wyatt died in Los Angeles in 1929, at the ripe old age of 80. He was one of the very few gunslingers to make it into old age, and perhaps unique in that he was able to enjoy his own burgeoning reputation. He was an intensely paradoxical man, one who had both upheld and manipulated the law: a speculator and gambler, who was also an able businessman and investor who knew the value of hard work. He was a loyal friend and partner, who also inspired great devotion from his friends, but also noted for his cool demeanor and lack of personal warmth.

Like all the old gunslingers, he had his tricks of the trade. Earp claimed that he only ever loaded five bullets into a six-shooter to 'ensure against accidental discharge.'

JOHN 'DOC' HOLLIDAY 1851-1887

John 'Doc' Holliday was unusual amongst the gunfighters, good and bad, in that he came from a well-to-do background. He was born in Griffin, Georgia to Henry Burroughs Holliday and Alice Jane Holliday, and was their eldest surviving child. Henry Burroughs Holliday was a Confederate Major in the Civil War, and was later elected Major of Valdosa, Georgia. But misfortune came quickly, John was intensely close to his mother, but she died in 1866. To compound his loss, his father remarried within an indecently hasty three months.

Soon after he gained his degree qualifying him as a Doctor in Dental Surgery from the Pennsylvania College of Dental Surgery in Philadelphia, a second blow fell. He was diagnosed with tuberculosis. Effectively, he spent the

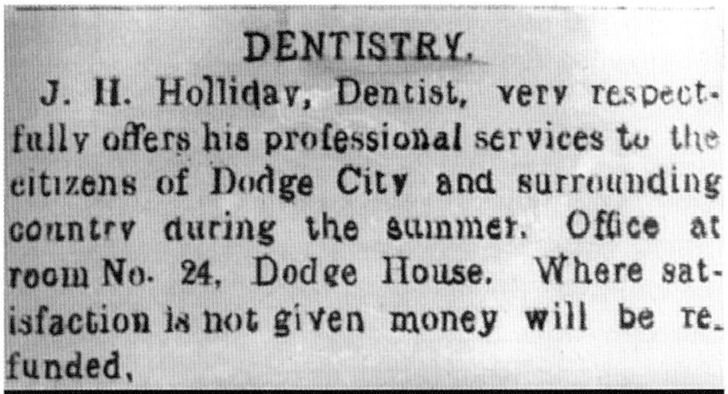

DENTISTRY.

J. H. Holliday, Dentist, very respectfully offers his professional services to the citizens of Dodge City and surrounding country during the summer. Office at room No. 24, Dodge House. Where satisfaction is not given money will be refunded.

Holliday began his professional life as a dentist, but when he discovered that he was terminally ill, he decided to follow a more glamorous career as a professional gambler and gunman.

balance of his life on borrowed time, and this may have accounted for the extremely cavalier way he led it.

He had begun to practice dentistry in various Western boomtowns, including Dodge City, but his illness necessitated a move west to hotter, drier climates. By now, he was too ill to follow his profession, so he headed west to Dallas, and like so many men of his type, he became a professional gambler. Fellow gunman Bat Masterson, and unequivocal good guy (also mentioned by L'Amour), later described Doc as being of a 'mean disposition and an ungovernable temper, and under the influence of liquor was a most dangerous man.' His unpleasant temper and vagabond lifestyle resulted in a corrosive cocktail of violence and murder. He went about armed with a gun in a shoulder holster, a gun on his hip and a long, wicked knife. His long list of killings started with the murder of a local gambler in Dallas, and a pattern of 'kill and run' established itself so that Doc never felt safe in any one place for too long. The most foolish murder he committed was that of a soldier from Fort Richardson, which brought him to the attention of the US Government. Doc escaped, but now had a price on his head, and was wanted by the law. He moved to Denver, remaining almost anonymous until he slashed a gambler, Bud Ryan, and almost killed him. At this time, he also became involved with the only woman that came into his life, 'Big nose' Kate. 'Big nose' was a madam and prostitute who worked in these professions by choice. She was also one of the most famous of the gunwomen of the West, and an excellent shot. Although she and Doc attempted to live together

'Doc' Holliday and his lady love, 'Big nose' Kate turned up in many Western boom towns, including Dodge City, Tucson, and Tombstone. He died young, ravaged by alcohol and tuberculosis.

respectably, the bright saloon lights were her natural habitat, and she returned to them time after time. Their relationship lasted, on and off, for many years, but was always volatile. On one occasion, 'Big nose' sprang Doc from jail in Fort Griffin, but when their relationship soured, she just as quickly turned him in.

The pattern of Doc's life was now set. Effectively, he was a professional killer. He rode with Wyatt Earp for some time, adding to his murder tally. In fact, one of his few redeeming features was his deep sense of loyalty to his friends, and to Earp in particular. Earp described him as a 'most skilful gambler, and the nerviest, fastest, deadliest man with a six-gun I ever saw.' But although Wyatt valued Holliday, he was also embarrassed by his behavior.

Although Doc claimed he had escaped nine attempts on his life – five ambushes and four hangings – he finally died in bed in Glenwood Springs, Colorado. His failing health had led him to this health resort, to try the sulphur spring water. He was just thirty-six years old, but contemporary accounts described his body as being so ravaged by drink and illness that he looked like a man of eighty. He took to his bed for 57 days, and was delirious for fourteen of them. Considering his style of life, this was a very strange way for him to die. His final words referred to this: 'This is funny,' he said.

THE DALTON GANG

Lewis and Adeline Dalton had a large family of fifteen children: ten boys and five girls. Most were born in Cass County, Michigan, where Lewis owned a saloon, but the family later settled on a farm outside of Coffeyville, Kansas. With no hint of what was to come, the eldest son, Frank, became a Deputy US Marshal, working in the dangerous Indian Territory. His younger brothers revered him, and the whole family were devastated when he was cruelly murdered. His younger brothers, Emmett, Grat, and Bob followed him into the service, but were soon disillusioned. Emmett described the work that was expected of them, 'Grafting as we of today know the term was a mild, soothing description of what occurred.' There was also some disagreement over unpaid expenses, and the brothers quit. They subsequently became involved in a little cattle rustling, and became outlaws, working on the wrong side of the law. This is a pattern that L'Amour often describes. The penalties for minor wrongdoing were so draconian that there was no way back for the perpetrators, and they were almost obliged to lead a life of crime. This is what happened to the Daltons.

They began a brief but flamboyant career of robberies and holdups, ultimately planning to break all records by pulling-off a double bank hoist in their hometown of Coffeyville. This was their first mistake. They rode into town, armed with pearl handled Colt .45s, disguised as a US Marshal and his posse. But the Dalton brothers were almost instantly recognized by a passerby, who alerted the marshal and townsfolk.

They had planned to rob the First National in the first place, and then go on to the Condon Bank. The first raid went off successfully, but as they left the Condon Bank, they were met by a hail of bullets from a group of armed citizens led by Marshal Charles T. Connelly. A massive gun battle ensued, in which Connelly and three townspeople were killed. After Connelly's demise, liveryman John J. Kloeher took over the attack and four members of the Dalton gang fell, shot in what is now known as Death Alley: Bob and Grat Dalton, Bill Powers and Dick Broadwell. Emmett was very seriously wounded but miraculously survived. The bodies of the dead gang members were treated with scant regards, photographed like trophies, and publicly displayed. For years, they lay in a grave unmarked, except for a rusty piece of iron pipe to which the gang had tethered their horses. Emmett erected a headstone some years later. He himself served fourteen years in the Kansas State Penitentiary, and went on to lead a blameless life upon his release. He was employed as a consultant on the 1909 film of the Dalton gang's last stand, and wrote several books condemning criminality. He died in 1937.

ABOVE: The ignominious end of the Dalton Gang. The corpses of Grat and Bob Dalton, Bill Powers, and Dick Broadwell, laid out like trophies outside the Coffeyville jail on October 5, 1892. They are handcuffed, even in death.

LEFT: The Condon Bank at Coffeyville, from a contemporary photograph. This was the second target (the first being the First National Bank) of the Dalton gang's raid on their hometown, which went so disastrously awry.

ROBERT CLAY ALLISON 'THE SHOOTIST' 1840-1887

Robert Clay Allison became increasingly deranged and was subject to violent mood swings and bizarre behavior. Here he is shown with his leg in plaster, having discharged his own gun before he drew. He died in a most unfortunate manner, being run over by his own wagon.

Robert Clay Allison was no gentleman gunfighter. He was a moody and vicious man who bred fear in all who knew him. He was born in Tennessee, and joined the Confederate Army at the beginning of the Civil War. But he was soon discharged due to 'personality problems.' His discharge papers described him as 'incapable of performing the duties of a soldier because of a blow received many years ago. Emotional of physical excitement produces paroxysmals [sic.] of a mixed character, partly epileptic and partly maniacal.' Clay worked as a cattle hand after leaving the army, and moved to the Texan Brazos River Territory in 1865. He worked as a trail hand, driving cattle to New Mexico. Things obviously went well for him, as by 1870, he had acquired his own ranch in Colfax County, New Mexico. But local newspapers were already reporting that he had despatched as many as fifteen men, and he had a grim reputation for violence, especially when he was drunk.

His first truly notorious, and grotesque, killing happened in late 1870. Allison was drinking in a saloon when a hysterical woman approached him. She told him that her husband had gone mad and killed a number of his own ranch hands at their cabin, together with their own infant daughter. Allison rounded up a posse, but they found no bodies at the ranch. However, a few days later, bones were discovered on the property, and the ranch owner was arrested and imprisoned. Enraged by the man's behavior, Allison broke him out of jail, lynched him, and cut off his head, riding twenty-nine miles to Cimmaron with this gruesome trophy on a pole, before displaying the head in a local saloon. This kind of behavior did nothing to endear people to Allison, who was clearly mad. His presence also attracted other killers who wanted to enhance their own reputations by adding him to their list of kills. Chunk Colbert coolly invited Allison out to dinner before trying to shoot him under the table. Fortunately, Allison beat him to it, just as coffee was served. When he was asked why he had accepted a dinner invitation from a man he knew was out to kill him, Allison responded that he 'didn't want to send a man to hell on an empty stomach.'

His behavior became increasingly deranged. When a dental appointment to cure a raging toothache went awry, and the unfortunate dentist began to drill the wrong tooth, Allison furiously bundled him into his own chair and ripped off half the man's lip in trying to extract one of the dentist's own teeth.

Another event that demonstrates Allison's bizarre view of the world is the Bowie knife grave affair. He had fallen into dispute with a neighboring rancher, and suggested that they should settle their differences by digging a grave big enough to hold them both. They should then climb into the pit, each armed only with a Bowie knife, and see which one of them survived to climb out. The victor would arrange a tombstone for the vanquished. But events overtook Allison, and this encounter never took place. Driving supplies back from Pecos, Texas, he fell from the wagon, and one of the wheels ran over his neck, killing him instantly.

This rather ignominious end was unusual for a 'shootist' at this time. Men of this ilk generally expired in a hail of bullets, or dancing at the end of a rope.

JAMES BUTLER 'WILD BILL' HICKOK 1837-1876

To this day, the reputation of Wild Bill Hickok epitomizes that of the gun fighting lawman; he was a 'genuine lover of law and order,' as well as a great showman and latter day duellist.

Hickok was born in Troy Grove, Illinois in 1837. He moved to Kansas in 1855, and was the town constable before reaching the age of 21. His career almost ended before it began when he inadvertently shot an unarmed man in his first killing. He was a contract scout, spy, and detective for the Union Army in the Civil War, and won the epithet 'Wild Bill' during this time. His reputation grew, and in 1871, the citizens of Abilene finally asked him to be their town marshal. Most of his predecessors in the job now lay in Boot Hill cemetery. They included the previous incumbent, pacifist Marshal Tom 'Bear River' Smith, who had been murdered by an axe-wielding homesteader. Not unreasonably, the weary citizens felt that a 'noted' and feared individual would stand a better chance of keeping the peace, particularly during the annual spring cattle drives. These generally resulted in the town being completely torn up by lawless cowboys. In fact, Hickok's reputation wasn't entirely deserved. He was a tremendous self-publicist who actively propagated the fiction that he had killed over a hundred white men – his tally was actually closer to ten. He had worked as a scout during the Civil and Indian Wars, and had been elected sheriff of Hays County in 1869, but it was his reputation for dealing with frontier desperados that attracted Abilene. Once installed as town Marshal, he proceeded to clean up the town, running Abilene from a card table in the Long Branch Saloon, and earning a massive $150 a month for his services. One cowboy described him as looking like a 'mad old bull' and he made every attempt to look as intimidating as possible. L'Amour describes his habitual costume 'black frock coat, a low-brimmed black hat, and two ivory-butted and silver-mounted pistols thrust behind a red silk sash.' In fact, the pistol handles were worn reversed to speed his draw. Hickok's larger-than-life presence kept a lid on much of the town violence.

He was also surprisingly successful in bringing gun control to the town, disarming even reluctant Texans. He posted a notice that disarmament would be vigorously

Hickok's predecessor as town marshal, Tom 'Bear River' Smith was killed by an axe-wielding homesteader, and now resided in Boot Hill cemetery.

enforced, and the Abilene Chronicle reported this. Their editorial comment ran: 'There's no bravery in a carrying revolvers in a civilized community. Such a practice is well enough and perhaps necessary when among Indians or other barbarians, but among white people it ought to be discountenanced.' Hickok's poster is reminiscent of Matt Coburn's 'NOTICE' in Confusion,

'To Thieves, Murderers,
and Short-card Artists
You are no longer welcome
in Confusion.
Those listed below can get out
or shoot it out,
And start any time they are ready.'

As Marshal, Hickok was also responsible for street cleaning, and kept the town roads clear of dead dogs and horses. He was also paid 50 cents for every stray dog he shot. On one occasion, he was called upon to despatch a mad Texas longhorn that was rampaging through the town. Hickok greatly enjoyed his time in Abilene, rooming with a succession of prostitutes, gambling, and drinking heavily. The famous painter, N.C. Wyeth painted a wonderfully atmospheric portrait of a dandified Hickok unmasking a card cheat in typical form. But his tenure in the cow town came to a disastrous end, when his deputy, Mike Williams, was killed in cross fire during a gunfight between Hickok and gambler Phil Coe. Hickok was devastated by Williams's death, weeping copiously as he laid his body on a snooker table in the Saloon. He paid for the deputy's funeral. After eight months of Hickok's 'cleanup,' Abilene town council decided not to renew his expensive contract, and banned the cattle drives instead.

Jobless, Hickok drifted East, touring in a melodrama staged by Buffalo Bill, 'The Scouts of the Plains.' But he was hopeless in his starring role. By this time, he was an unsteady drunk, and had a surprisingly high, girlish voice. He also threatened to shoot the stagehands. Broke, he

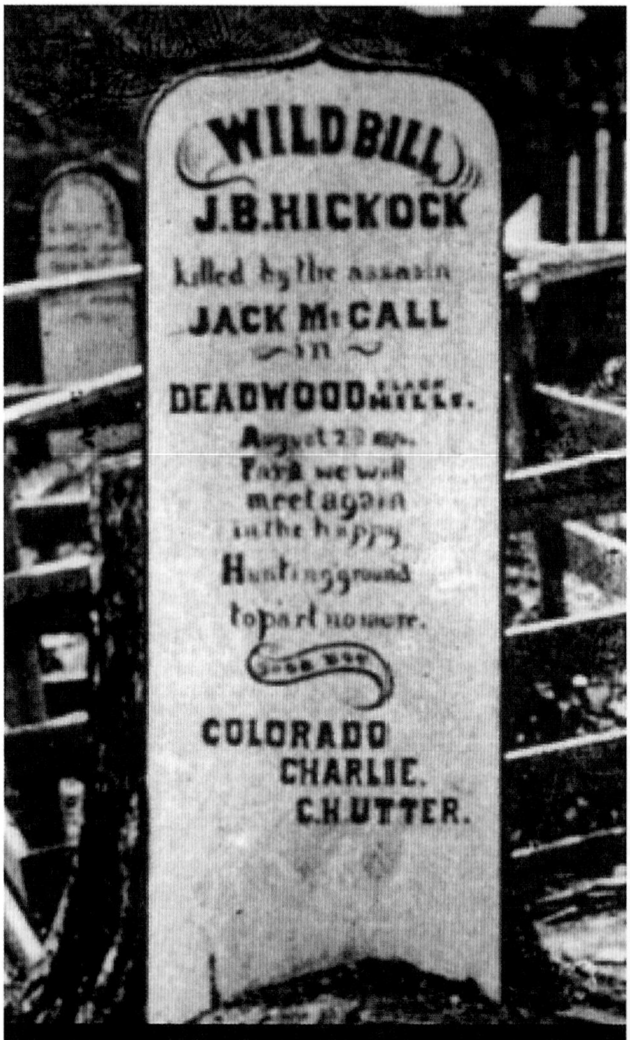

Jack McCall murdered the half-blind Bill Hickok on August 2, 1876, to general public revulsion. Hickok's tombstone bears Charley Utter's moving epitaph, together with his incorrectly spelled name.

Wild Bill was known for his dandified appearance.

drifted to Deadwood, trying to disguise his failing eyesight. A gold mining venture failed, so he returned to his old profession at the poker tables. In fact, he had owned a couple of gambling joints at one time or other, in Junction City and Hays City. This was how he met his end, shot in the back by the cowardly Jack McCall, who wanted a share of Hickok's reputation. As he fell, his hand of cards scattered on the table—the ace of spaces, ace of clubs, eight of clubs, eight of spades and queen or jack of diamonds—this is known to this day as the 'Dead man's hand.'

His contemporary obituary in the in the Cheyenne Daily Leader was scathing. It implied that he was an obsolete figure from the 'lawless times' of the past, and that he had degenerated into a 'tame and worthless loafer,' his constitution ruined by 'wine and women.' But his Deadwood grave is visited to this day, and his legend is undiminished. Any gunman would have done well to listen to his professional advice, given in an interview of 1865, 'Take time. I've known many a feller slip up for shootin' in a hurry.' He maintained that he valued accuracy rather than speed, but then he was one of the fastest draws ever known in the West.

JESSE WOODSON JAMES 1847-1882

Jesse was born in Clay County, Missouri, a younger brother by four years to Frank James, whom he came to dominate throughout his life. Jesse fought, notionally, on the Confederate side during the Civil War, but was actually embroiled in a parallel guerrilla campaign. This mostly involved raiding, stealing, and murdering civilians, although his commander noted that he was the 'keenest…fighter in the command.' This period in Jesse's life formed his outlook for life. His father, Robert James (a Baptist minister), had been murdered by Kansas raiders; and his formidable mother, Zerelda James Samuel, was imprisoned for spying against the Union. He himself had been badly wounded in a shootout with a party of Union cavalry. This all led to an enduring hatred of everything that reminded him of the 'oppressive' North, including banks and trains. When he returned home from the War, Jesse formed a family gang of outlaws, together with his brother Frank and four younger half-brothers.

At first, as they confined their attacks to the aforementioned banks and trains, the James gang had some public support, despite the fact that they often killed innocent bystanders during their raids, including a schoolboy in Liberty. John Newman Edwards, the famous Missouri editor, referred to Jesse as 'America's Robin Hood' who had a 'chivalry of crime.' In fact, perhaps James's most enduring claim to fame is that he and his gang invented the bank robbery and staged the first large-scale train hold-up in the country's history. James played along with his press image, handing a press release to the conductor of a train the gang had just raided. It helpfully described their attack as the 'Most Daring Robbery on Record,' and he considerately left blanks for the newspapers to fill in with the value of their spoils. Finally, the banks grew tired of the gang's activities, and brought in the Pinkerton Detective

'I am tired of this life of taut nerves, of night-riding, and day-hiding…tired of seeing Judas on the face of every friend I know.'

Agency. Despite their motto, 'We Never Sleep,' the gang successfully gunned down several agents who tried to infiltrate their home territory. Frustration finally led the Pinks to mount a grenade attack on the James' family home in 1875. This backfired disastrously. Frank and Jesse's nine-year-old half brother was killed, and their mother's arm was so badly shattered that it had to be amputated. The Agency was roundly condemned for this barbaric behavior, and the James gang were very nearly awarded an amnesty.

The gang continued their spree of thieving and murder until the tables were finally turned on them in 1876. They attempted to hold up the First National Bank in Northfield Minnesota, but the bank staff and several townspeople retaliated, and a massive gun battle ensued. Three members of the gang were gunned down, and three of the James brothers were captured. Frank and Jesse escaped, but Missouri Governor Thomas Crittenden offered rewards of $10,000 (reputedly on the advice of Allan Pinkerton) for turning in either Jesse or Frank. Pressure tightened on the brothers, and the threat of betrayal hung around their necks like a millstone. Jesse hardly ever took off his guns, and never turned his back to a door or window if he could help it.

This early photograph of Jesse James makes him look fresh-faced and innocent, but his gang initiated an unrivaled sixteen-year spree of murder and theft, and invented the bank robbery and train hold-up. Despite his paranoid precautions, two members of his own gang ultimately betrayed him.

Ultimately, the reward led to Jesse's betrayal. Gang members Robert and Charley Ford gunned him down in his own St. Joseph home. He had very unwisely put down his gun, just for a moment, to adjust a crooked picture. But the Fords were forced to share the reward with several officials, including Crittenden, and were shunned and ridiculed as back-shooting cowards. Charley couldn't stand this treatment, and committed suicide. Robert was condemned to the even worse fate of reenacting the shooting every night in a stage show, where he was often booed off stage. He was finally shot to death in a tent saloon in Creede, Colorado.

ABOVE: **The James gang held up and robbed any number of trains during their career, and even left press releases to publicize their wrongdoings.**

BELOW: **Jesse James was one of the West's most wanted men, and could not afford to put his gun down.**

His ruthless campaign of murder and pillage, which had lasted for sixteen years, was finally over. Jesse's death concluded one of the most serious crime waves ever to hit the West.

Jesse's rather bizarre and fiercely protective mother insisted that he was buried in the yard of the family home, where she charged visitors 25 cents to see his tombstone, which read:

Jesse W. James
Died 3 April 1882
Aged 34 years, 6 months, 28 days
Murdered by a traitor and a coward
whose name is not worthy
to appear here.

Frank James couldn't take any more of the claustrophobic outlaw life, so accurately described by Louis L'Amour, without his brother to boss him around. He turned himself in, saying 'I am tired of this life of taut nerves, of night-riding, and day-hiding...tired of seeing Judas on the face of every friend I know.' N.C. Wyeth brought this paranoiac tension to life in his portrait of the James gang in hiding: tension is etched into each face; each man nervously holds his gun. A strangely sympathetic Missouri jury refused to convict Frank, and he gave up his life of crime, spending the

It was on Saturday night, Jesse was at home
Talking to his family brave
Robert Ford came along like a thief in the night
And laid poor Jesse in his grave.

It was Robert Ford, that dirty little coward
I wonder how he does feel
For he ate of Jesse's bread and he slept in Jesse's bed
Then laid poor Jesse in his grave.

rest of his life in various humdrum jobs.

Even during their lifetime, the James gang were the subject of many dime novels, and their personality cult really took off after Jesse's death. There were many post mortem sightings of him, just as there would be for Elvis in the twentieth century. But his death also signalled the fact that the 'era of the badman' was drawing to a close. Better methods of law enforcement meant that outlaws felt more and more exposed and were forced to hide in more and more remote regions to escape detection.

HENRY McCARTHY ANTRIM ALIAS 'BILLY THE KID' 1859-1881

Billy The Kid, the teenage outlaw, was one of the most colorful figures of the Old West. He was a controversial figure in life and in death. He is considered by some observers to be a cold-blooded, psychopathic killer, while others see him as boy who 'loved his mother devotedly' and was led on by adults to a life of criminality. But in both versions of his life story, he is credited with at least six killings, though his ballad states, 'He'd a notch on his pistol for twenty-one men.'

Billy was born on New York's east side in November 1859. His father died when he and his brother Joseph were very young, and his mother, Catherine, died in 1874, just a year after remarrying. By this time, the family were in Silver City, New Mexico, where they had gone to seek a cure for their mother's tuberculosis. Billy's stepfather didn't want the two boys, so he put them into foster homes where The Kid washed dishes to earn his keep.

Billy's juvenile life of crime started at this time, when he stole some butter from a rancher, and went on to steal laundry. Unfortunately, being locked up for this minor misdemeanor scared him so much that he decided to escape —up the chimney. For the next couple of years, he tramped around working as a ranch hand and gambler, trying to avoid brushes with the law. But everything went down-hill rapidly after he shot killed a bully who was teasing him. Now unable to get honest work, he reluctantly joined a gang of rustlers known as 'The Boys.'

Involvement with these criminals ultimately led to him changing sides, and getting legitimate work with English rancher John Tunstall. At this point, The Kid staged a kind of bizarre 'rebirth,' by assuming a new alias, William H. Bonney. Many believe that Billy looked upon his employer, as the father he had never had, and that he was a reformed character. Unfortunately, Tunstall was murdered, and his killing sparked the Lincoln County War. When this violent feud finally wound up, The Kid's involvement on the side of the Regulators (who had been responsible for at least two murders) led to a life outside the law again. He was once more unable to find lawful employment, so he drifted about, gambling and cattle rustling. Knowing that the new Governor of the territory, Lew Wallace, wanted to re-establish order in Lincoln, The Kid turned himself in, offering to turn states evidence against other participants in the hostilities, an offer which was accepted by Governor Wallace. But when he realized that the court was loaded against him, Billy decided to escape once more.

I'll sing you a true song of Billy the Kid
I'll sing of the desperate deeds that he did
Way out in New Mexico long, long ago
When a man's only chance was
his own forty four.

When Billy the Kid was a very young lad
In the old Silver City he went to the bad
Way out in the West with a gun
in his hand
At the age of twelve years he first
killed his man

Now this is how Billy the Kid met his fate
The bright moon was shining,
the hour was late
Shot down by Pat Garrett,
who once was his friend,
The young outlaw's life had now
come to its end.

By now, he was a celebrity, and his activities were widely reported in the newspapers, who coined the soubriquet 'Billy The Kid.' The Kid was reputedly fed up with having every murder in the West attributed to him, but admitted that 'I don't know, as anyone would believe anything good of me.' He managed to avoid capture for two years, but when he was framed for the murder of deputy James Carlyle, Pat Garrett was charged with bringing him in. Garrett finally caught up with The Kid on December 23, 1880, in a cabin in Stinking Springs. After a brief standoff, Billy surrendered. He was charged and sentenced for the murder of Sheriff Brady during the Lincoln County War, and was taken back to Lincoln to await his hanging. The Kid was fully aware that there could now be no reprieve so he made his final escape, killing guard J.W. Bell and taking time out to gun down Robert Olinger, who had bated him during his prison stay, with his own shotgun. The Kid reckoned that he wouldn't have shot Bell, except for the fact that he tried to run, but offered no apology for Olinger's dispatch.

Public opinion now swung against the Kid, and Pat Garrett was charged, once again, with bringing him to justice. It took him three months to catch up with Billy in Fort Summer. At the very moment that Garrett was pumping boarding house owner Pete Maxwell for intelligence about the Kid's movements, Billy walked in to get a steak for dinner. Garrett felled the youngster with two bullets from his .45 caliber, single-action Colt, one of which lodged in his heart. The Kid spoke fluent Spanish, and his rather pathetic final words were 'Quien es? Quien es?'—'Who is it?' 'Who is it?'

Fair Mexican maidens play guitars
and sing
A song about Billy, their boy
bandit king

Billy the Kid looks slightly simple in this contemporary photograph, but must have had a certain charisma to generate such a massive personality cult.

Billy's brief but colorful career as a gunman and outlaw was over. He was reputed to have gambled with Doc Holliday, dined with Jesse James, and gone target shooting with Bat Masterson. But his advice to those that would follow in his footsteps was, 'Advise persons never to engage in killing.' Many of his friends and acquaintances mourned his passing very sincerely, praising his sense of humor, loyalty to his friends, extreme bravery, and kindness to his horses. He looks a little simple in his portrait, but others spoke of his intelligence and cunning. Many also spoke derisively of Pat Garrett's self-interest. He gained the office of sheriff of Lincoln County for his work in killing The Kid, and wrote the best-selling biography, *The Authentic Life of Billy the Kid: The Noted Desperado of the Southwest.*

Billy was certainly no 'good bad man.' By the time of his death, he was pretty bad through and through, and many believed he was a cold-hearted murderer. But the teenage outlaw of the Southwest has left probably the biggest legend of any gun-slinging wrongdoer of the West, fueling a huge tourist industry in New Mexico.

COLT FRONTIER 1878

Louis L'Amour liked to interject interesting guns into his plots. When we meet the mysterious stranger, Jonas, in opening chapter of *The Man Called Noon*, J.B. Rimes tosses him a gun, 'The gun was new, a Frontier model, and the weight of it on his hip was comforting.' Jonas appears to be suffering from memory loss caused by a bullet wound to the head. But Rimes can tell that he is used to bearing a weapon from the deft way that he catches the gun, checks it, and holsters it instinctively. This is the modus operandi of a gunfighter.

The 'Frontier model' in question is a Colt Frontier or Double Action Army Revolver. The company launched the model in 1878. Caliber was .44-40, with the barrel available in various lengths. Shorter barrels were more easily concealed and therefore of interest to plainclothes lawmen

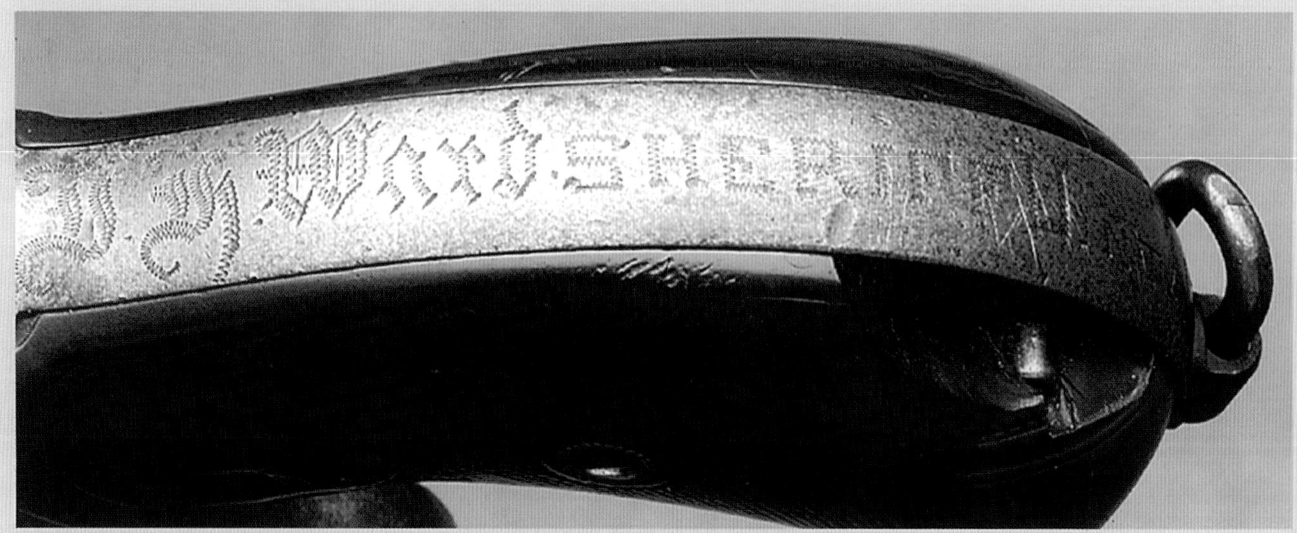

SPECIFICATIONS	
CALIBER: 0.44-40	GRIPS: Hard Rubber
LENGTH OF BARREL: 4 inches	ACTION: Double
BARREL SHAPE: Round	YEAR OF MANUFACTURE: 1878
FINISH: Blue/gray mixed with surface rust	MANUFACTURER: Colt

LEFT: The design of the Frontier really set the pace for Colt revolvers for the next 100 years.

BELOW LEFT: The owners name, J. H. Ward, is emblazoned on the backstrap. Ward was the Sheriff of Vinta, Colorado.

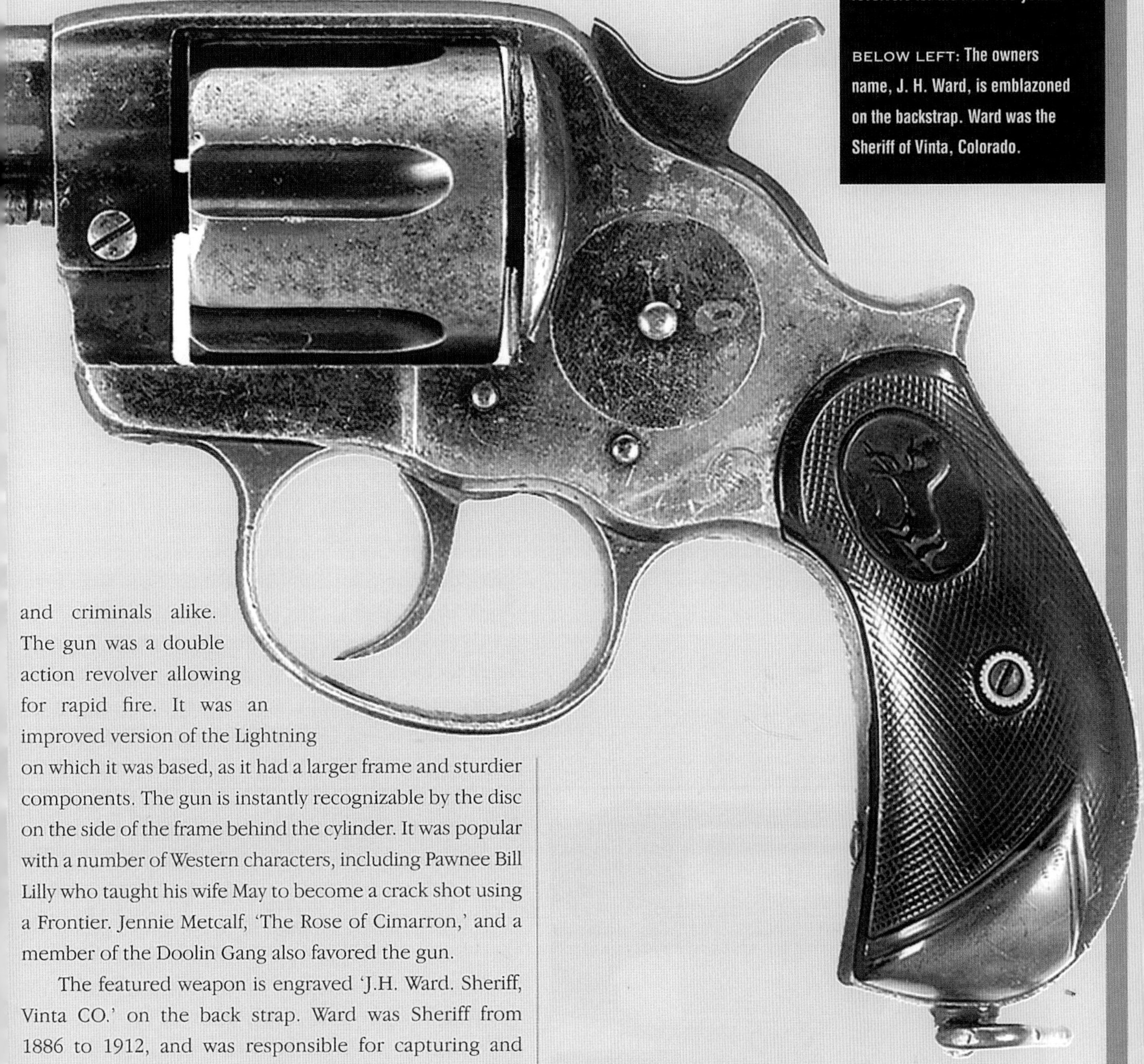

and criminals alike. The gun was a double action revolver allowing for rapid fire. It was an improved version of the Lightning on which it was based, as it had a larger frame and sturdier components. The gun is instantly recognizable by the disc on the side of the frame behind the cylinder. It was popular with a number of Western characters, including Pawnee Bill Lilly who taught his wife May to become a crack shot using a Frontier. Jennie Metcalf, 'The Rose of Cimarron,' and a member of the Doolin Gang also favored the gun.

The featured weapon is engraved 'J.H. Ward. Sheriff, Vinta CO.' on the back strap. Ward was Sheriff from 1886 to 1912, and was responsible for capturing and bringing in Butch Cassidy. Significantly, he was also a party to Cassidy's parole.

REMINGTON 1863 NEW MODEL ARMY REVOLVER

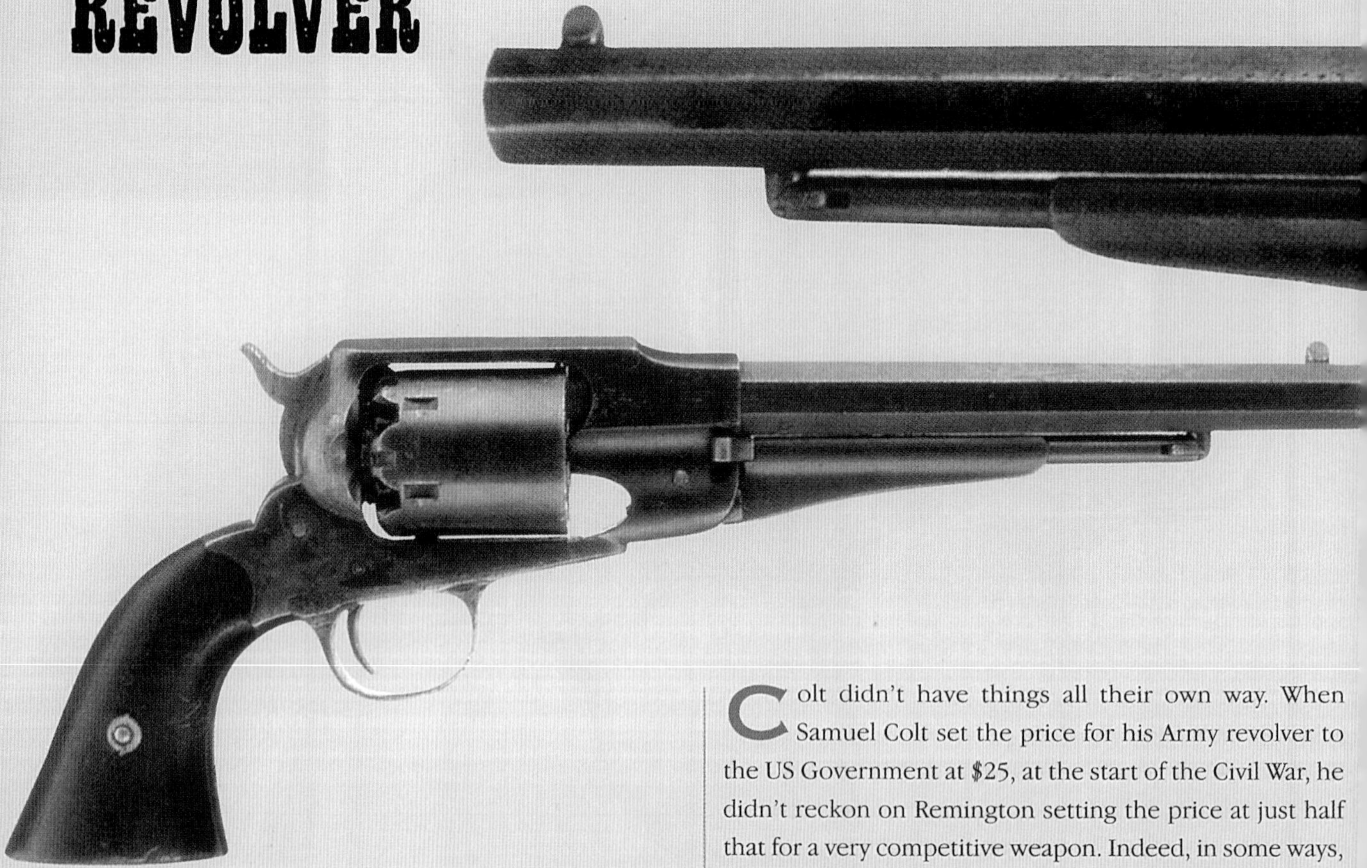

Detail of the finely machined cylinder and hammer, both of which display a good amount of the original blue steel finish.

Colt didn't have things all their own way. When Samuel Colt set the price for his Army revolver to the US Government at $25, at the start of the Civil War, he didn't reckon on Remington setting the price at just half that for a very competitive weapon. Indeed, in some ways, the Remington New Model scored over the Colt. It had a solid frame making for a more rigid barrel and cylinder under fire. The pistol was based upon a design by Fordyce Beals and was introduced to the market in 1861. It matched the Colt at a caliber of .44 (designed to suit the Union army), and was a weapon highly valued by soldiers and civilians alike. It was a similar model to the Navy, which was a .36 caliber weapon; 122,000 examples of the Remington Army revolver were delivered from the company's plants at Ilion and Utica between 1861 and 1875, making it second only to the Colt in popularity. This meant that were many examples still in use on the frontier when the Civil War was over.

George Maddox, 'a cold-blooded killer' and member

LEFT: The Remington New Model Army Revolver was a major competitor to Colt as the Civil War approached. Its shape, while less elegant than Colt's Army, demonstrated many of the same specifications and proved to be a reliable weapon in action.

BELOW LEFT: The Remington revolver had a solid frame, which gave the gun good rigidity when firing.

of the Quantrill gang, was famously photographed with a loaded pair of .44 Army revolvers. These were clearly his weapons of choice! But somehow, this gun never found its way into the legend of the West in the way that the Colt did, despite its good points. Many of Louis L'Amour's characters carry unspecified 'pistols' and it is under this heading that the Remington must fall. probably remain.

SPECIFICATIONS

CALIBER: 0.44	ACTION: Single
LENGTH OF BARREL: 8 inches	YEAR OF MANUFACTURE: 1863
BARREL SHAPE: Octagonal	MANUFACTURER: Remington Arms Company, Ilion, New York
FINISH: Blue	
GRIPS: Walnut	

THE MORMONS

Louis L'Amour quite often refers to Mormons in his stories. Like so many other Westerners, they made the trek West for the sake of freedom, and in their case, to escape religious persecution. The first group of 'Saints' had crossed the Mississippi River in February 1846, on the first stage of the 'exodus' West. Brigham Young, who had read Fremont's description of the Valley of the Great Salt Lake, inspired their 1,400-mile long trek, and its destination. This trek would dominate the Church's history for the rest of the century. At first, the Mormons used covered wagons, then handcarts when their dray animals froze to death. But the journey to their final settlement in Utah was long and extremely hazardous and many pioneers died en route—seven hundred in the first year alone. Once they reached their 'New Zion' in Utah, the Mormons imposed their civic order on the wild landscape in a very Eastern style, with wide streets and substantial buildings in stone, brick, and wood. They also established other Mormon colonies throughout a substantial swathe of the West, in Utah, Arizona, Nevada, and Idaho.

Many American literary figures have held a low

The first waves of Mormon pioneers entering the Great Salt Lake Valley.

A romantic depiction of the Mormon 'Saints' crossing the Mississippi around 1846, on the first stage of their journey West.

Many Mormons perished on their way west, in the harsh winter of 1856.

opinion of Mormons. Mark Twain openly despised them (though he was forced to describe Salt Lake City as having 'a general air of neatness, repair, thrift and comfort'), and early Western writer Zane Grey often used them as his 'villains.'

But Louis L'Amour demonstrates a far higher regard for the sect, and so do his characters. Utah Blaine advises Mary Blake to take refuge in the nearby Mormon settlement, obviously believing them to be decent and reliable. Borden Chantry reinforces this view. When he

A typical Mormon wagon train crossing the prairie.

and Tyrel Sackett wonder if Mormons could be involved in the recent spate of hold-ups (strangely, Utah has been spared), he discounts the theory, saying, 'Most Mormons I've known were law-abiding folks.' Indeed, they are far more likely to be the victims of crime. Some of Ben Curry's gang have to be restrained from raiding their well-stocked farms.

Indeed, Mormons made a good living from helping other Westerners on their way, especially the forty-niners. For some L'Amour characters, such as Mike Bastian, Salt Lake City is their only taste of civilization. Bastian also expresses admiration of their excellent tracking abilities. Mountain man Linus Rawlings has also visited 'Deseret,' saying that the Salt Lake was the most water he has ever seen.

The Mormons established way stations, such as Cove Fort, to provide shelter for early pioneers heading West.

An early view of Salt Lake City.

WINCHESTER 1866 CARBINE

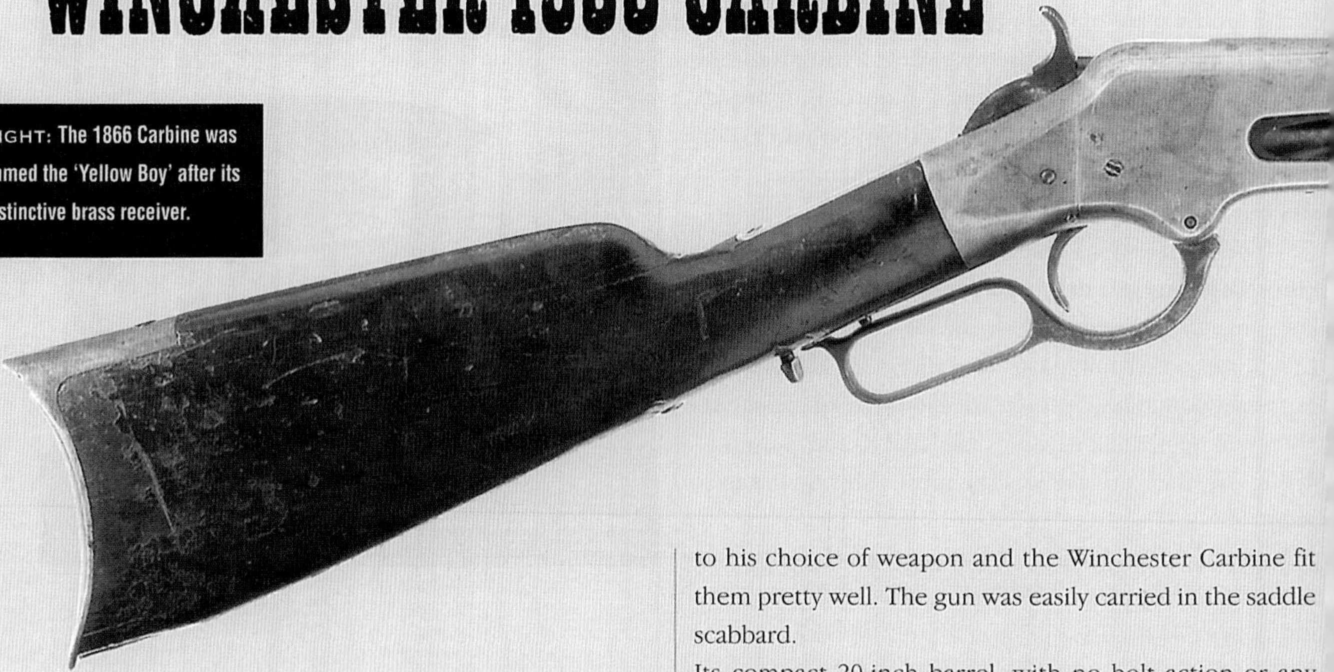

RIGHT: The 1866 Carbine was named the 'Yellow Boy' after its distinctive brass receiver.

Throughout the L'Amour novels we find ourselves in the company of cowpunchers. This tough and individualistic breed grew up to service the big herds that were driven north from Texas in the years after the Civil War. The cattle were originally raised to feed the growing population of the West. But after the War, the majority were transported East via a growing railroad network. A transcontinental route was completed in 1869, and a whole rail system was built in the following decade. A hungry East Coast market was waiting for Texan beef.

The Cowboy had very particular needs when it came to his choice of weapon and the Winchester Carbine fit them pretty well. The gun was easily carried in the saddle scabbard.

Its compact 20-inch barrel, with no bolt action or any other encumbrance, made it swift to draw and just as easy to stow. It featured a saddle ring on the left side of the frame for extra security and front and rear swivels for carrying on a sling. The polished brass frame and receiver gave its nickname 'Yellow Boy.'

The .44-inch rim fire cartridge had its limitations when it came to ultimate power, but this was more than compensated for by its accuracy and ease of use. With fourteen shots and a quick reload action you could put two bullets into your intended target in the time that it took to aim a higher-powered single shot rifle. This was tremendously useful for a wide range of targets—game along the trail, a sick maverick, a gang of rustlers or a hunting party of Indians.

Indians also aspired to Winchester ownership, as it put them one step ahead of their adversaries in the United States Cavalry. For the most part, cavalrymen were still using Civil War issue, single shot weapons. Indians acquired the weapons either by capturing them from settlers, or from unscrupulous white traders. Indian versions were customized with brass and nickel-plated

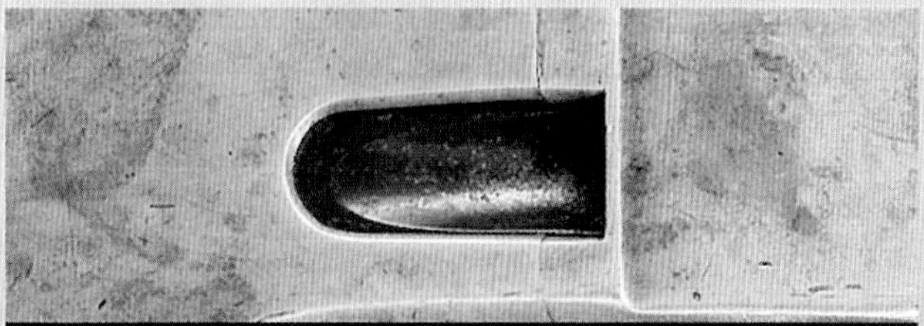

The familiar port in the side which received bullets. Normal loading was by thumbing the shells in.

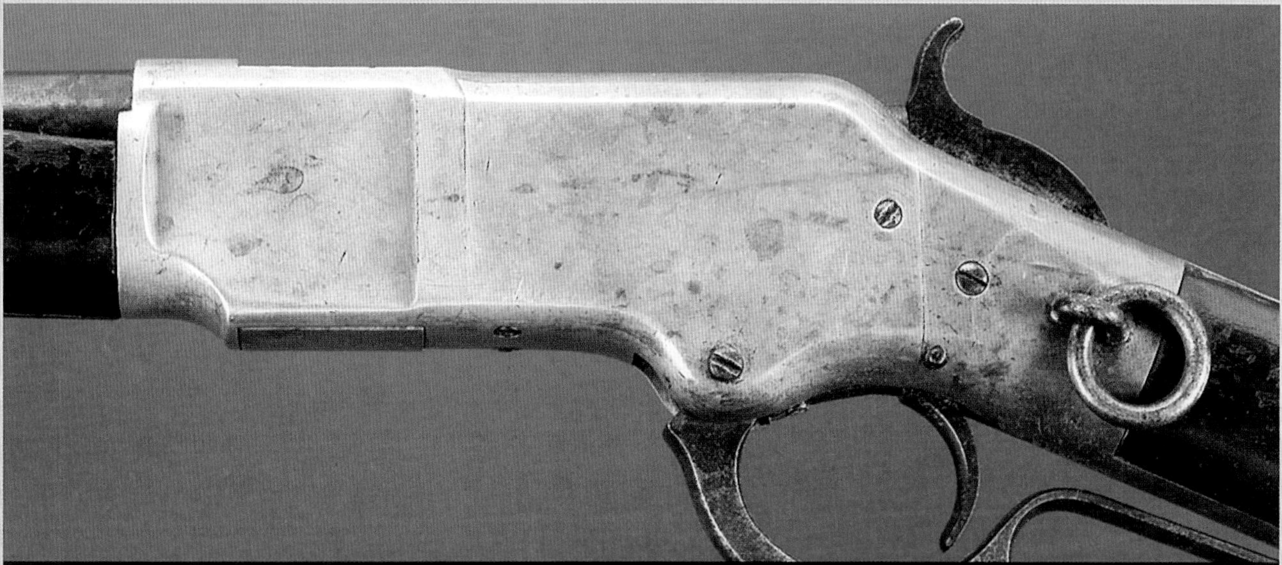

Left side view shows carbine ring. At $40, cowhands weren't about to lose this gun.

studs hammered in to the stock and fore grip, together with rawhide tassels and beadwork. Many examples have survived.

John Wayne also immortalized the weapon in the film *True Grit*. His version was modified with a loop under lever. In the film, Wayne demonstrates the technique of riding, firing, and reloading with one hand, and one eye! It is however debatable how many cowboys could afford this excellent gun because it was priced at a swingeing $40 – the exact monthly stipend of a 'forty-a-month cowhand.'

SPECIFICATIONS	
CALIBER: 0.44 rim fire cartridge	ACTION: Under lever repeating with 14 shot magazine
LENGTH OF BARREL: 20 inches	
BARREL SHAPE: Round	YEAR OF MANUFACTURE: 1866-91
FINISH: Blue Steel Barrel, brass frame and receiver	MANUFACTURER: Winchester Repeating Arms Company, New Haven, Connecticut
GRIPS: Walnut	

COWBOYS AND INDIANS

CHARLES GOODNIGHT 1836-1929

Oh, he would twirl that lariat and he didn't do it slow
He could catch them forefeet nine out of ten for any kind of dough
And when the herd stampeded he was always on the spot
And set them to milling, like the stirrings of a pot.

Nearly all L'Amour Western novels feature cowboys. He had a great respect for these men, and insisted that they were often intelligent romantics attracted to the perceived freedom of life on the Western trails. The term originally derived from the Spanish 'vaqueros,' and their equipment, clothing, and techniques of cattle management were greatly influenced by this connection.

A cowboy attempts to round up the cattle, mouth covered against the dust.

Charles Goodnight, the greatest Western cowboy of them all. His story influenced many Louis L'Amour characters.

ABOVE AND BELOW: A romantic evocation of the tough outdoor life of the cowboy.

Although L'Amour accurately portrays the hard lives of his 'forty-a-month-cowhand(s),' forced to work themselves 'half dead with tiredness,' he also credits them with a great deal of dignity, resourcefulness, and 'cow savvy.'

I've circled, herded, and night-herded too
But to keep you together is what I can't do
My horse is leg weary, and I'm awful tired
But if you get away I am sure to get fired
Bunch up, little doggies, bunch up.

L'Amour's father was involved in the cattle industry at one time, working as a state livestock inspector for the railroad in the family hometown, Jamestown. This was a hub of the Northern Pacific route. Louis and his brothers encountered many cowboys in this way, travelling West, back to their ranches in North Dakota, or travelling East

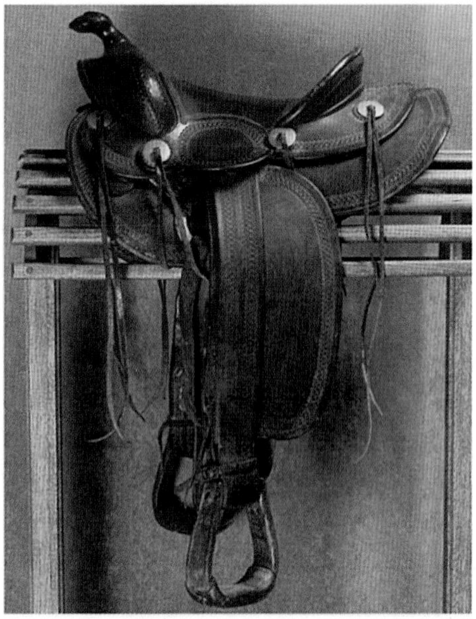

ABOVE AND LEFT: Fine Western Saddles. Top is a Powder River Saddle made by the Denver Dry Goods Company. The blankets are Mexican and Navajo. Bottom has tooled leather with four plated tie down conchos on both sides and matching girth rings.

with stockcars full of cattle.

The greatest Western cowboy of them all was undoubtedly Charles Goodnight, the pioneer cattle king, whose larger-than-life story inspired L'Amour's cowpoke heroes. Goodnight's real-life fame spread throughout the West and inspired hundreds of men to try their luck in cattle ranching.

Charles Goodnight was born in Illinois in 1836, but his father decided to trek his family West in 1846—The Year of Decision. The young Charles was obliged to ride bareback for seven hundred miles, as his family couldn't afford a saddle for him.

He and his stepbrother quickly grew up to become cowhands, and as they were paid in calves, soon built up a small herd of some 180 head of cattle. But the outbreak of the Civil War virtually wiped them out. Charles became a Texas Ranger in 1857, fighting and scouting for the Confederacy in the Texas Panhandle. Years later, he described his situation, and that of the entire Texas cattle industry, when the hostilities were over, 'I suffered great losses. The Confederate authorities had taken many of

Pair of tooled leather saddlebags. What few possessions the cowboy owned were consigned to them.

them (his cattle) without paying a cent. Indians had raided our herds and cattle thieves were branding them, to their own benefit without regard to our rights.' He joined in the Texas-wide roundup of stray cattle that became known as 'making the gather.'

Goodnight realized that he needed a business partner, and hitched up with Oliver Loving. Twenty-five years older than Charles, Loving was an experienced cattleman who had driven Texas longhorns all the way to Chicago.

Looking for a good business opportunity, the partners decided to drive their herd around the Comanche-infested Texas Panhandle to supply government agents in New Mexico. These agents were charged with feeding 8,000 reservation-bound Navajo, who were virtually starving for the lack of meat. It was 1866 when they set out on this very risky escapade. To avoid the threat of Indian attack, they took the longer, completely arid route

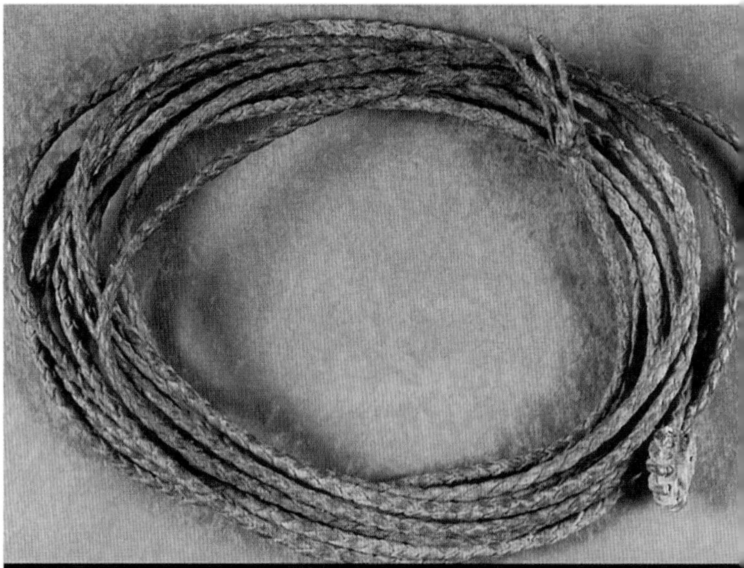

THIS PAGE: In the words of the song, 'Rope and brand 'em.' The special lariat (the word is derived from the Spanish 'la reata') and branding irons were tools of the cowboy trade.

through the 'the most desolate country.' Three hundred cattle died in the heat and a hundred more thirst-crazed beasts drowned in a stampede at the Pecos River when they finally got there. Goodnight and Loving sold half the surviving herd to the reservation agents, and then continued on into Colorado, selling the remaining animals in Denver. The whole escapade netted the partners the huge sum of $24,000.

Not only did the pair forge the Goodnight-Loving trail, which became one of the most heavily used in the Southwest, but Goodnight also invented and constructed the first chuck wagon, drawn by oxen. The wagon was equipped with a chuckbox, whose hinged lid dropped down to become a cook's worktable. Inside the box were various drawers and compartments that contained the staples of the trail diet—flour, beans,

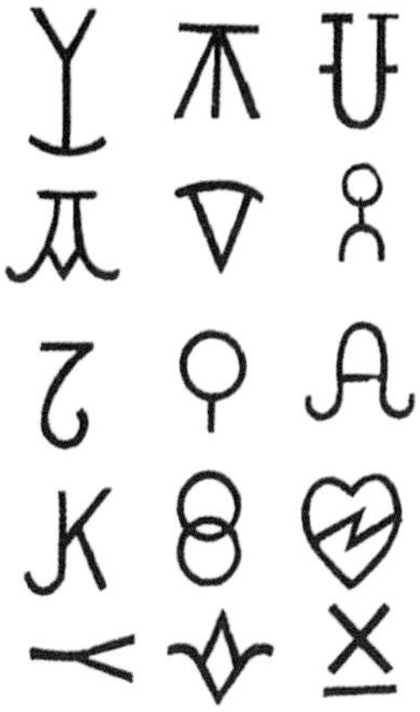

Goodnight's chuck wagon was the epicenter of life on the range.

ABOVE: **Vital equipment for the trail.**

BELOW: **Duster Wyman wears Levis in *Hanging Woman Creek*.**

coffee, pork, and canned tomatoes. The chuck wagon became the most critical piece of equipment used on the trail drives for decades, and a modern form remains in use on the larger ranches of today. L'Amour often refers to the chuck wagon—food (and especially hot coffee) was obviously hugely important to sustain the grindingly hard work of the trail. L'Amour's cowhands even describe themselves as 'riding the grub lines,' and Barney Pike remembers how he would 'crawl out of bed on a chilly morning…(and) stagger half blind to the chuck wagon.' Barney even suggests that Eddie should put his cooking skills to good use as a trail cook. In fact, these men were quite well paid. Good food was highly prized by the trail bosses, as it could stop cowboys defecting to other outfits.

Goodnight also worked to perfect a unique method of driving cattle. He put the trail boss out in front, the horse herd and chuck wagon behind him, followed in turn by the point riders and lead steers, with the bulk of the herd coming next, kept together by flank riders, with drag riders coming up the rear, preventing stragglers from falling behind.

Loving decided that the next step should be for him and Goodnight to win government beef contracts at Bosque Redondo. Unfortunately, the Comanche caught up with Loving on the open plain, wounding his wrist and side. Despite being rescued, gangrene set into the wounds, and Loving died as Goodnight reached his bedside. Goodnight described him a 'one of the coolest and bravest men I have ever known, but devoid of caution.' Grief-stricken, he constructed a special casket from discarded tin cans to carry the body of his friend back to Texas, to honor his dying wish.

L'Amour shows several examples of this close emotional bond between male 'partners' working the trails. Perhaps Barney Pike and Eddie Holt are his supreme example of this kind of relationship, which vastly increased the likelihood of survival for both men. They

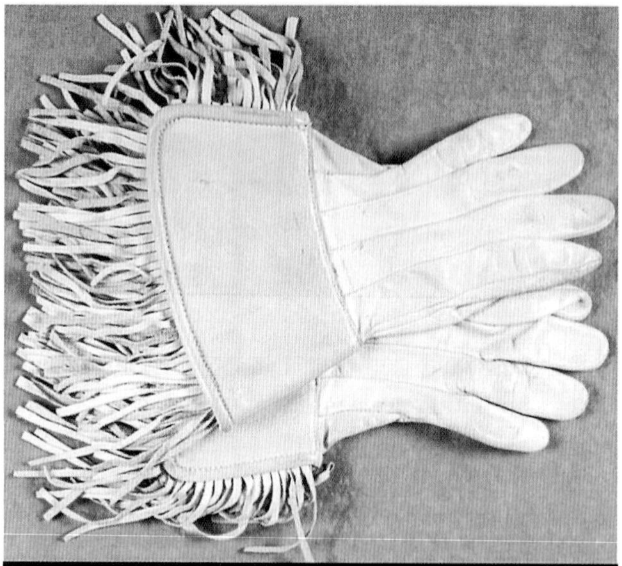

Hide gloves were practical and rather dandyish.

John Batterson was the inventor of the Stetson, originally known as the 'Boss of the Plains.'

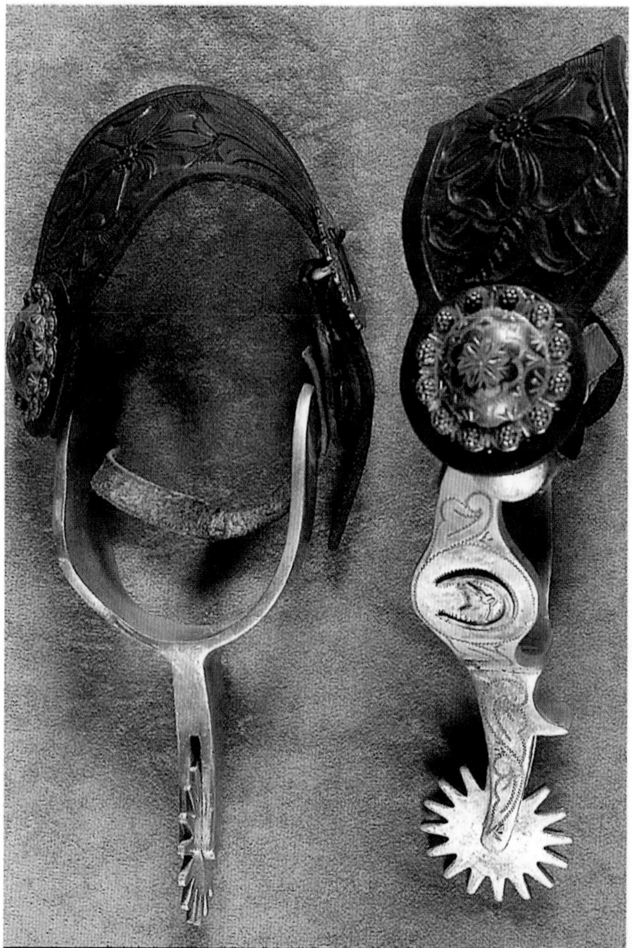

Jangling spurs were music to a cowboy's ears.

play to each other's strengths and watch each other's backs. They even seem to have a rather cosy domestic life together; Barney greatly appreciates Eddie's good home cooking.

Goodnight married Mary Ann Dyer in 1869, and like many L'Amour heroes—including Utah Blaine—decided to settle down at this point in his life. As he said 'After I married I thought I would no longer follow my wild trail life. I concluded to settle down and take up ranching instead.' He duly bought land in Colorado, but like many L'Amour characters, he missed the freedom of the trail, the excitement, coffee from the chuck wagon... sourdough biscuits.

Goodnight took the opportunity of running his own spread to learn a good deal about land management. Overgrazing was a serious hazard of ranching, and Barney Pike, L'Amour's archetypal cowhand, discusses how different types of grass stand up to this. 'Blue gama... mixed with buffalo grass. It'll stand a lot of grazing, and it re-seeds itself.' Goodnight also pioneered work in cattle breeding; crossbreeding the tough Texas longhorn with Herefords to achieve financially lucrative animals. He also interbred buffalos with domestic cattle to produce 'cattalos.' Like many of his class, he was also active in enforcing vigilante justice against cattle rustlers and horse thieves.

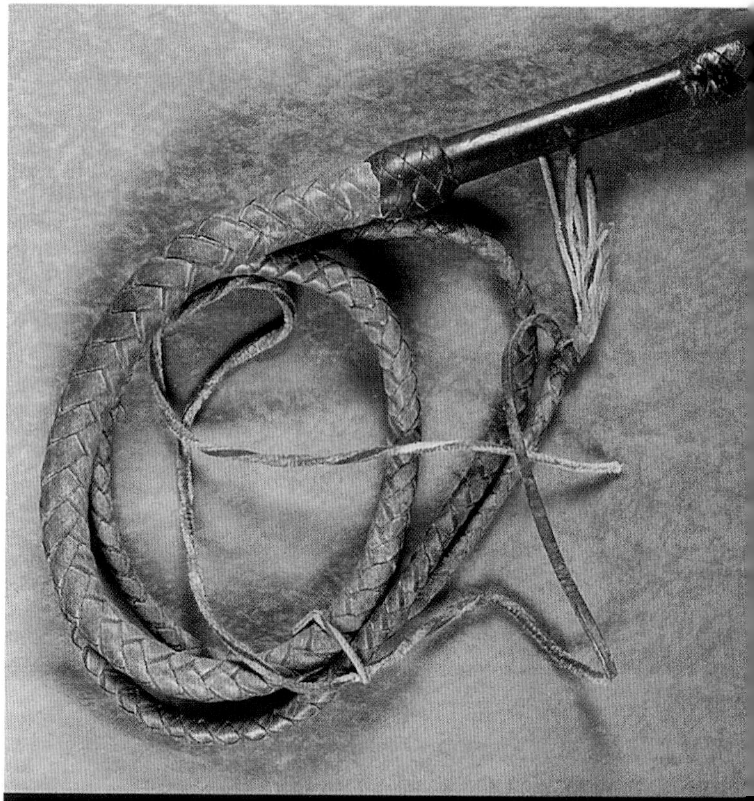

A trail manager's whip.

A cowboy's best friend was his horse.

But, for the second time in his life, Goodnight was financially wiped out in the 'Panic' of 1873. He found that all he had left to his name were 1800 longhorns. Never one to give in, he formed a business partnership with Irishman John G. Adair, who backed him to set up the JA Ranch, the first in the Comanche-Kiowa buffalo land. By this time, the Comanches had all but given up the struggle, and Goodnight felt it was safe to move back to the Panhandle. Goodnight established the new ranch in the legendary Palo Duro Canyon, where an abundant supply of sweet, fresh water meant that the grass was always green. The importance of this find could not be overestimated. As L'Amour says 'to the cattlemen water and grass were their very life blood.'

The partnership between Goodnight and Adair lasted for eleven years. By the time Goodnight decided he wanted to have his own land again; they had built up a herd of 100,000 head of cattle grazing a one million acre ranch. Goodnight described how 'to care for them (the cattle) over such an extensive range we employed a little army of men called 'cowboys'.' For the first time, the word had come into general usage. Goodnight had a very paternal relationship with these men, forbidding them to drink, gamble, swear, or even play cards in the bunkhouse. Unfortunately, this meant that when they hit town, his 'cowboys' were completely out of control, and developed a dismal reputation.

Goodnight made a cool half million dollars from his venture with Adair. Just like Tom Gatty in *Hanging Woman Creek*, he had started off as a cowpuncher, and ended up a rich and powerful man through herding cattle. He now established a ranch on land along the route of the Fort Worth and Denver City Railroad. A town bearing his name duly sprang up. The cattle business had used the railroad from its earliest introduction into the West. By this time, cattle ranching rivalled mining as the dominant industry of the region, and exploited every possible advance to become more profitable. Barney Pike explains how trail bosses rode the trains to explore new pasture, and to get ahead of migrating herds. Finished cattle were shipped on the hoof from railhead towns like Abilene (America's first cow town, where Illinois businessman J.C.

Goodnight and Adair built up a herd of 100,000 cattle.

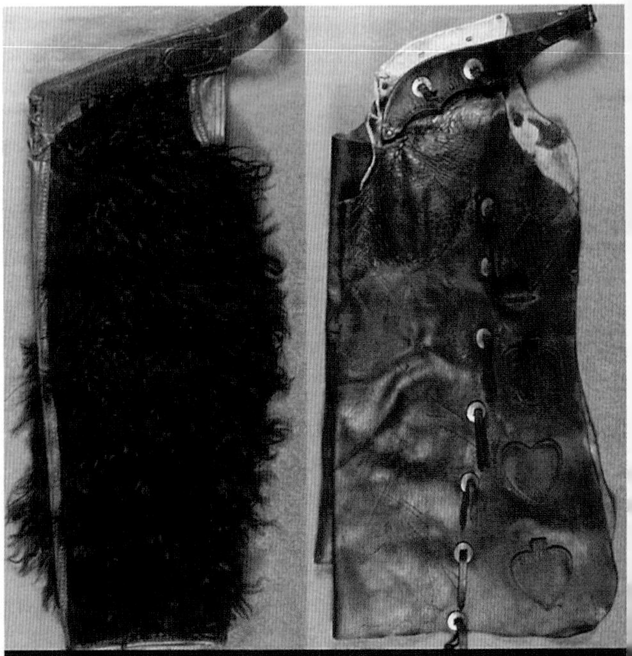

A pair of buffalo chaps. Eddy wears a pair that he has from his days in a Wild West show.

A romantic view of cowboy life.

McCoy built his cattle market in 1867), Ellsworth, and 'Jimtown' (Jamestown). The stock was then railed to Eastern hubs such as Chicago, St. Louis, and Rock Island. By the 1880s, the advent of refrigeration cars meant that Western beef could be transported all the way to Europe. Barney and Eddie also ride the Iron Horse, carrying their saddles, looking for their next cowhand jobs.

It was at this, Goodnight's last ranch, where the inveterate plainsman died at the age of 93, having survived for years on a trail diet of coffee, beef, and Cuban cigars.

Goodnight was not only the father of the Western cowboy, but he had lived their legend to the fullest. He was the first and last of the great frontier cattlemen.

Cattle being driven into stock pens at a rail head.

HENRY RIFLE

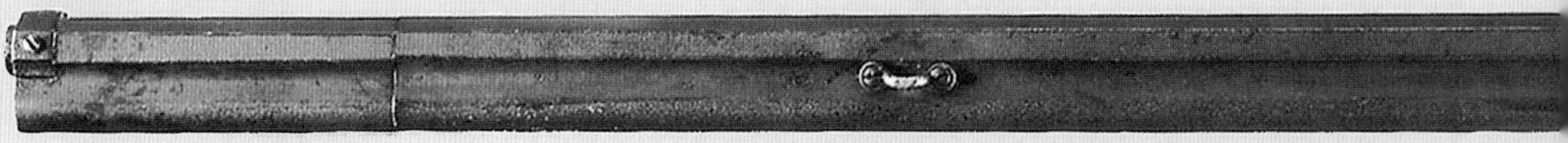

Oliver Winchester appointed Benjamin Tyler Henry as plant superintendent at the New Haven Arms Company in 1858. One of his key tasks was to develop reliable cartridges for the failed Volcanic lever action rifle. The result was not only improved cartridges, but also a completely new gun design patented by Henry on October 16, 1860. This new rifle was a 15 shot repeater with lever action, which used a .44 rim-fire copper cartridge. This fired a round-nosed, grooved lead bullet propelled by 26-28 grains of black powder. Muzzle velocity was 1200 feet per second, a huge improvement over the 700 fps of the Volcanic. The gun had a standard 24 inch barrel, apart from a few experimental models, which had shortened barrels. This latter innovation was an attempt to reduce the 9 pound weight of the weapon. The frame was made from either iron or brass.

In six years of production, 14,000 examples were manufactured, including 1,731 purchased by the army at the end of the Civil War.

The Henry is the rifle of choice in L'Amour's *Over on the Dry Side* (1975). Both Doby Kernohan, a young settler and the novel's hero Owen Chantry, use them. Doby reflects, 'I never had but just the rifle. I'd always wanted me one of them pistols, but we never had the money for it. I had me a rifle and a good one too—a Henry. I also carried a Bowie a man could shave with, it was that sharp.' So the Henry is seen as a standard element of western gear, just like the Bowie knife. This was the kind of equipment that kept frontier men alive.

Our featured weapon bears a relatively high serial number and is believed to have been part of the military

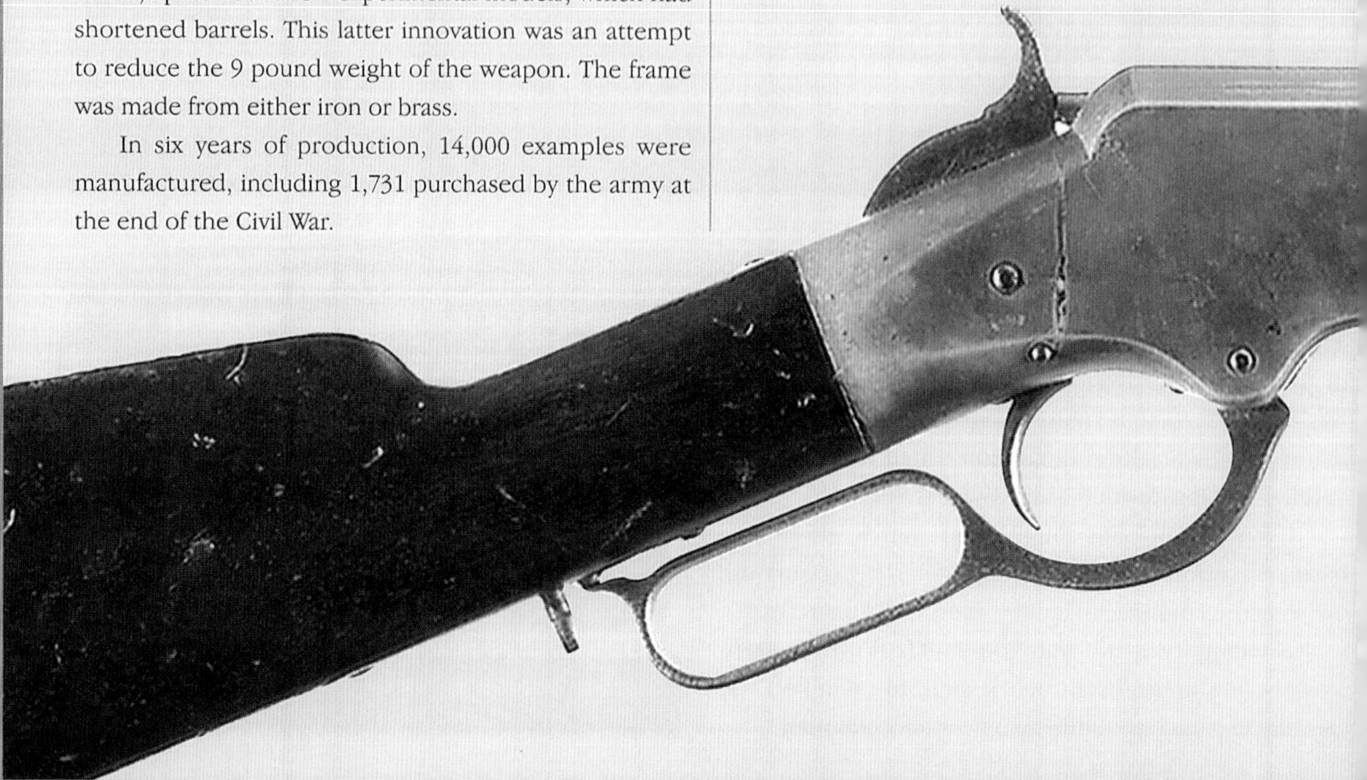

BELOW: The Henry Rifle clearly shows its resemblance to the later Winchester production models.

BOTTOM: The brass frame is noticeably devoid of the side receiver slot and the heavy octagonal barrel – both features that identify this as a Henry.

issue and to troops on guard duty in Washington D.C. towards the end of the war. Many of these guns then found their way back into the civilian hands of frontiers people when the War was over. It has a polished brass frame, and is stamped 'H' for Henry on the lower tang. Unlike the later 1866 Winchester, the magazine is loaded from the front of the tube under the barrel, and not through the familiar loading gate on the right side of the frame. Nelson King developed the side-loading system. He was later a plant superintendent.

'H' for Henry is stamped on all the major components.

SPECIFICATIONS

CALIBER: 0.44	ACTION: Lever Action 15 shot repeater
LENGTH OF BARREL: 24 inches	YEAR OF MANUFACTURE: 1864
BARREL SHAPE: Octagonal	MANUFACTURER:
FINISH: Brown patina	New Haven Arms Company, New Haven,
GRIPS: Walnut	Connecticut

LOUIS L'AMOUR'S INDIANS

'We did not give our country to you; you stole it.'

SITTING BULL

A Sioux Indian scalped and killed Louis L'Amour's maternal great grandfather in North Dakota, so it is hardly surprising that a slightly ambiguous view of the original Westerners permeates his novels. In *Hanging Woman Creek*, he refers to the tribe as the 'scalp-hunting Sioux.' Nor does he pull any punches when describing Wa-ga-su taking a Seneca scalp (*To the Far Blue Mountains*), 'with his knife (he) made a quick circular cut, then grasping the hair he jerked off the scalp.' In fact, he was extremely knowledgeable about the history and customs of the Indian peoples and had met many 'real' Native Americans in his youth, when they sat on the porch of his grandfather's house drinking tea and coffee.

Sitting Bull sports a magnificent war bonnet.

Native American Indians came to the US across the frozen Bering Strait, first arriving up to 40,000 years ago. They were from Asia, of Mongolian stock, and supported themselves by hunting. They were soon impressed with the abundant livestock of their new world. Waves of immigrants continued to arrive in the East, pushing the original settlers further and further West and South, until the entire continent was thinly populated. Louis L'Amour describes how just like the later white settlers, the new incomers populated the land by 'pushing out other Indians.'

They will appear
– may you behold them!
They will appear
– may you behold them!
A horse nation will appear.
A thunder-being nation will appear.
They will appear, behold!
They will appear, behold!

KIOWA

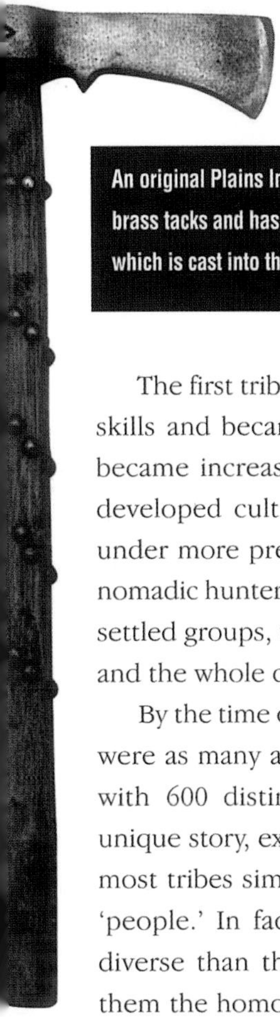

An original Plains Indians tomahawk. The shaft is decorated with brass tacks and has a drilling along its length to allow the pipe, which is cast into the back edge of the blade, to be smoked.

The first tribes to arrive developed agricultural skills and became maize-growing farmers. They became increasingly civilized, with more highly developed cultures. Groups arriving later were under more pressure, and remained warlike and nomadic hunters. But as they conquered the more settled groups, they gradually adopted their ways, and the whole cycle began again.

By the time of the first European settlers, there were as many as three million American Indians, with 600 distinct societies. Each had its own unique story, explaining how it came to exist, and most tribes simply referred to themselves as the 'people.' In fact, they were far more culturally diverse than the ignorant Europeans who gave them the homogenous name of 'Indians.' By this time, the tribes living in the region we know as the West had developed widely different cultures and lifestyles. These reflected the conditions of the territory they occupied. The region was vast, and the climate varied hugely from the icy north to the sweltering south. As Zeb Rawlings says in *How the West Was Won*, 'before the coming of the white man, (the Indian) had adapted himself to his surroundings to a remarkable degree.'

The Plains, or red, Indian is perhaps the closest to the recognizable cliché of Western films, complete with impressive war bonnet and pony. In reality, the people of the Plains were semi-nomadic and non-agricultural, living mainly in semi-permanent villages on the edge of the plain lands. The main tribes of this area were the Assinboine, Arapaho, Kiowa, Kiowa-Apache, Sarsi, and Teton-Dakato. All of these tribes were completely dependent on the buffalo for their clothing, tepees, cooking utensils, tools, and weapons and lived on a diet that consisted, almost exclusively, of buffalo meat. They had originally hunted on foot, but their lives were revolutionized when white men introduced the horse to America. Plains Indians had no wheels, but had developed the 'travois' method of hauling meat and supplies. This was a tough sheet of rawhide mounted on two poles, first pulled by dogs, then horses.

Sitting Bull, leader of the Hunkpapa Sioux who routed Custer's Seventh Cavalry at the Battle of the Little Big Horn.

The Rocky Mountain plateau region was mainly settled by the Flathead, Kutenai, Nez Perce (who later helped Lewis and Clark and their way West), Paiute, Ute,

Arikara warrior Bear's Belly, clad in a grizzly bear hide. They were close cousins of the Pawnee and very warlike.

and Yakima tribes. Some of these Native Americans were hunters; others were hunter-gatherers. Other tribes looked down on the latter, derisively terming them 'diggers.'

The Pueblo Indians of the Southwest were more successful, developing all kinds of intricate crafts such as pottery, cotton weaving, and turquoise jewelery-making. They had sophisticated religious rituals, lived in stone houses, and traded with tribes in Mexico. But the Pueblos ultimately fell victim to the other tribes of the region—the warlike Navahos and Apaches, who lived from raiding and hunting.

The benign Californian climate meant that Indians from this region (such as the Modoc and Penutian Family) were able to retain a very simple existence. They only wore clothes in the winter, and lived off a diet of acorn flour. They also constructed primitive balsa rafts of bundled rushes, but their only claim to dexterity was their refined basket weaving.

A war dance.

By complete contrast, the Tlingit people of the Northwest had such an abundance of food (especially salmon) in the rivers and the ocean, and a profusion of cedar wood, that they were able to construct a very

The stone houses of the Pueblo people, whose descendents still live in the Southwest.

A Cheyenne warrior with war bonnet beautifully crafted with ermine drops and beaded brow band. His sash is also beaded with a star motif.

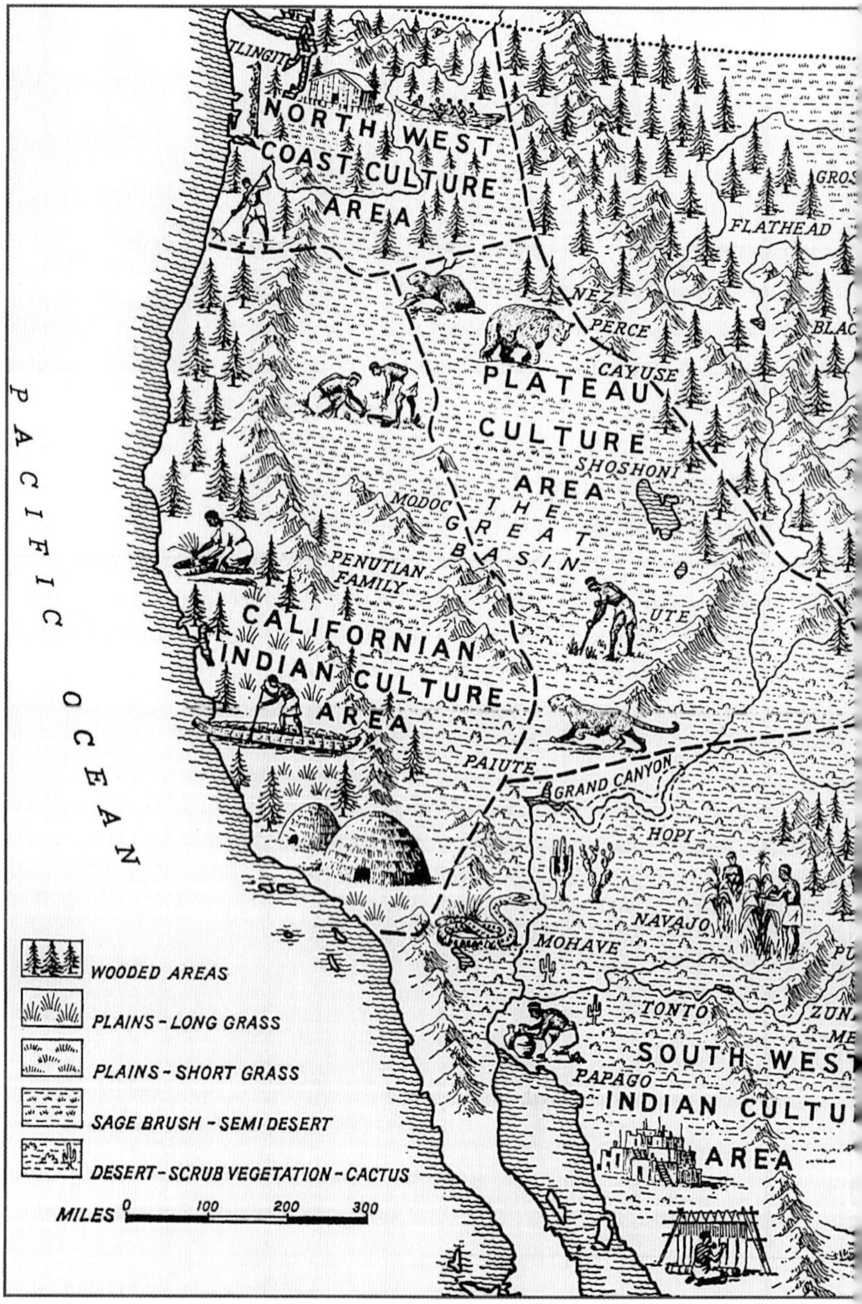

sophisticated society. They lived in elaborate wooden halls up to five hundred feet long, held 'potlachs' (ritual feasts), celebrated complex religious ceremonies, and each family carved itself an intricate totem pole. They were also a sea-going people, building fabulous cedar canoes that held up to fifty people.

But the Mexican Aztecs were the most advanced Indian society that the white invaders came upon. The Aztecs had conquered the original Mayan and Toltec peoples to establish a quasi-military state in the fourteenth century,

and had developed wonderful crafting abilities. In many ways, it is clear that Louis L'Amour and several of his heroic characters view the Indians and their tribal

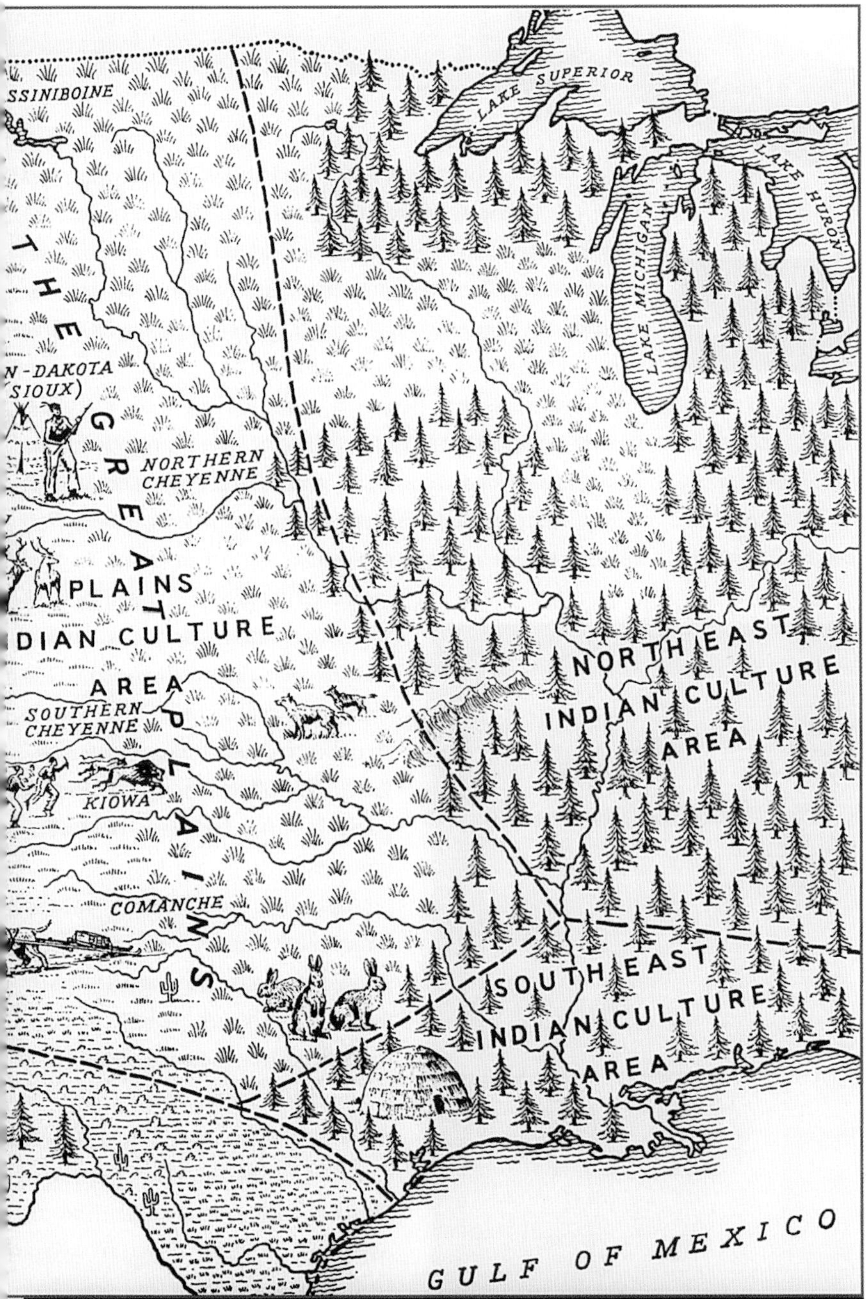

A map showing the distribution of the Native American tribes at the time of the expansion West.

Yellow Shirt, a Sioux warrior, holding the sacred Horse Dance stick in his right hand and a beaded pipe and tobacco bag in his left.

knowledge as the key to the new world. In *To the Far Blue Mountains*, Barney Sackett acknowledges that he will 'learn much from them about this country.' He accurately describes their simple way of life, 'mostly hunting and gathering berries, roots and nuts, they need much land to support only a few... some of the tribes...plant corn... (but) mostly they live by hunting, fishing, and gathering, so they move from time to time, going to new areas where they can find more game, and more food.' Although his party suffers from Indian attack, Indians also help the Sacketts to survive their first winter in the New World, teaching them how to make buckskin clothes and moccasins, and how to live off the land.

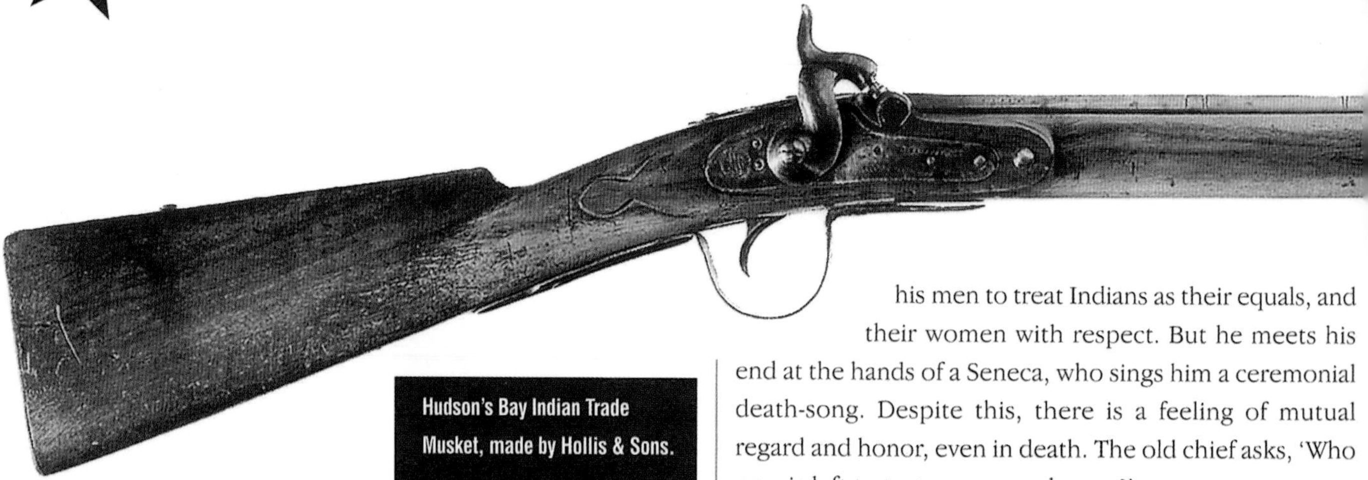

Hudson's Bay Indian Trade Musket, made by Hollis & Sons.

L'Amour uses Barney Sackett's experience to illustrate his unsentimental view of the Indian. On the one hand, Barney has an Indian friend—the Eno, Potaka—and rescues Wa-ga-su from the brutal Tuscarora. He instructs his men to treat Indians as their equals, and their women with respect. But he meets his end at the hands of a Seneca, who sings him a ceremonial death-song. Despite this, there is a feeling of mutual regard and honor, even in death. The old chief asks, 'Who now is left to test our young braves?'

Indian stories, legends, and history are a thread woven throughout L'Amour's books. There are numerous examples of how true plainsmen have espoused Indian ingenuity, to work with, rather than against, the land. Utah Blaine makes a pot out of bark, an 'Injun trick,' to boil water to tend the dying Kelsey's wounds, and grinds a maize poultice for Timm's wounds. 'This was, he recalled, an Indian remedy that he had seen used long ago.' Later, he collects 'a stack of herbs used by the Indians to doctor wounds.'

This beaded hide shirt demonstrates the exquisite artistry of the native peoples.

Tracking, a highly valued plainsmen ability ('To a Western plainsman, a track was as easily read as a road sign') is also recognized as an Indian skill. Utah Blaine is so able a tracker that he is described as 'an Injun on the trail,' while Mike Bastien (*Son of a Wanted Man*) can 'track like an Apache.' Indeed, Bastien wears Indian moccasins for tracking work, getting as close as possible to nature, 'skilled in the arts of the wilds.'Linus Rawlings, another L'Amour character who is deeply in touch with nature, 'had great respect for the Indian. He knew

him, not as a poor heathen of whom the white man took advantage, but as a fierce fighting man who lived for war and Horse-stealing.' It is almost as though the Indians are seen as an organic element of the Western landscape itself, which was 'sacred to the Indians, (with) the great peaks they revered.'

To some extent, this view of the native plainspeople means that L'Amour is able to avoid dealing with any moral issue about white settlement. This he generally represents as a good thing, as taming the 'wild country.' In *How the West Was Won*, L'Amour unsentimentally catalogs how the tribes were 'forced to move West during the Indian removal.' But his hero Zeb Rawlings, a soldier charged with protecting the railroad workers from Indian attack, has a surprisingly positive view of the Native Americans. 'Like many another soldier who served on the frontier… (he) had developed a sympathy for the Indian…he did not believe them a pack of savages to be killed off like so many mad dogs.' L'Amour takes this a degree further, equating bad treatment of the Indian with moral bankruptcy. Men who disregard the Indians, like railroad boss Mike King, are men of a lower caliber. He only values what he regards as the 'superior culture' and technical skill of the white man, 'I don't have any love for the noble red man, and never did.' Men like him have only come to the West to exploit it. King's greed and folly lead him to break his word, and push the 'blazing and iron trail for the Iron Horse' through the Arapahoe hunting grounds. This brings death and destruction down on his own people, including Zeb's uncle, tracklayer Sam Prescott.

Throughout the novels, the incursion of white settlers into the West is more or less opposed and repulsed by the native peoples. Zeb Rawlings' post-army career flounders when he loses half his cattle during a pitched battle with the Kiowa, who also drove Matt Coburn off his ranch. Roger Morgan's wagon train is attacked by Cheyenne. Arapahoe braves, with faces 'painted with streaks of black'

The 'travois' was used to haul meat and supplies. It was originally pulled by dogs.

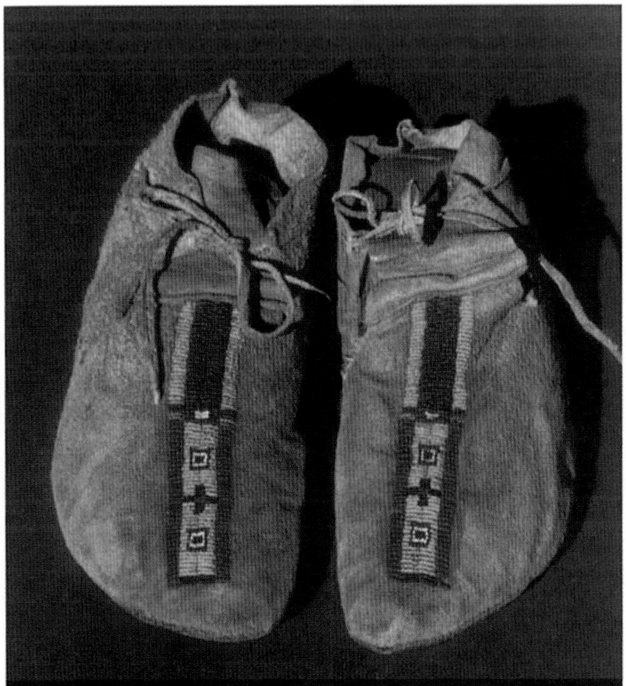

A beautiful pair of beaded soft hide moccasins. Mountain men also adopted these.

Blackfeet Indians set John Colter free, but nude, assuming that he wouldn't last for long in the desert. They were one of the most aggressive tribes, and were opposed to the mountain men defiling their lands.

attack the settlers' town, while 'a bad Indian, the Tonkawa Kid…killed and robbed a farming family.'

L'Amour carefully categorizes the degrees of antagonism displayed by the differing tribes. Some like the Shoshones and Flatheads can co-exist with the frontier people. The Nez Perce even boast that they have never killed a white man. Other groups, like the Sioux, Cheyenne, and Arapahoe are more opportunistic, while L'Amour describes the Ute, 'next to the Blackfeet no tribe was more trouble to the white man.' That is, if you discount the Seris, said to be cannibals, one of whom trails Catlow through 'meat hunger.' The Iroquois are also described as 'very savage,' and Catlow refers to the land of the Comanches, Apaches, Tonkawa, and Tamahumara as being full of 'wild animals and wilder Indians.'

L'Amour also describes the gradual integration of several tribes into the settled Western lands—a real-life phenomenon. He describes the 'Five civilized tribes – the Cherokees, Choctaws, Chickasaws, Creeks, and Seminoles. Most of them lived like white men. A good many had education, a good many were veterans of the war, and others had ancestors who had fought with or against Jackson.'

Indians draw buffalo into a canyon to make for an easier kill.

Geronimo of the Apaches. Like many Indians, he seems curiously diminished by ordinary western clothing.

SHARPS BUFFALO RIFLE

The Sharps Buffalo 'Gun' was a legend in the West. Its long distance accuracy is celebrated in a classic Hollywood movie scenario. The bad guy is confidently riding off into the sunset, the good guy takes aim leisurely, touching the foresight with spit to provide a gleam of light, carefully adjusting the vernier backsight. The audience is convinced that his adversary has escaped, when 'good guy' squeezes the trigger. The gun booms loudly, the barrel bucks from the explosion of the heavy .50 caliber cartridge exploding. Then silence returns. We watch 'bad guy' continue his ride into the distance for several long tantalizing seconds. Suddenly, almost in slow motion, his back explodes and he slumps from his mount.

In *The Man Called Noon*, Ruble Noon reflects on the gun's prowess as Ben Janish and John Lang pursue him into the mountains. We are not told what kind of rifle Noon has at this point but we believe it to be a Winchester, as he reloads by 'thumbing' the shells as you would into the right hand side of the frame. 'He got up slowly reloading the rifle as he did so. He had done better shooting, and he thought of Billy Dixon at Adobe Walls, who had knocked an Indian from his horse at just under a mile…but that was with a Sharps buffalo gun, a big .50.'

Our featured gun has a classic 30 inch barrel. It is smaller than the big .50, but at .45-70, it is still an extremely potent example of the breed. The .45 inch lead slug was propelled by a 70 grain charge. Even the standard Winchester, at only .44-40 (with 40 grains at its disposal), was still a weapon to be reckoned with. But by comparison

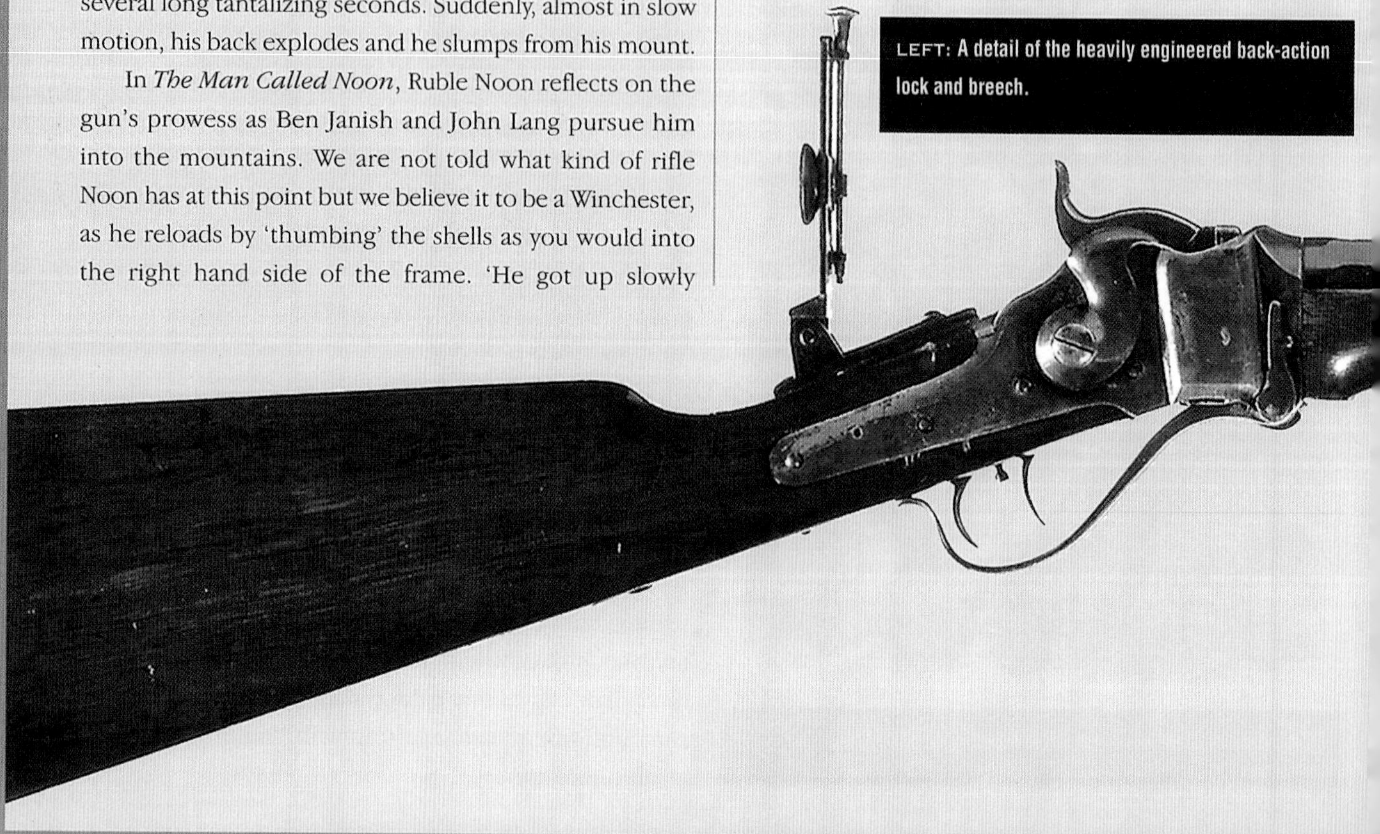

LEFT: A detail of the heavily engineered back-action lock and breech.

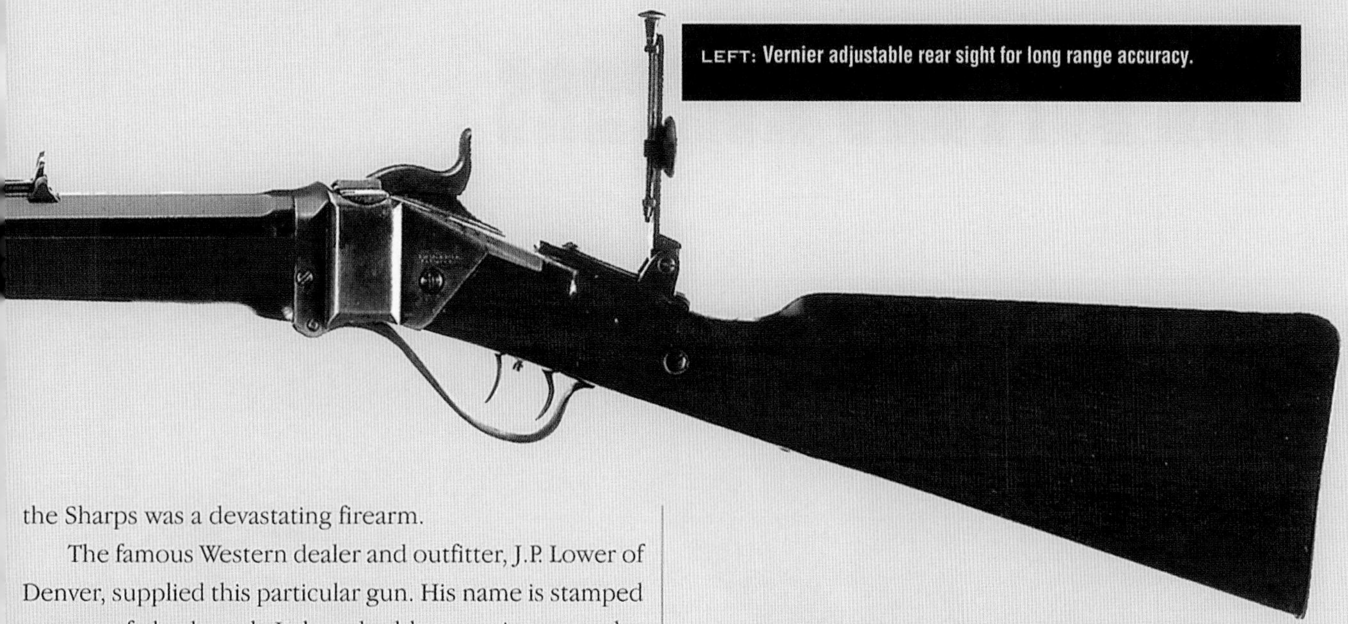

LEFT: Vernier adjustable rear sight for long range accuracy.

the Sharps was a devastating firearm.

The famous Western dealer and outfitter, J.P. Lower of Denver, supplied this particular gun. His name is stamped on top of the barrel. It has double set triggers and a shotgun butt plate. The gun also has his special 'Rocky Mountain' buckhorn sight that Lower himself designed and had made up by Sharps. The tang sight is a modified sporting sight with a vernier staff added for extra range. The gun went by the soubriquet 'old reliable.'

ABOVE: Set trigger arrangement, which gave hair trigger firing accuracy. The rear one set and the front one released.

BELOW: Well polished foregrip in nicely aged walnut.

SPECIFICATIONS

CALIBER: 0.45-70	ACTION: Single shot/breech-loading
LENGTH OF BARREL: 30 inches	YEAR OF MANUFACTURE: 1874
BARREL SHAPE: Octagonal	MANUFACTURER:
FINISH: Blue casehardened	Sharps
GRIPS: Walnut	

THE BUFFALO HUNTERS

From the early part of the nineteenth century, the Plains were gradually stripped of their herds of buffalo. Early pioneers like the mountain men killed them to provide food as a means of survival, as the Indians had done to supplement their diet, and to provide clothing and shelter.

However, these small inroads into the population of the herds were nothing compared to the wholesale

A Buffalo Hunter's kit believed to be the best preserved and most complete to have survived from the days of the Frontier.

Mountain men pursue the herd on horseback to get a close range shot.

slaughter that occurred following the Civil War. Western expansion led to the view that everything was there to be exploited and as a result the mighty herds were hunted down and slaughtered to the gates of extinction. Many of the hides and meat was shipped back east to the ready markets but an increasing proportion went to sustain life in the growing frontier towns. To fulfill this need, a breed of professional hunters came into being—men who killed to sustain the 'market' for Buffalo products, and who killed coolly and scientifically with the modern weapons at their disposal in the latter half of the nineteenth century. In the early days of smoothbore flintlocks—the only weapons available in the early years of the century—killing game as large as a Buffalo required skill. A close

The herds are now re-established after virtual extinction.

Early hunters used every means at their disposal to hunt Buffalo. This group is setting fire to the prairie in order to stampede the herd toward a group of well armed trappers.

shot was necessary to penetrate the animal's thick hide, which meant careful stalking.

As weapons technology developed—largely during the Civil War—more powerful breech loading rifles became available, which made mass slaughter of the herds a reality. Our spread (pages 122-123) shows a complete Market Buffalo Hunter's outfit which comprises a Sharps Model 1874 'Old Reliable' hunting rifle in its original Buffalo fur covered travelling box. With it is a complete collection of butcher knives in fur covered wooden blocks, and also a cylindrical water canteen with a wire handle. Three photos survive with the collection: one of Buffalo skinners, a mounted Buffalo head, and a studio portrait of the hunter's brother. It is believed from the excellent condition of this equipment that it would have been carefully transported on a wagon to the scene of the hunt and only then removed from the protective boxes in the immediate vicinity of the herd.

Western conservation in the twentieth century enabled the herds to be reintroduced and they can now be seen grazing in growing numbers (bottom left), a scene which harks back to that witnessed by the first western explorers.

SPENCER SPORTS OR BUFFALO RIFLE

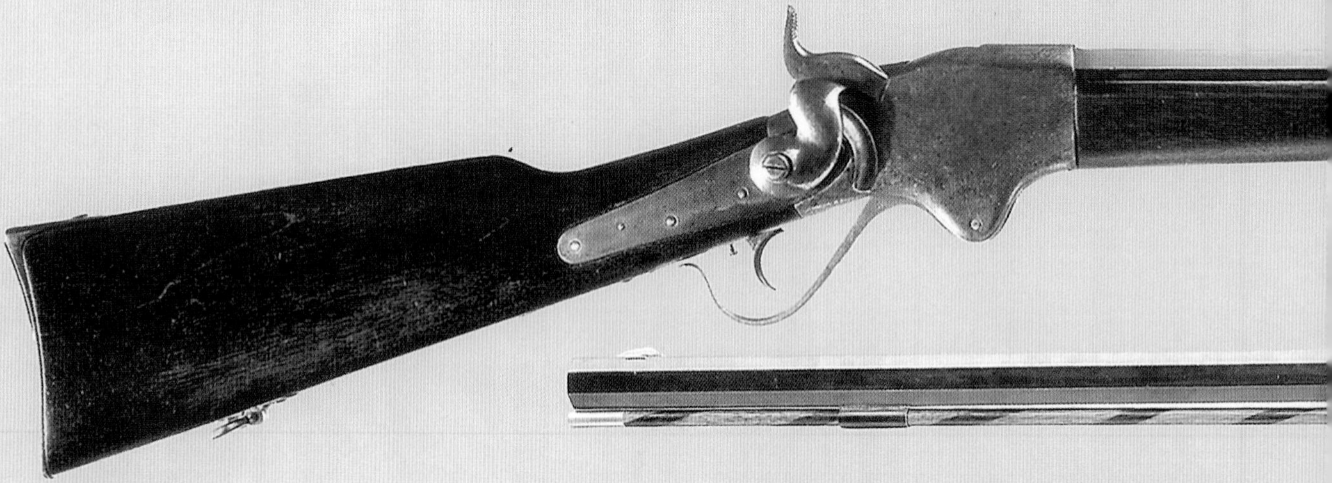

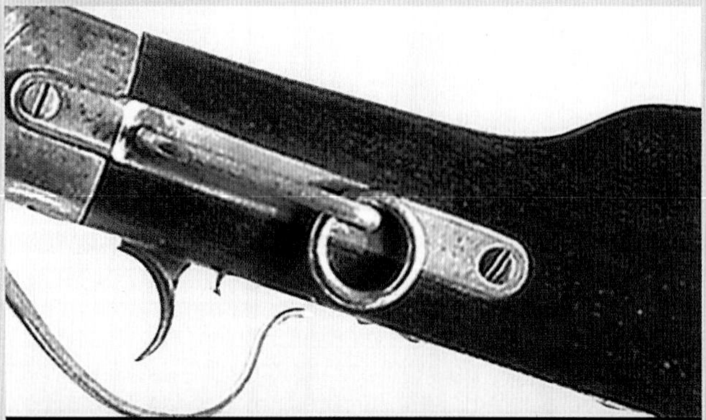

The sliding carbine ring was a leftover from the original carbine version of the gun.

L'Amour features the Spencer in *Utah Blaine*. The grasping Nevers is intent on seizing Mary Blake's B-Bar Ranch, and rides out with twenty of his hands. In contrast, only three men, Rip Coker, Dan Timm, and the novel's hero, Utah Blaine, defend the B-Bar. Timm packs the Spencer. He is a trusted older hand, who was a friend to Mary's murdered father. During the nighttime standoff, Coker is armed with a Winchester rifle but he passes this off as the even more fearsome Colt Revolving Shotgun. But as L'Amour points out 'The Spencer .56 was no bargain either.' Timm stays out of sight, 'bedded down by the stone well in the vague light. "Yeah," Timm's voice came from the well coping. "You hombres make a right tempting target.

SPECIFICATIONS	
CALIBER: 0.45	ACTION: Seven–shot repeating rifle
LENGTH OF BARREL: 32 inches	YEAR OF MANUFACTURE: c1872
BARREL SHAPE: Octagonal	MANUFACTURER:
FINISH: Brown	A. J. Plate, San Francisco, California
GRIPS: Walnut	

BELOW: Right side detail shows Civil War carbine action lock coupled with heavy duty octagonal

BELOW: Left side with tiger striped ramrod, silver side nail covers and swivel on base of butt for sling carrying.

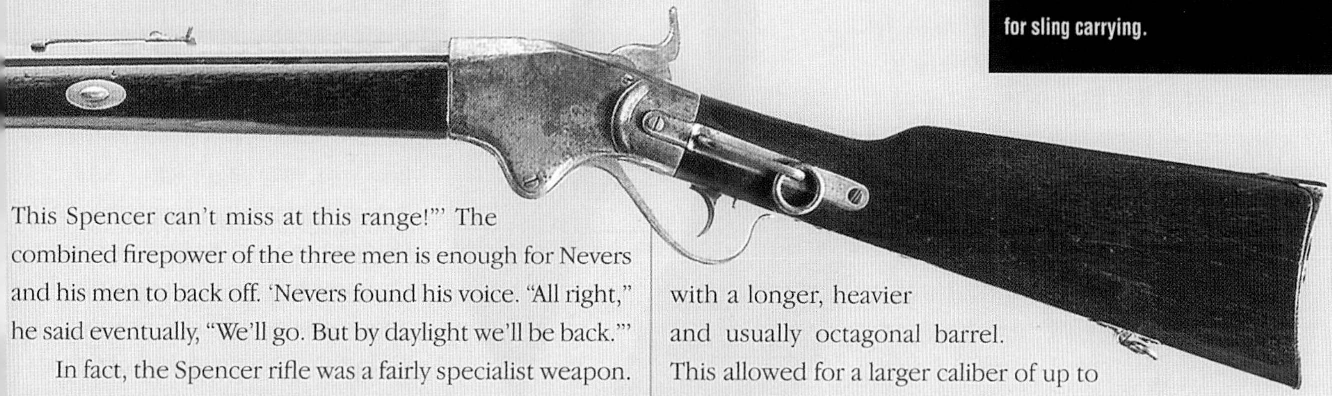

This Spencer can't miss at this range!"' The combined firepower of the three men is enough for Nevers and his men to back off. 'Nevers found his voice. "All right," he said eventually, "We'll go. But by daylight we'll be back."'

In fact, the Spencer rifle was a fairly specialist weapon. It was based on the well-proven military version used by both sides in the Civil War. It could be employed as both a carbine and a rifle. The seven–round tubular magazine used a rim fire cartridge and was a great improvement, both in terms of speed of loading and handling, over the muzzle loading rifles that both sides started out with.

When adapted for Western use, the gun was equipped with a longer, heavier and usually octagonal barrel. This allowed for a larger caliber of up to .56 of an inch, and had the effect of reducing the kick on firing. These modifications greatly improved the gun's effectiveness at long range and its ability to stop a Buffalo—or a man—made it a good choice.

The famed Western gun dealer A. J. Plate of San Francisco rebuilt this particular example. Plate's name is stamped on the barrel.

GREAT INSTITUTIONS OF THE WEST

THE TEXAS RANGERS: MEN WHO COULD NOT BE STAMPEDED

In Louis L'Amour's West, law enforcement ranges from judicial law upheld by appointed officers, right through to lynch mob justice. The closest thing to an official police force in the West (as opposed to individual lawmen) was the outfit known as the Texas Rangers. L'Amour mentions these elite men many times. His marshals and sheriffs have often served with the Rangers. Indeed, the Rangers' tracking and detective methods formed the blueprint for professional law enforcement on the frontier.

In the absence of any real protection from the Mexican government, Austin ('The Father of Texas') recruited ten good men to protect the new territory. They became the nucleus of the Texas Rangers.

For example, in *How the West Was Won*, ex-army officer Zeb Rawlings serves two years in the Texas Rangers, following a disastrous stint ranching. He ends up as a deputy US marshal, operating in the Indian Territory. Zeb is the kind of lawman that Louis L'Amour admired, and it's significant that his post-army career in enforcement begins with the Rangers.

But the harshness of Western conditions, and the many temptations on offer meant that the barrier between the law officer and criminal was more permeable than it is today. Men crossed and re-crossed this divide in real life, and do so in L'Amour's novels. In *Catlow*, L'Amour describes several Texas Rangers who have switched to the other side, becoming professional man hunters, putting their renowned tracking skills to work for personal gain. Hired gunmen and killers often started out with respectable backgrounds in the army and as officers of the law, just like Matt Giles who had 'begun his killing as a mere boy in the Moderators and Regulators wars of northeast Texas, and had graduated to a sharpshooter in the Confederate Army' before going irredeemably bad.

The origins of the Texas Rangers stretch back to the earliest days of Anglo settlement in Texas, and the organization is now the oldest law enforcement agency in North America with statewide jurisdiction. At the beginning of the nineteenth century, the territory of Texas was controlled by Mexico, and the Austins (father and son Moses and Stephen) were hired by the Mexican government to recruit settlers for the new land. But Mexico soon proved to be completely unable, or unwilling, to protect the new settlers from Indian attack. In 1823, Stephen Austin recruited a fledgling force of ten men 'to act as rangers for the common defense.' This was a positively revolutionary idea for the time, when Western law enforcement was at best patchy and informal.

This original force of 'ranging' officials is credited with being the forerunner of the contemporary Texas Rangers. They went on to become not only an effective force for law enforcement, but one of the most mythological elements in the history of the Old West, a focus of

Remember the Alamo. The 'Last Stand' defense of this mission fort against overwhelming Mexican forces took place in 1836. This was the year in which Texas declared itself to be an independent republic. The defense of the Alamo became a patriotic symbol of American resistance to the domination of foreign powers.

traditional values. They 'ranged' the length of the new colony, protecting the white settlers from attack by a whole roster of Indian tribes, including the Comanche, Karankawa, Waco, Tehuacani, and Tonkawa. When no threat was apparent, the men returned to their own land and families.

A Corps of professional, full-time Rangers was established a few years later, whose members were paid $1.25 a day (for 'pay, rations, clothing and horse service'). In this way, the men were responsible for providing their own arms, mounts and equipment and many Rangers carried examples of the newly introduced Colt revolving pistols, from the recently established company.

Before the involvement of the Austins, only a tiny number of colonists had made it to Texas by 1821 (an estimated 600-700). But despite attempts by the Mexican government to limit the number of settlers coming into Texas via the US, an estimated 50,000 Americans settled in the state between 1823 and 1836. Inevitably, this led to a schism of opposing interests opening up between the new American Texans and the Mexican government. This bad feeling led to the wrongful imprisonment of Stephen F. Austin for over two years in Mexico City (accused of 'inciting revolution' against the Mexican regime), when he tried and failed to negotiate improved rights for the white settlers. Not unnaturally, this experience converted Austin (the 'Father of Texas') from a moderate man willing to negotiate with Mexico to a fervent believer in the Texas Independence movement. He went on to become a volunteer commander in the Texas Revolution.

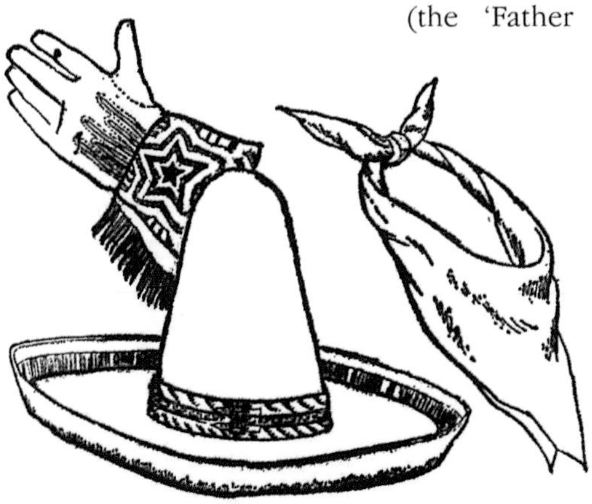

The Rangers' costume owed more than a nod to traditional Mexican dress.

When a provisional 'rebel' government, (known as the Permanent Council) was established by the 'Consultation of 1835,' one of its first acts was to recruit twenty-five professional Rangers under the command of Silas M. Parker. Their primary duty was to 'range' the frontier between Brazos and the Trinity. This force grew to consist of three companies of 56 men, each commanded by a captain together with first and second lieutenants with a major in overall charge of the force.

In the heat of the Revolutionary war, men often served as both soldiers and Rangers. Some Rangers were drafted into cavalry regiments, and were known as dragoons. The Gonzales Ranging Company of Mounted Volunteers, for example, was the only fighting force to answer Colonel Travis's desperate plea for assistance in defending the mission fort of the Alamo (1836) from the overwhelming force of 5,000 Mexican troops. The Rangers died heroically alongside the other defenders, who included famous scout, hunter, and Indian fighter Davy Crockett.

'The Last Stand' became a potent symbol of American resistance to foreign domination and was instrumental in Texas joining the Union in 1845. Several other Rangers were captured by the Mexican commander, General Santa Anna, and were amongst the 350 people that he ordered to be slaughtered on Palm Sunday 1836, in fields just outside Goliad. This massacre, and that of the Alamo, became the focus of Texan revolutionary fervor, and the origin of Sam Houston's famous battle cry 'Remember the Alamo, Remember Goliad.'

The Tumlinson Rangers were also involved in the struggle, fighting a rearguard action to protect the shattered Texan army as it retreated in the 'runaway scrape.'Other Rangers served as scouts for the Texan military forces, and won a tremendous reputation for their brilliant tracking skills. Individual Rangers, such as Jack

The Gonzales Ranging Company of Mounted Volunteers was the only fighting force to answer Colonel Travis's desperate pleas for assistance in defending the Alamo from over 5,000 Mexican troops. The Rangers died heroically alongside the other defenders.

Hays, Ben McCulloch, Samuel Walker, and 'Bigfoot' Wallace became famous as frontier fighters. They were also getting better equipped. In 1839, the Rangers became the first civilian force to be armed with Colts. The Texas Government bought 180 holster-sized pistols (these were saddle, rather than belt holsters) for their use. These weapons were five-shot, .36 caliber, nine-inch barrelled, revolving pistols of the type that Colt had first patented in 1835. Samuel Walker, a contemporary Ranger who rode for Captain Jack Hays, wrote to Samuel Colt in England, 'The pistols which you made…have been in use by the Rangers for three years…. In the summer of 1844, Col. J. Hays with 15 men fought about 80 Camanche [sic] Indians, boldly attacking them on their own ground, killing and wounding about half their number…. Without your pistols we would not have had the confidence to have undertaken such daring adventures.'

Ultimately, the Texan forces' policy of attrition won the day, and the current border between the two countries was established. But there were continual skirmishes along the Mexican side of the Rio Grande for the next ten years. In fact, Rangers were making punitive strikes into Mexico well into the twentieth century. In one battle of 1917, it is thought that the Rangers may have killed as many as twenty Mexicans. Despite this, Mexicans and Indians have both been counted amongst the ranks of the Rangers. As early as the 1830s, an Indian nicknamed 'Bravo Too Much' rode with the most famous early Ranger, John Coffee ('Jack') Hays.

Once Texan independence had been achieved, the next step was to re-tame the colony – by establishing the rule of law, and repelling Indian attack. The Rangers proved to be a cost-effective way of achieving both of these aims. Their role became more inward looking, and although they had been known as 'los diablos Tejanos' (The Texas Devils) for their effectiveness against Mexican guerrillas, the responsibility for defending the international border gradually devolved upon the US army. In response to this, the number of Rangers began to dwindle.

The Texas Rangers also played an important role in the Civil War. Many enlisted in 'Terry's Texas Rangers' (commanded by the brilliant Colonel E. Terry) and were a great boost to the strength of the Confederate Army. Despite seceding in 1861, and for the duration of the Civil War, Texas was readmitted to the Union in 1870.

During the post war period of reconstruction, the role of the Rangers was assumed by the highly political and widely disliked State Police, who were charged with the implementation of the deeply unpopular 'carpetbagger' laws. This resulted in the institution falling into disrepute amongst war-weary Texans. But following the repeal of the

The Texas Rangers used the first Colt revolvers in their defense work. They effectively neutralized several Indian tribes with the weapon.

ABOVE AND BELOW: The newly enclosed Texan ranges often fell victim to fence cutters and rustlers. The Rangers were their only defense against these miscreants.

carpetbag rule in 1873, the service was reformed.

The Texas Legislature ordered the formation of two Ranger forces in 1874; the Frontier Battalion, led by Major John B. Jones and the Special Force, led by Captain Leander McNelly. At this time, an increased level of external security had led to a huge upsurge in internal lawlessness, so the Rangers developed a different role as law enforcers, while continuing their fight against insurgents. They effectively neutralized the formerly powerful Comanche and Kiowa, by fighting such famous skirmishes as the Battle of Plum Creek. But the new Rangers also brought over 3,000 Texan desperados to justice, including the train robber Sam Bass (in 1878) and the gone-to-the-bad gunfighter Wesley Hardin. Hardin was reputed to have killed thirty-one men, but was captured single-handed by Ranger John B. Armstrong, wielding a long-barrelled Colt .45, shouting 'Texas, by God!'

The legislation of 1874 was a defining moment in the history of the force, whose members were now officially officers of the peace, rather than fighting men serving in a semi-military organization. Despite this, if a Ranger was fighting an outside force, such as Mexicans or Indians, he

continued to be judged as a soldier. But when he was enforcing the Texan criminal law, he was considered a detective or policeman. The Ranger's role often involved bringing the rule of law to the massive Texan ranches, combating fence cutters and cattle rustlers. The Rangers' authority was acknowledged state wide, without reference to city or county boundaries.

Between 1894 and 1895, the Rangers scouted 173,381 miles, made 676 arrests, returned 2,856 head of cattle to their rightful owners, assisted the civil authorities on 162 occasions, and were brought in to guard jails thirteen times.

The Frontier Battalion nomenclature was abolished in 1901, the name fading into history along with the frontier itself. The Rangers were now seen purely as a law enforcement agency; an elite group of officers brought in to support local lawmen. Unfortunately, the Rangers had been so effective that they now seemed redundant. Their numbers declined to a mere four companies of twenty men each.

This tiny force was completely overwhelmed by the dramatic events at the beginning of the twentieth century – prohibition, the Mexican Revolution, and the Texan oil boom to name but three. Rather than beef the force up, it was even further depleted to four companies of only fifteen men.

But it gradually became apparent to the State legislators that Texas badly needed an elite force to handle some of its toughest crimes. In 1935, the Rangers became the cream of the Texas Department of Public Safety (which

Senior Ranger Captain Frank Hamer and his colleague Manny Gault finally tracked down Bonnie and Clyde Parker, after 102 days. The Rangers had hoped to take the dangerous duo alive, but gunned them down when they reached for their weapons.

The Rangers were active in enforcing prohibition between 1920 and 1933. They located and destroyed many stills.

also contained the Texan Highway Patrol). This force was the true forbear of the modern-day Texas Ranger, developing more modern and subtle approaches to the sophisticated crime of the modern era.

The Rangers gradually swapped their horses for cars, responding to a different criminal profile. One of the most famous Rangers of this era, Senior Ranger Captain Frank Hamer, trailed Bonnie and Clyde for 102 days, together with his Ranger colleague Manny Gault. The Rangers finally caught up with the dangerous duo in Louisiana's Bienville Parish, setting up an ambush on a rural Louisiana road. The Rangers had planned to take the couple alive, but gunned them down when they reached for their weapons. They ended the pair's killing spree of at least thirteen murders, including police officers.

A falling off in standards took place in the 1920s, when Governor Ferguson allowed some men to be inducted in the service who were not worthy of the honor, including some ex-convicts. This indignity resulted in forty Rangers, including Hamer, resigning. Between 1920 and 1933, National Prohibition forbade the sale of alcohol, and Rangers worked closely with Federal agents to destroy stills and confiscate illegal alcohol smuggled in from Mexico. They co-operated in shutting down liquor distribution networks, illegal gambling dens, and speakeasies.

A general cleanup of the service was instigated in 1934, following a Texas Senate inquiry. This recommended the establishment of the Department of Public Safety, an institution that still survives to this day, which would operate the Ranger service. This was to be cut down to a meagre 36 men, but would benefit from state-of-the-art crime-fighting techniques and a vastly improved communications network. In these early years as part of the DPS, Rangers were furnished with an updated version of the Colt .45, together with a lever action Winchester .30 rifle. They still had to provide their own horse and saddle, though these were now driven long distances in state-supplied horse trailers.

During World War II, the Rangers were part of the internal Texan security network, screening air raid warning training films and tracking down escaped German POWs. By 1945, the force was again on the increase, to 51 men. Their duties continued to evolve, and during the 1950s, Rangers calmed incidents of civil disorder, kept an eye on the cattle rustlers, and shut down illegal gambling dens.

Always a semi-military force, the Rangers took a strong interest in weaponry.

The service continued to increase in size, and in 2012, the modern Texas Rangers Division has 160 members. This includes 134 Commissioned officers, 1 Forensic artist, 1 Fiscal analyst, and 24 Civilian support personnel. Their role is now totally one of law enforcement, including a diverse range of criminal investigations. The personnel are distributed between six field headquarters, located throughout Texas, in Houston, Garland, San Antonio, Midland, Waco, and Lubbock. The Rangers also have an Unsolved Crimes Investigation Team based in San Antonio.

Unsurprisingly, considering their illustrious reputation, it takes a special kind of person to be accepted as a Texas Ranger. On paper, the requirements are: being a citizen of the United States, being in excellent physical condition, having eight years' experience as an officer of the law with a bona fide law enforcement agency, and being currently employed by the Texas Department of Public Safety. Very little recruitment is necessary – it is not unusual for around 40 applicants to apply for each opening. The Rangers continue to add to their legend to this day.

PINKERTON'S NATIONAL DECTECTIVE AGENCY

Allan Pinkerton founded Pinkerton's National Detective Agency in 1852. Pinkerton was a Scottish immigrant who became one of the greatest figures in American legal history, a man famous for his 'great power of observation and courage.' The organization he founded was the first detective agency in the US, and became the forerunner of the modern FBI. Pinkerton also invented many methods of investigation and evidence gathering that are still in use today.

From the beginning, Pinkerton agents were a huge force in bringing effective law enforcement to the US, nowhere more so than the (definitely wild) West. Louis L'Amour acknowledges their massive contribution to the 'taming' of the territory in his Western novels, and as the stories unfold, several of his characters turn out to be 'Pinks.'

Allan Pinkerton was a Scottish immigrant. He was a man of the highest ethical standards who infused his agency with his personal enthusiasm and dedication to law enforcement.

Pinkerton was born in Glasgow, Scotland in 1819, the son of police sergeant William Pinkerton. When his father was killed in a political riot, Allan went to work as an apprentice at the McCauley Cooperage Works as a barrel maker, soon becoming one of their most valued craftsmen. But he also became involved in the embryonic labor movement as a Chartist (an early form of trade unionist). Belonging to the labor movement was very controversial at this time, and Pinkerton was obliged to flee from Scotland (with his new wife Joan Carfrae) to avoid arrest. The Pinkertons lost everything on the voyage to their original destination, Canada, when their ship was flooded in a near shipwreck. Worse was to come. When they waded to shore, the survivors were accosted by Indians demanding trinkets, and Joan lost even her precious wedding ring.

Whether this unpleasant welcome put them off settling in Canada is uncertain, the tales of the thriving American city of Chicago appealed to Allan's entrepreneurial nature. He was sure that there would be a need for skilled craftsmen like him. His supposition was absolutely correct. Pinkerton soon had work, and subsequently opened his own factory, 'Pinkerton's One And Original Cooperage of Dundee.' By now, he also had three children, William, Robert, and Joan. Interestingly, Allan was a staunch abolitionist, and was an active member of the underground network that helped former slaves escape to the North.

Pinkerton's curious and inquiring nature soon led him to become involved with helping local law officials track down a gang of counterfeiters. He also arranged a covert 'sting' to flush out the quasi-respectable gang-leader. His partner in the operation, Sheriff Yates, was so impressed with his intelligence, courage, and tenacity that he offered Allan his first job in law enforcement – as deputy sheriff of Kane County. He later became the first professional detective in the Chicago Police Force. By the end of 1848, Pinkerton had achieved the highest number of arrests for murder and burglary in the entire force.

Chicago's role as a railway hub between the East and West had led to a great influx of people into the city. Inevitably, some of them were criminals, and the incidence of violence, theft, and rape in the city rose dramatically. There was little to stem this, with a police force of less than a dozen men expected to control more than 30,000 citizens. This convinced Allan that there was a need for a second dedicated team of investigators for the use of private companies and individuals. This belief led him to establish his own detective agency in 1850. Pinkerton's National Detective Agency opened its first office at 151 Fifth Avenue, Chicago.

One of Pinkerton's first major clients was the Rock Island and Illinois Central Railroad, whose attorney was none other than the young Abraham Lincoln. In *Hanging Woman Creek*, L'Amour describes how Pinkerton man Jim Fargo is trying to track down the murderous Van Bokkelen, to the surprise of main character Barney Pike. Pike says that he thought 'Pinks usually only hunted train robbers and the like.' It was certainly true that this formed a good part of the Agency's early work. Pike later reflects that Pinkerton

Pinkerton is credited with saving President Lincoln from at least one assassination attempt, and became very important to the Union cause during the Civil War.

agents are also hired by cattle ranchers, or by companies like Wells Fargo. This (rather controversially) suggests that contemporaries believed Pinkerton agents were only interested in law enforcement when financial concerns are involved. Interestingly, though, Jim Fargo is also a deputy US marshal.

As well as acute powers of detection, Pinkerton offered high standards of ethical behavior by himself and his operatives. He was an excellent PR man, coining the company slogan 'We never sleep' and its trademark 'eye.' This emblem is the root of our modern phrase 'private eye.' The agency itself was colloquially known as 'The Eye.' All his agents were expected to maintain high personal standards, and he handpicked them himself. Some of the famous original 'Pinks' were George H. Bangs, Francis Warner, and Kate Warne. Kate was the first female detective in America, and her 1856 appointment was particularly groundbreaking. The police didn't employ women officers until 1891, and didn't use women as investigators until 1903.

Through Pinkerton's good offices, and intelligence network, Lincoln survived long enough to be inaugurated as President. He blamed himself for the final, successful attempt on the President's life, as he had left Washington by this time.

Some Pinks were reformed criminals, and used their knowledge of lawbreaking to assist their detective work. In *The Man Called Noon*, J.B. Rimes turns out to be a Pinkerton agent. L'Amour describes him as an ex-outlaw, who had been recruited by the Agency to catch a train robber. But Rimes is now firmly on the side of the law, and ends up by bringing the vicious Peg Cullane to justice.

From the very beginning, the Agency used the most up-to-date technology to facilitate its investigations, employing telegraph and weapons experts. Pinkerton was also an early exponent of psychology. He once hired a double for a murdered bank clerk to stalk the perpetrator until the man completely broke down, convinced that his victim was haunting him. By the 1870s, the Agency had the world's largest collection of mug shots and an extensive database of criminals. Pinkerton's methods were progressively adopted by the police force itself.

The Agency gradually became a household name, particularly after its involvement in a series of high profile cases, such as the Adams Express Job, where Allan was able to return $39,515 of a stolen $50,000.

But perhaps Pinkerton's most famous coupe was his defeat of an assassination plot to kill his old friend Abraham Lincoln, the newly elected President. Lincoln's strong pro-abolitionist stance during his campaign had earned him a good deal of hostility in the South, and there were serious concerns that civil war would break out if he were to be elected. While guarding the route of the Philadelphia, Wilmington, and Baltimore Railroad – the main rail artery to the South – Pinkerton agents picked up intelligence about a plot for a Confederate group, the Knights of the Golden Circle to murder the incumbent President at Baltimore's Calvert Rail Station. Even the local chief of police was implicated in the conspiracy. But Pinkerton managed to spirit 'Abe' away, and save his life long enough to be sworn in.

Later in that year of 1861, the dreaded civil war did indeed break out. Convinced by his own experiences as to the efficacy of intelligence work, President Lincoln summoned Pinkerton to the capital. He called upon him to organize a secret service in Washington to flush out Confederate spies. In effect, this was the first ever government-sanctioned spy ring in the US. Pinkerton employed some of his most trusted agents on this work, including Kate Warne, who divided her time between Virginia and Tennessee, posing as a Southern belle. In fact, women agents were used on both sides. One of the Confederate agents flushed out by Pinkerton's spies was Rose O'Neil Greenhow who had passed vital plans to the South. Once exposed, she was lucky to escape hanging. Pinkerton agent Elizabeth Baker successfully discovered the existence of a Confederate-built early submarine. This information effectively prevented the Confederacy from breaking the Northern Blockade. The Pinks also foiled a plot to break out all 8,000 prisoners of war being held at Camp Douglas.

Allan Pinkerton and his son William were both actively involved in undercover work in the South. Allan worked in Tennessee, Georgia, and Mississippi, with an assumed Southern identity as Major E.J. Allen. On one occasion, he only just escaped being lynched when his cover was blown. But to Pinkerton's horror, one of his first and most valued agents, Timothy Webster, was exposed, caught, and hung by the Southern authorities. Allan was so devastated by Webster's loss that he had the agent interred in his own family burial plot.

As well as acute powers of detection, Pinkerton offered high standards of ethical behavior by himself and his operatives

But mounting criticism of Pinkerton and his methods led him to leave Washington. This was a move he was to regret bitterly, believing that he would have been able to prevent John Wilkes Booth's successful attempt on Lincoln's life in 1865.

During the Civil War, two other Pinkerton offices had been opened, in New York and Philadelphia. Allan's second son, Robert, had also joined the agency. Unlike his brother William, who was actively involved with detective work, Robert was an administrator —but hugely valuable as such. He established the card-file system still used by the FBI, and originated the concept of the 'mug shot.' Pinkerton agents scoured every possible outlet—including newspapers and wanted posters—for news of criminal activity, and proactively monitored places where criminals gathered, such as racecourses. Pinks also compiled a glossary of criminal slang, to gain entry into the lawless underworld.

Between 1865 and the early 1900s, the Pinkerton agents based in the West played a part in bringing some of the most infamous frontier criminals to justice.

A fascinating chapter in the agency's history opened up in the Post-war period. America was now moving West, and so was crime. Pinkerton opened a network of offices all over the new territory, covering the ground from Kansas to California and from Texas up to Canada. William Pinkerton did a lot of frontier detection work, assisted from time-to-time by his father. Between 1865 and the early 1900s, the Pinkerton agents based in the West played a part in bringing some of the most infamous frontier criminals to justice. These included the James gang, Cole Younger, Butch Cassidy and the Sundance Kid's 'Wild Bunch' (in a classic Western shootout), 'Black Jack' Tom Ketcham, the Burrow Gang, Hillary Farrington, the six Reno brothers, and William Randolph.

Pinkerton agents had tracked ex-Confederate guerrillas, the James brothers, around the Smoky Mountain foothills for years, but the brothers had always eluded them. Louis L'Amour describes the gang's miserable, hunted lifestyle during this period. 'In their sixteen years as outlaws, few of the James gang even made a decent living…most of that time they were on the dodge, hiding out in caves, barns and shacks, poorly fed, poorly clothed, suspicious of each other.'

Finally, the frustrated Pinks engaged in a risky strategy —one of the few operations undertaken that brought the Agency into disrepute. A grenade attack on the James family home backfired horrendously, leaving the brothers' mother, Zerelda, needing one of her hands amputated, and the James's nine-year-old half-brother dead. There was a huge public outcry against the actions of the Pinks, even though Allan strenuously denied that his agents were responsible for the devastating explosion. In fact, he was indicted for murder (although no warrant was ever served) and the Missouri legislature called for an official investigation into the affair. But the Pinkertons had their revenge. They were instrumental in the intelligence that led to the final stand of the gang in Northfield, Minnesota, wiring the townsfolk to let them know that the gang was on their way. The Agency also recommended that a reward should be offered for Jesse James 'dead or alive'—a massive $10,000. Ultimately, this led to James being gunned down by fellow gang members Robert and Charley Ford. Poetic justice as it turned out, for as L'Amour explains '(James) had already murdered two of his own gang and was planning to kill others.'

The Pinks were involved in other rather ambiguous cases. In 1875, Pinkerton agent James McParland worked undercover as a miner, alongside Irish immigrant coal miners who were suspected of being involved with the murderous gang, the Molly Maguires. At the time, the mine owners believed them to be responsible for several deaths amongst the 'bosses,' but now there is a tendency to believe that most of the men were only trying to achieve better working conditions. Either way, several of the 'ringleaders' exposed by McParland were executed.

Although Allan Pinkerton himself died in July 1884, his sons ably continued his work. The Agency survived the

Butch Cassidy's Wild Bunch – in a reflective moment. Bill Carver, Kid Curry, Harry Longabaugh ('The Sundance Kid'), Ben Kilpatrick, and Leroy Parker (Butch Cassidy). The Pinkerton Agency brought the gang to justice in a classic western shootout. They were just some of the criminals called to account by the 'Pinks.'

nineteenth century by standing by his sacred precepts of honesty and toughness. As he had written 'with hands clean and with a clear conscience—you are sure to win.' Pinkerton believed that essentially, 'the right is mighty and must prevail'—with a little help from the Pinkerton Detective Agency, of course.

Reformed safebreaker George White interesting expressed the criminal's view of the Agency when writing his memoirs. He had hated them for interrupting his 'professional duties' but also held them in grudging esteem, and was forced to 'acknowledge that they were honest and it was dangerous for a crook when a Pinkerton was on his trail.'

The agency survives to this day, as Pinkerton Consulting and Investigations, still using a modern, graphic representation of Allan's 'eye' as their company logo.

COLT LIGHTNING 1877

THESE PAGES: Three versions of the Colt Lightning, one with traditional black rubber grips, one with fancy New York style factory engraving on a nickel plated finish, and one with pearl grips.

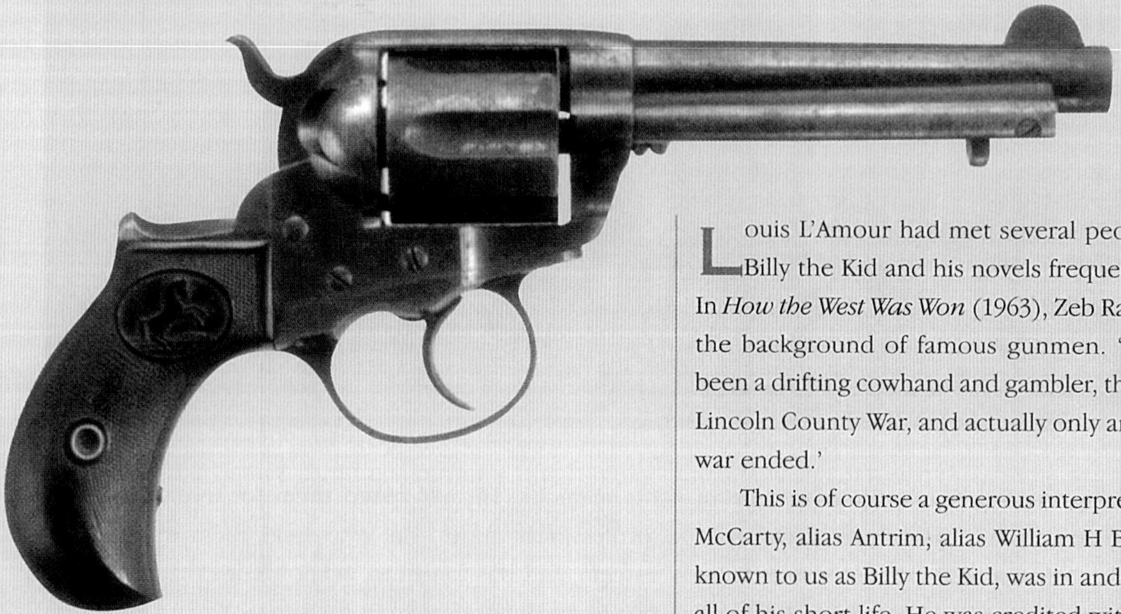

Louis L'Amour had met several people who had met Billy the Kid and his novels frequently mention him. In *How the West Was Won* (1963), Zeb Rawlings talks about the background of famous gunmen. 'Billy the Kid had been a drifting cowhand and gambler, then a feudist in the Lincoln County War, and actually only an outlaw after that war ended.'

This is of course a generous interpretation, and Henry McCarty, alias Antrim, alias William H Bonney, but better known to us as Billy the Kid, was in and out of scrapes for all of his short life. He was credited with the killing of 21 men—one for each year of his life—but his actual total was nearer to six.

In his line of work, a rapid-fire revolver would have been a valuable asset, and the aptly named Colt Lightning

SPECIFICATIONS	
CALIBER: 0.38	ACTION: Double
LENGTH OF BARREL: 4 inches	YEAR OF MANUFACTURE: 1877
BARREL SHAPE: Round	MANUFACTURER: Samuel Colt, Hartford, Connecticut
FINISH: Gray with traces of original blue	
GRIPS: Hard Rubber	

ABOVE: The Colt Lightning clearly shows it roots in the Peacemaker, but with the added speed of double action.

is on record as being Billy's favorite weapon—in the .38-inch caliber. Indeed there was strong demand for a double action weapon, and the early models of 1877 strongly resembled the Peacemaker on which they were based. Double action was achieved by adding a strut, which connected the trigger movement to the hammer. This allowed the trigger to slip past the strut at the top of the cycle, thus releasing the hammer. It could also be cocked manually and fired like a single action. This did have its disadvantages. The trigger pull was necessarily stronger and there were more parts to wear out. But this did not seem to deter Billy, or indeed any of the other 165,999 purchasers of the gun. It was a popular weapon in the final years of the Frontier.

COLT BUNTLINE SPECIAL

SPECIFICATIONS	
CALIBER: 0.45	ACTION: Single Action Revolver
LENGTH OF BARREL: 16 inches	YEAR OF MANUFACTURE: 1876
BARREL SHAPE: Round	MANUFACTURER:
FINISH: Blue/casehardened	Colt, Hartford, Connecticut
GRIPS: Walnut	

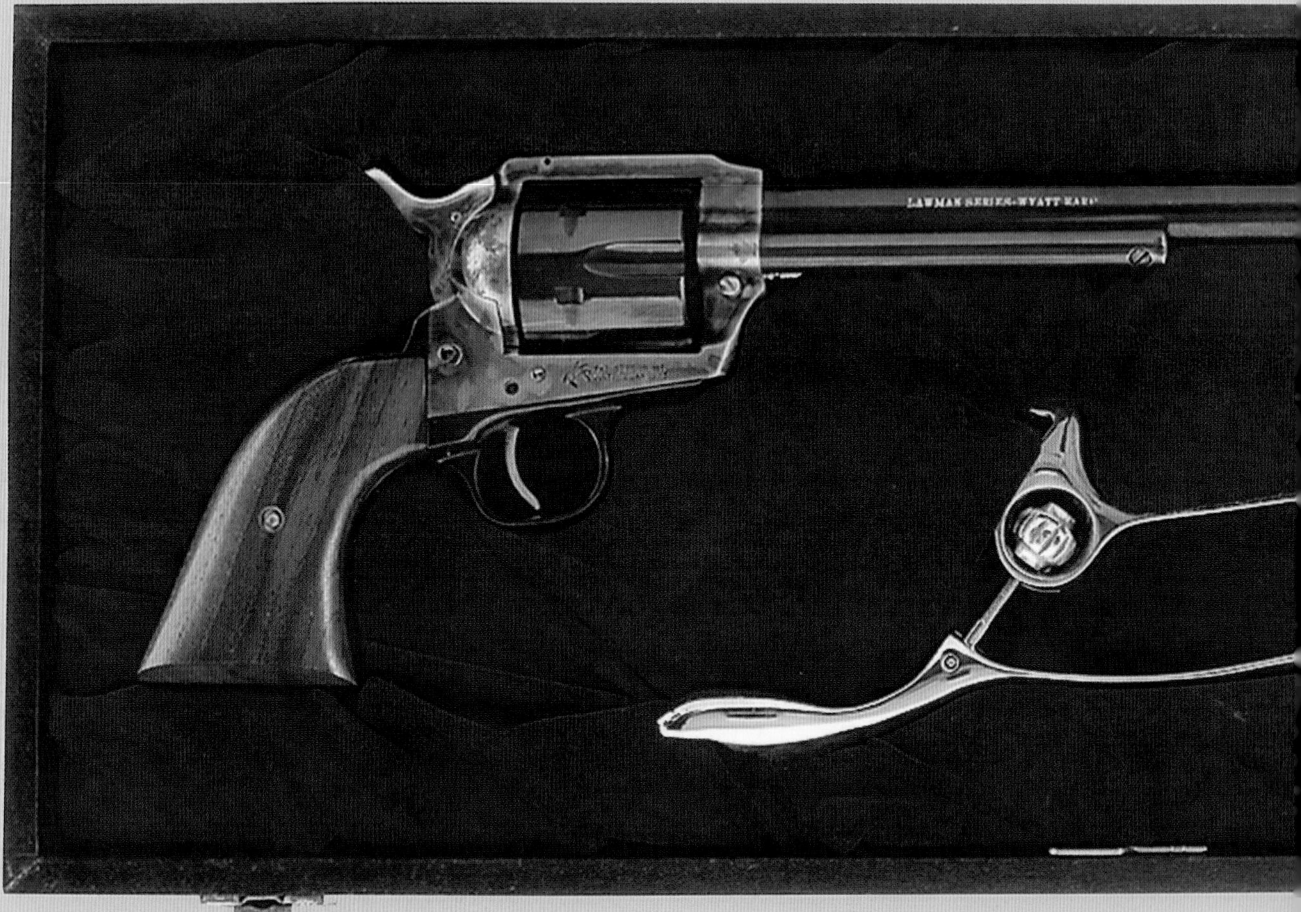

An exciting innovation to the Colt Single Action appeared at the Philadelphia Centennial Exhibition of 1876, when the weapon was offered with a 16 inch barrel and a skeleton shoulder stock. Only thirty examples were originally offered. The gun acquired its legendary association with Wyatt Earp when (it was claimed) dime novelist Ned Buntline (Edward Judson) ordered five Colt Special .45 revolvers to equip the Dodge City Peace Commission, of whom Earp was one. This is how the guns got their name, the Buntline Specials. It is not known if Earp actually carried a Special, but Buckskin Frank Leslie, a Tombstone gambler and bartender, ordered a 10–inch version in 1881. This was the year of the Earp brothers' famous gunfight at the O.K. Corral.

Clearly these experimental modifications would have turned the single action into a very useful weapon. Fired down a sixteen-inch barrel, the .45 cartridges would have been extremely accurate and have had great stopping power at range. The nickel-plated skeleton stock would have meant that the shootist could have held the gun extremely steady and would have enabled them to take careful aim before squeezing the trigger.

The gun could also be fired without the stock, and the extra weight of the barrel would have ironed out any tendency to kick from the extra length.

The gun went on to be manufactured for many years after 1876, and is still available in presentation cases.
Louis L'Amour cites Wyatt Earp as the gunman to beat in many of his Western novels, and he has helped to keep alive the legend of the West's greatest gunman.

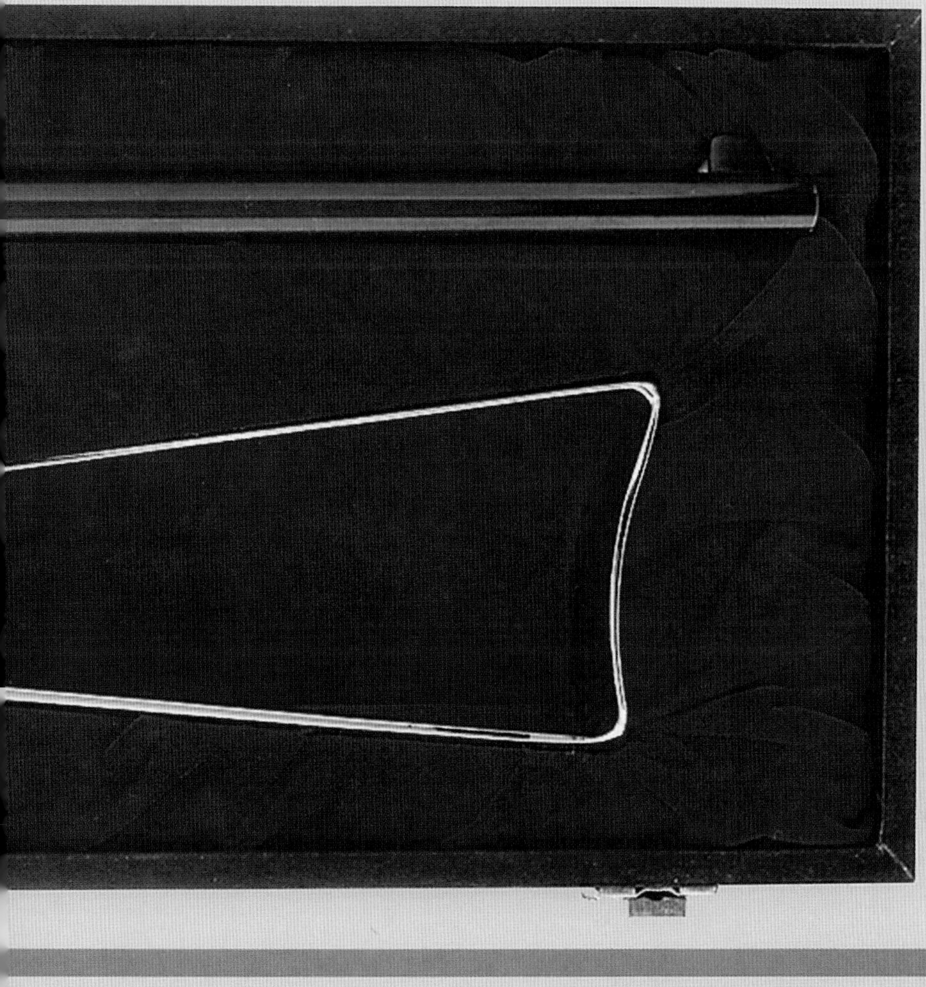

A modern reproduction of this legendary arm, complete with skeleton stock and silk lined presentation case. Such weapons are highly prized by collectors.

THE CIVIL WAR

'A house divided against itself cannot stand. I believe that government cannot endure, permanently half slave and half free.'

ABRAHAM LINCOLN

The Civil War was ignited by the issue of slavery, but with the secession of several pro-slavery Southern states, an even bigger issue became paramount—the preservation of the Union itself. When Lincoln became President, control of the nation's government passed to the North for the first time in several generations, and hostilities seemed inevitable. When it came, the conflict touched almost every American family in some way or another, including that of Louis L'Amour, whose grandfather fought in the War. The ripples of the conflict can be felt in many of his Western novels, and in the lives of both his real and imaginary characters.

Brigadier General J. E. B. Stuart, a great Confederate commander.

Although much of the West was left pretty well unscathed by the actual fighting, the spark that ignited the nation-wide conflagration happened in the territory in the fall of 1855. The new states of Kansas and Missouri were bitterly divided by the issue of slavery, and this led to the murder of an abolitionist settler by his pro-slavery neighbor. This in turn resulted in a miniature 'civil war' between the 'free-soiler' abolitionists and the pro-slavery movement. This preceded the events of the nationwide conflict by several years. In fact, some of the bitterest fighting of the War, between the so-called Jayhawkers and Bushwhackers, tore the region apart. Their vicious and barbaric methods were epitomized by such men as the brutal 'Bloody Bill' Quantrill, for whom Jesse James fought. His specialty was the murder and pillage of innocent civilians and their homes.

As the major hostilities broke out, other Western states became part of the theater of war. Texas and Arkansas declared for the Confederacy. Kansas was on the Unionist side. Missouri was a border slave state. But

The Battle of Shiloh.

loyalties did not necessarily follow state lines, and like many parents, Eve Prescott Rawlings worried that her sons could end up on different sides of the conflict. Her mountain man husband, Linus, died at the great battle of Shiloh in April 1862, where he and his son Zeb fought on the side of Grant and Sherman against Johnston's confederate forces. In a cinematic moment typical of L'Amour, Zeb Rawlings prevents a Texan from killing Grant, and unwittingly turns his back on the dead body of his father. He returns home, only to find the graves of both of his parents. As for many, sorrow is his underlying motive for the trek West.

Despite that fact that Valverde in New Mexico saw the farthest westerly battle of the War, virtually every aspect of Western life was affected by the conflict in some way or other. For example, many Plains Indians became swept into the hostilities. Although Lincoln attempted to persuade the tribes to remain neutral, the withdrawal of the US military was seized upon as an opportunity by warlike tribes like the Apache and Navajo who began a

A stone bridge on the Warrenton turnpike near Bull Run. It became a symbol of Union losses.

Colonel Michael Corcoran and the officers of the 69th New York State Militia gather around an artillery piece at Fort Corcoran.

The field at Gettysburg, scene of the most costly military action ever to take place on American soil.

campaign of raids against frontier settlers.

Lawfulness in general was often a victim of the conflict, as many officers, including those of the Texas Rangers, were obliged to join the military forces on both sides. Once the fighting was over, there were a lot of experienced men available to work on the side of justice, and just as many dispossessed desperados ready to break the law.

President Ulysses S. Grant, one of the greatest Union commanders.

The Sheridan doctrine of destroying confederate property, so that 'The people must be left with nothing but their eyes to weep with,' meant that the economy of the South was ruined. Texas was left particularly battle-scarred and impoverished. Ironically though, the thriving industrial towns of the North, such as Chicago, were hungry for meat, and Texan beef was in huge demand. Cattle were selling at as much as $30 to $40 a head in the northern meat markets. This high demand gave cattle entrepreneurs like Charles Goodnight and his ilk an opening they did not fail to exploit.

When Robert E. Lee surrendered on April 9, 1865, victory celebrations were held all over the West. For the frontier region, the end of the war heralded a new wave of immigrants. The collapse of the Southern economy, the loss of many personal fortunes, and general war fatigue, encouraged many to make their way West for a fresh start—just as the Sackett brothers do in *The Daybreakers*. Not only men braved the challenge of the frontier. In *The Cherokee Trail*, Mary Breydon has been burnt out of her Virginia home and widowed, and needs to make a new life for herself and her little daughter. She becomes the manager of a stagecoach station, and turns it into a vital stop on America's Westward journey.

At the cost of over 620,000 lives, the Union had been saved, and America was restored to nationhood. The democratic Republic, created in 1776, survived. But the victorious Lincoln had precious little time to access the harrowing cost of the War. He lost his life to a murderous Confederate Marylander, John Wilkes Booth, who was incensed that former black slaves would now become citizens.

The Civil War created the greatest schism in American society since the foundation of the Republic. Sometimes North against South led to brother against brother.

COLT DRAGOON

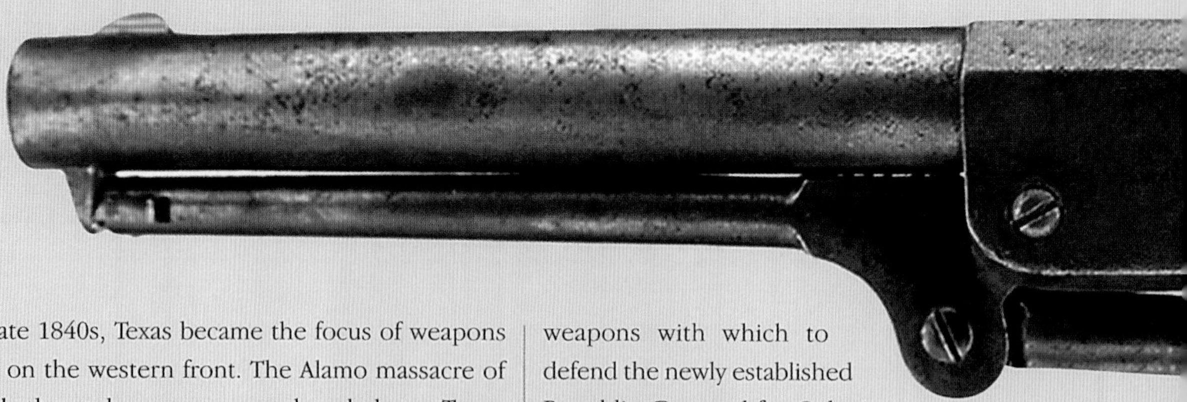

In the late 1840s, Texas became the focus of weapons activity on the western front. The Alamo massacre of 1836, and the subsequent war that led to Texan independence, resulted in a heavy demand for advanced weapons with which to defend the newly established Republic. Demand for Colts in particular was stimulated by the notable success of the Texas Paterson Colt revolvers at 'Hays Big Fight.' Captain Jack Hays and a detachment of 15 Texas Rangers defeated over eighty Comanche using the weapon. The Indians had rushed the small force of Texans after their first volley of shots, thinking that the Rangers had paused to reload. But instead, the repeating handguns continued to fire, with devastating affect.

The Rangers were enlisted into the US Cavalry when the war

Detail of the cylinder showing the honest patina of age. Originally many of these weapons had intricate engravings of combat scenes on the cylinders.

SPECIFICATIONS	
CALIBER: 0.44	ACTION: Single action 6 shot repeating revolver
LENGTH OF BARREL: 8 inches	YEAR OF MANUFACTURE: 1848
BARREL SHAPE: Round	MANUFACTURER: Samuel Colt, New York City
FINISH: Gray with traces of blue	
GRIPS: Walnut	

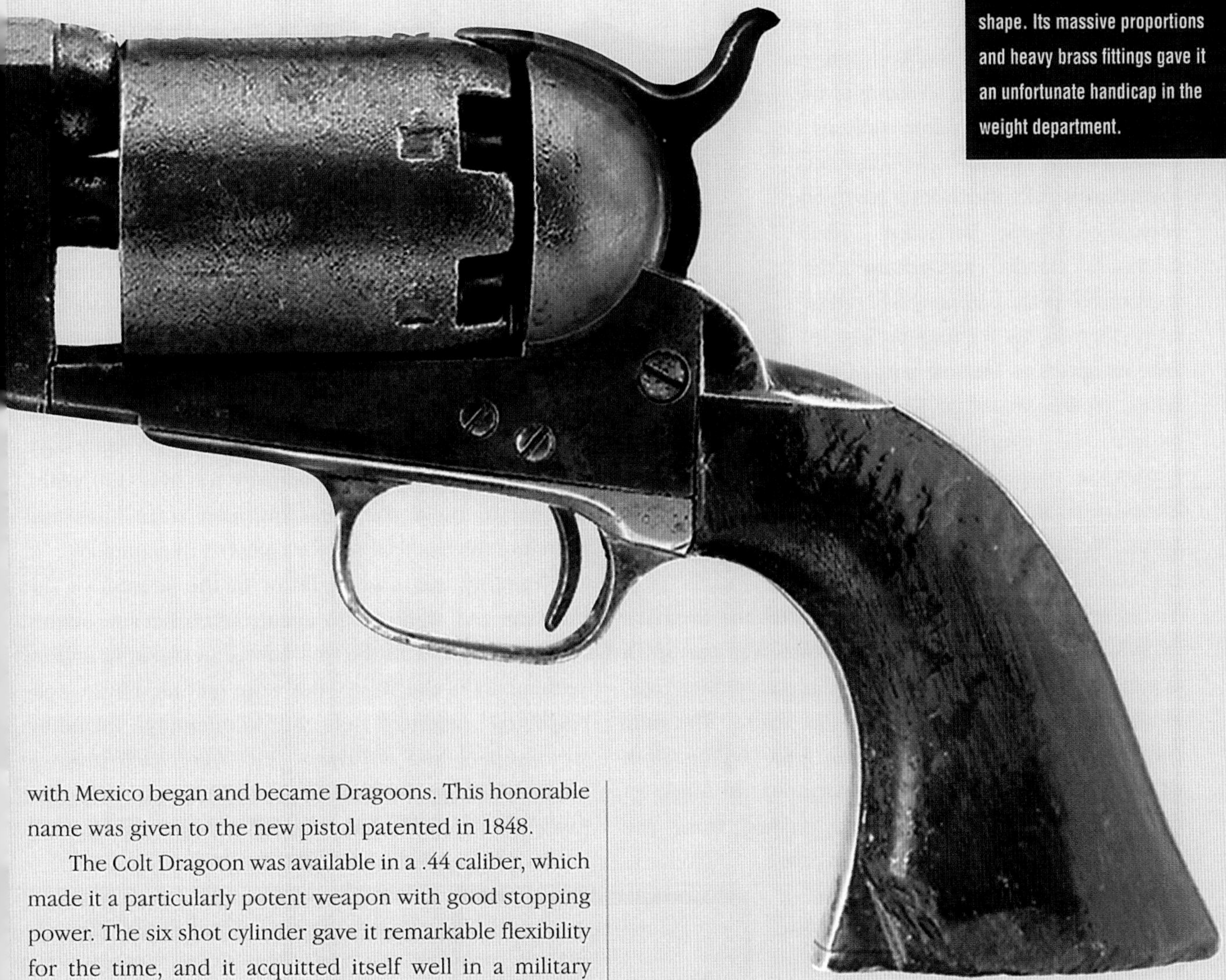

LEFT: The Colt Dragoon is one of the first models in what is regarded as the classic Colt shape. Its massive proportions and heavy brass fittings gave it an unfortunate handicap in the weight department.

with Mexico began and became Dragoons. This honorable name was given to the new pistol patented in 1848.

The Colt Dragoon was available in a .44 caliber, which made it a particularly potent weapon with good stopping power. The six shot cylinder gave it remarkable flexibility for the time, and it acquitted itself well in a military capacity against Indians and Mexicans alike. It's introduction was also well timed for use in the 1849 Gold Rush, when the demand for weapons of self defense rose alarmingly. Nobody was going to jump your claim staring down the barrel of a .44 Dragoon! However, the gun did have its drawbacks. Weighing in at a considerable four pounds, two ounces, it was the second largest Colt revolver ever made. This weight meant that the gun was supplied with a pommel holster rather than a belt type. Later models also had a shoulder stock, enabling it to be fired like a carbine. Many examples were factory engraved with Texas Ranger and Indian fight scenes, in honor of its pedigree.

Despite later advances in pistols, the Dragoon was carried for many years on the Frontier. Over 20,000 examples were made.

WELLS FARGO & CO.

Wells Fargo was one of the great institutions of the West, and was a positive force for the civilizing of the Wild Frontier. Its very name conjures a thrilling image of a six-horse stagecoach loaded with gold, thundering across the romantic plains landscape. Louis L'Amour clearly recognized the importance of the company, and refers to it often in his Western novels. In fact, its activities became part of the fabric of the American West, serving people of every background and profession, and actively seeking to control lawlessness, although as Clyde points out in *The Empty Land*, 'Wells Fargo does not build towns nor enforce the law…except along the stage routes.'

Henry Wells and William Fargo founded the company in 1852, and the company's first office was set up in downtown San Francisco at 420 Montgomery Street, right in the heart of the tent city of the '49ers. The new company offered banking (buying gold, selling bank drafts) and express, secure carriage for all kinds of cargo, especially gold dust and bullion from the newly sunk mines. Right from the beginning, there was also a thread of altruism in the company culture. Wells Fargo offered their services to all 'men, women, or children, rich or poor, white or black.' Indeed, they ran their business for all the settlers and frontiers people of the West, including blacks, whites, and Spanish-speaking Hispanics. William Wells was also an early proponent of sexual equality, later founding Wells College for Women in New York with the slogan, 'Give her the opportunity!' Several women were agents by the 1880s, sometimes taking over from their husbands as company employees when they were widowed. Veterans of the US Army have also worked for the company for over 150 years, helping to build the great overland stage lines and founding the financial service aspect of the company.

Integrity was a great factor in the success of the business and Wells Fargo agents often became highly respected figures in the new towns and volatile mining settlements of the West. They were recruited from well-respected members of the community, including storekeepers and attorneys, and were each given a certificate of appointment by the company. As well as the Express service, the agents also offered basic banking and financial services.

The company started their overland stagecoach line in the 1860s, and was

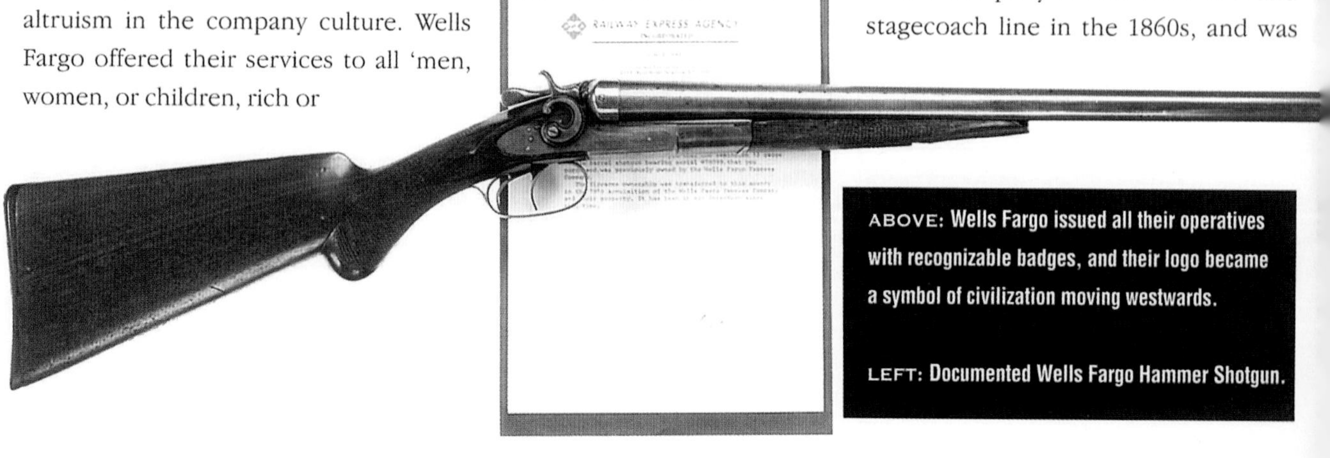

ABOVE: Wells Fargo issued all their operatives with recognizable badges, and their logo became a symbol of civilization moving westwards.

LEFT: Documented Wells Fargo Hammer Shotgun.

Wells Fargo stagecoaches often rode with a shotgun outrider for protection. The company established their business to serve all the frontiers people of the Western territories.

Madison Larkin was a Wells Fargo Messenger and shotgun guard, and would have worked for one or other of the local agents. He is photographed at Phoenix in 1877.

The Wells Fargo stagecoaches were often subject to hold ups, from desperados attracted by the gold and valuables they often conveyed, but armed guards usually protected these shipments.

also partly responsible for the Butterfield Overland Mail Company established in 1858 (which they later took over). They sent the mail by the fastest means possible, stagecoach, steamship, railroad, pony rider or telegraph, and their operatives often brought the mail through at dreadful personal risk. Wells Fargo also employed detectives to investigate fraud and any other illegal practices in connection with their business, together with armed escorts and shotgun riders to discourage theft and hold ups. They were reputed to carry cut down shotguns, which were easy to conceal under the seat of a wagon, and lethal at close range.

This modus operandi daunted many would-be villains. Ben Curry's gang (*Son of a Wanted Man*) didn't risk stage hold ups carrying large shipments of money or bullion precisely because these consignments would have shotgun guards. German Bayles (*The Man Called Noon*) rode as a Wells Fargo shotgun guard before going to the bad, and 'His activities had seesawed back and forth on both sides of the law.' L'Amour character J.B. Rimes (*The Man Called Noon*), became an outlaw by shooting a Wells Fargo agent in a disastrous hold up, but he redeems himself and goes on to become a Pinkerton detective. Matt Coburn (*The Empty Land*) is another Wells Fargo employee who goes on to represent the law. He started his illustrious career in enforcement by working as a shotgun messenger for the company. His would-be employer, Newton Clyde, also 'had the reputation of being one of Wells Fargo's best men, and had survived a few gun battles himself.' Clyde is well aware of the many stagecoach hold ups around the West—down in Arizona, on the Black Canyon run, and in Oregon, California and Colorado—and tries to hire Matt to run Confusion's gold bullion out of town.

Despite all their precautions, the company inevitably fell victim to crime and hold-ups from time to time, all of which were all widely covered in florid detail by contemporary newspapers (in sharp contract to the

Wells Fargo inscription above the barrels of the Wells Fargo Remington shotgun featured on page 152.

The distinctive Wells Fargo logo became a symbol, not only of the company, but also of the outside world in remote Western towns. It was an endorsement that the town had a future.

company's own concise and business-like notes). From 1877, Wells Fargo posted a standing reward of $300 for information about robberies and crimes against the company.

Ironically, in some bizarre circumstances, holdups could be good news for the passengers. L'Amour tells the story of how Joss Ringgold defended the stage he had just robbed from Apache attack. A petition was then circulated asking for a pardon for Ringgold. 'I think every employee of Wells Fargo signed it.'

By 1866, Wells Fargo was operating the major overland stagecoach lines west of the Missouri, and soon drove on to Salt Lake City. They gradually took over the routes of the Pony Express, and their stages eventually rolled over 3,000 miles of territory. The stagecoaches used by Wells Fargo were constructed by carriage builder J. Stephens Abbot, and master wheelwright Lewis Downing, in their Concord, New Hampshire, factory. The unique feature of the coach was its suspension, which rested on bullhide leather 'thoroughbraces,' giving the coaches a rolling gait rather than a jarring motion. Mark Twain accurately characterised the Wells Fargo coach as 'an imposing cradle on wheels.' The coaches weighed in at around 2,500 pounds, and decked out with a damask cloth interior, cost a stiff $1,100.

A modern re-creation of a Wells Fargo coach rolling into town.

Wells Fargo used many different kind of locks, mostly manufactured by Ayers, Climax, and Romer.

The stagecoaches were initially integrated into the railroad network. But as the rail barons pushed the railroad West, trains became an increasingly vital part of the Wells Fargo network. By 1888, the railroad enabled Wells Fargo to offer an 'Ocean-to-Ocean Service' through twenty-five states. The company was now divided into three departments, 'P' Pacific, 'C' Central, and 'A' Atlantic.

Wells Fargo continued to run the Express business, delivering valuable cargoes of every kind, up until 1918 when it was taken over as part of the government war effort.

It must have been pretty dusty on top of the traditional stages.

WINCHESTER 1873

When Bill Justin of the Bar J ranch discovers that he is losing stock to rustling, he looks for a couple of men to keep watch at his *Hanging Woman Creek* line camp. Pronto Pike and Eddie Holt are two drifters looking for a job, and fit the bill perfectly. Their new boss equips them with a wagon full of supplies, guns, and ammunition. Eddie is the first to discover the weaponry: ' "Pronto you come see this here." What he was showing me were two brand-new Winchester 73s and boxes with about 500 rounds of ammunition. And with them a note, scrawled on paper greasy with gun oil. "I been missing stock." '

Pronto waits to sight in the rifle, as he is dubious of hitting anything with the Colt .44s packed in the wagon.

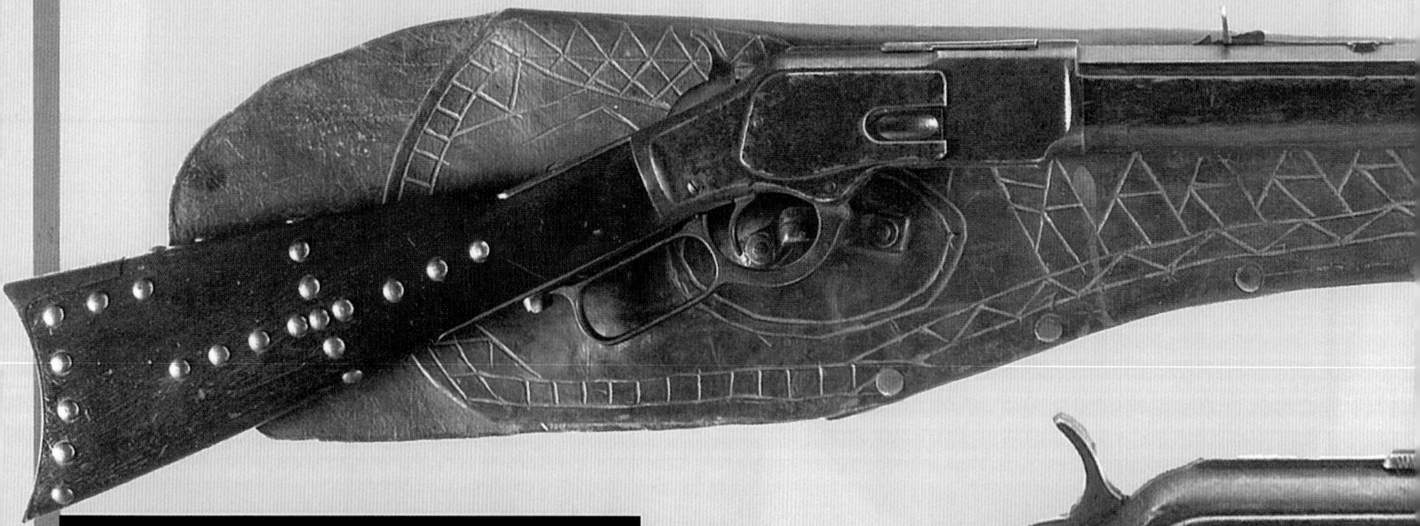

ABOVE: Example with personalized nickel tacks favored by Indians.

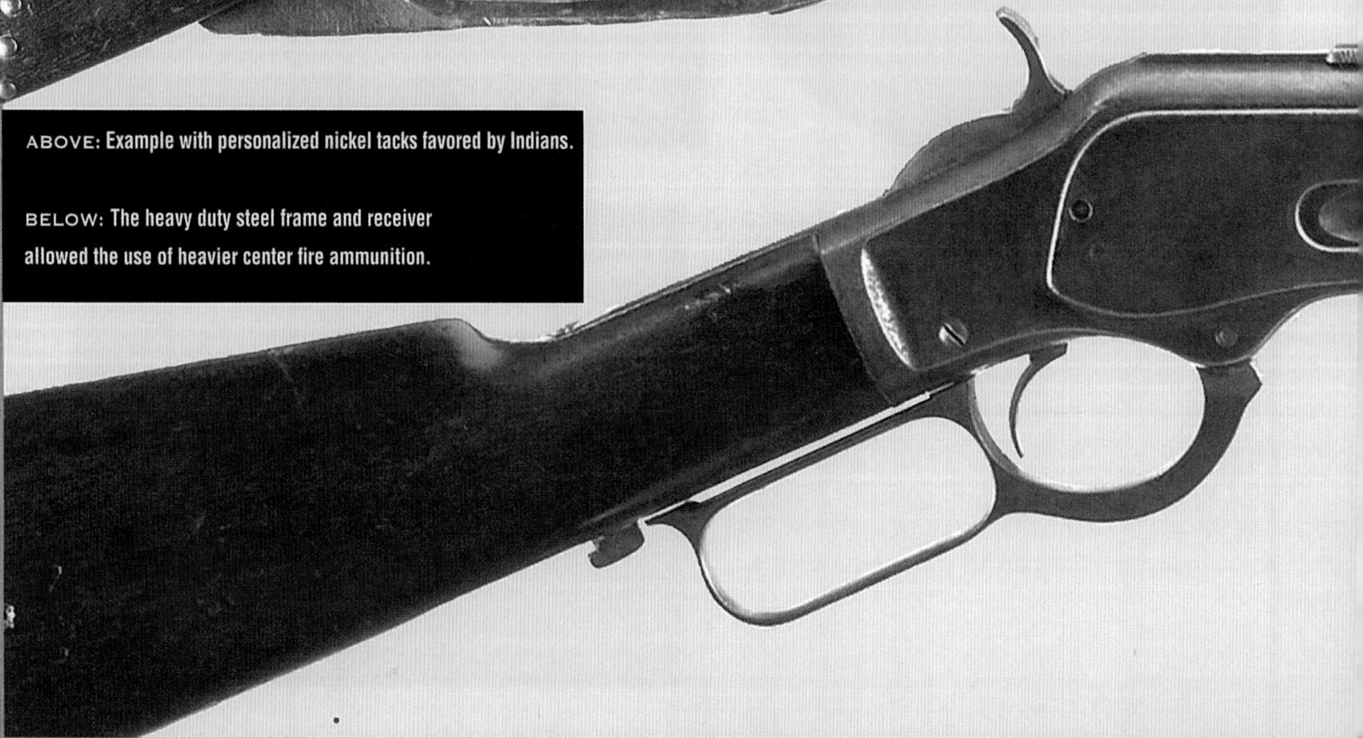

BELOW: The heavy duty steel frame and receiver allowed the use of heavier center fire ammunition.

He says that he has never owned a handgun because they are too expensive, even second-hand. He has been wont to carry a Winchester 'but that was a meat gun, and a man never knew when he would have to brush off a scalp-hunting Sioux.' Along with the Colt Peacemaker, the Winchester shared the reputation of being the 'gun that won the west.'

In reality, the frontier was all over by 1890 and the gun remained in production until 1919. This put the greater part of the model output well outside the period on which its fame rests.

The 1873 was an advance over the 1866 model, as its frame and receiver were made from stronger, lighter steel instead of brass. Gone was the pretty 'yellow-boy' look. This enabled the use of the more powerful center fire cartridge designated as .44-40. This was a .44 inch caliber bullet propelled by a cartridge containing 40 grains of black powder. It was a potent combination.

Colt launched the Peacemaker the same year and wisely offered the gun in the same range of calibers as the Winchester rifle. This meant that the ammunition was interchangeable and a man needed to carry only one sort of cartridge.

We show two models, both with 24 inch barrels. The second has a tooled leather scabbard. This gun was the property of a cowboy, Hug Brown, and it bears his initials.

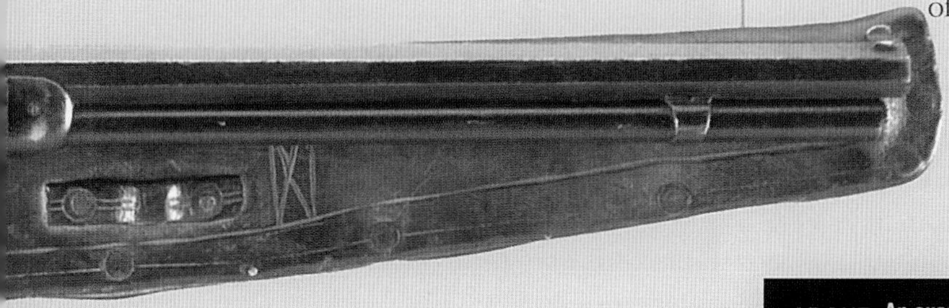

ABOVE: An example of a hand-made leather tooled saddle scabbard.

BELOW: Classic Winchester lines make this one of the most recognizable Western arms.

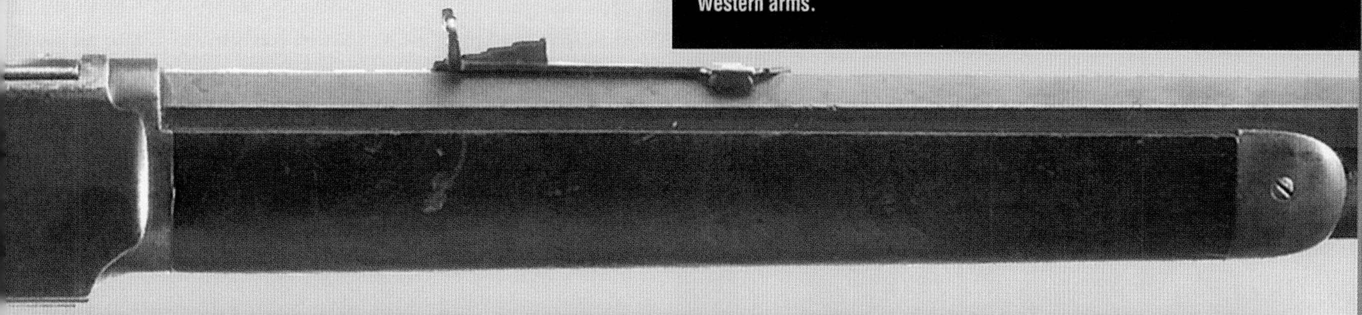

SPECIFICATIONS

CALIBER: 0.44-40	**ACTION:** 15 shot lever action
LENGTH OF BARREL: 24 inches	**YEAR OF MANUFACTURE:** 1890
BARREL SHAPE: Octagonal	**MANUFACTURER:** Winchester Repeating Arms Company, New Haven, Connecticut
FINISH: Blue/casehardened	
GRIPS: Walnut	

GOLD DIGGERS

The California gold rush started on January 24, 1848, when James Marshall (who was building a sawmill for his wealthy employer John Sutter), found gold nuggets glittering at the bottom of a ditch. 'It made my heart thump,' he said. In *The Empty Land*, animal tracker 'Jim' had had a similar experience back in 1824, picking up a gold nugget in a remote mountain gully in western Utah. Little does he know that 'within its tiny golden heart lay something explosive and violent (that) would one day shatter the Nevada-Utah nights with gunfire.'

Initially, it appeared that the surface gold was widely spread, and a huge influx of men came West to exploit it—the forty-niners. Some were equipped with little more than tin spoons. Louis L'Amour describes them on their way in to gold rush town Confusion, 'Hundreds of belted men were coming up the trail, men booted, unshaved and wild, coming up the highroad to hell. If they did not find their ticket in this town they would in the next.' Soldiers and sailors deserted to join the gold rush, and immigrants flocked to the El Dorado of America. Americans usually came across the long and dangerous Overland Trail, while overseas immigrants came by sea to San Francisco, often abandoning their boats in the harbor. As L'Amour said, among them were 'some good minin' men, but they'll be outnumbered by the rowdies, the gamblers, the killers, the sneak thieves, short-card artists, and cutthroats.'

Gold towns all had a Registry Office for staking claims and valuing finds.

Panning for gold was a hard and often thankless task. Many gold miners died in the filthy conditions.

The discovery of gold led to a massive demographic shift to the West. Men came from every corner of the earth in the thousands, from Europe, Hawaii, China, Peru, Mexico, and Chile. This gave a cosmopolitan feel to the West Coast that is still evident today. The Chinese immigrants were particularly active in importing their cultural traditions, setting up Chinese restaurants and laundries. Over 90,000 people flooded into the area in that first year, and San Francisco grew from a town of 2,000 citizens in 1848 to become the West's first city, with a population of 35,000, by the following year. In fact, the gold rush resulted in more immigrants flocking to California than to the rest of the States combined.

Many of the miners were desperate men; ex-convicts

from Australia, escaping slaves and dispossessed Indians. Their 'character' spilled over in the kind of violence and lawlessness Matt Coburn is hired to control. The miners lived a hard and filthy life, and many died in the goldfields, their health undermined by the dreadful living conditions, and corrosive disappointment. Gold camps like Confusion sprang up overnight, and many died just as quickly when their claims were worked out. But some survive to this day.

The flood of immigration also affected the wider life of the Plains. In 1849, there was a devastating outbreak of cholera that killed many immigrants and frontiers people, and infected many of the native tribes. L'Amour's gold-finding trapper, Jim, was now running a tavern and livery stables in a Missouri town. Serving diseased immigrants on their way West resulted in the tragic death of his wife and son. Indirectly, this devastating experience leads him to tell Dick Felton and co. about his long-forgotten nugget, and to his own death as he tries to retrace his steps to where he found it. Felton et al. soon find the gold, and the cycle is perpetuated. Ignorance and greed also led immigrants to decimate and disrupt the wildlife of the Plains, which in turn led to starvation for many Indians.

For many, the journey West to 'see the elephant' (a euphemism for the gold rush experience) was hellish, according to one of the disappointed hopefuls, 'death is in the pot.' Gold fever left many men broken and bitter. Many returned empty-handed to the East, and to New England in particular. But many others stayed on in the West, on the lookout for other ways to make a living.

By 1852, most of the surface gold deposits were worked out, (just like Lilith Prescott's worthless inheritance), and only wealthy investors could afford the heavy machinery and labor necessary for deep shaft mining. Zeb Rawlings and his sons Prescott and Linus explore such a mine in *How the West Was Won*. In fact, the most lucrative activity was often supplying the miners' requirements, rather than the often futile gold digging. Mormon Sam Brannan set up an impromptu general store right next to the original Sutter dig, and made far more money out of the strike than Sutter himself. Storekeeper Gage of Confusion is part of this lucrative supply network.

An early tin type of Black Bart, one of the most notorious gold field robbers. His respectable appearance belies his true profession.

Louis L'Amour's attitude is always rather ambiguous to gold, and to wealth in general. Greed for both is often at the root of persecution (such as that inflicted on the original Barney Sackett in *To the Far Blue Mountains*), or moral corruption, like Peg Cullane's murderous lust for Fan Davidge's treasure. To him, the real wealth of the West lay in the land itself.

COLT REVOLVING SHOTGUN

Louis L'Amour really demonstrates his knowledge of Western armaments in *Utah Blaine*, and the book is a rich source of exotic weaponry. During a nighttime standoff at the Bar B Ranch the three defenders Utah Blaine, Dan Timm, and Rip Coker 'advertise' the prowess of their weapons for the benefit of the opposition. Rip Coker, an ornery hand who has thrown in his lot with Blaine despite the odds against him, uses positive psychology to outwit Russ Nevers and his men. He is armed with a Winchester rifle, which he manages to pass off as a Colt Revolving Shotgun in the dark. 'Wish you gents would make up your minds to die,' Coker commented casually. 'This here Colt shotgun is loadin' my arms down.' If it had been the Colt, it would have been a big gun. The gun barrels were between 30 inch (with a round profile) and a massive 36 inch (when the profile was part octagonal). The cylinder held four chambers of 10 gauge shot, which would retain its velocity for a

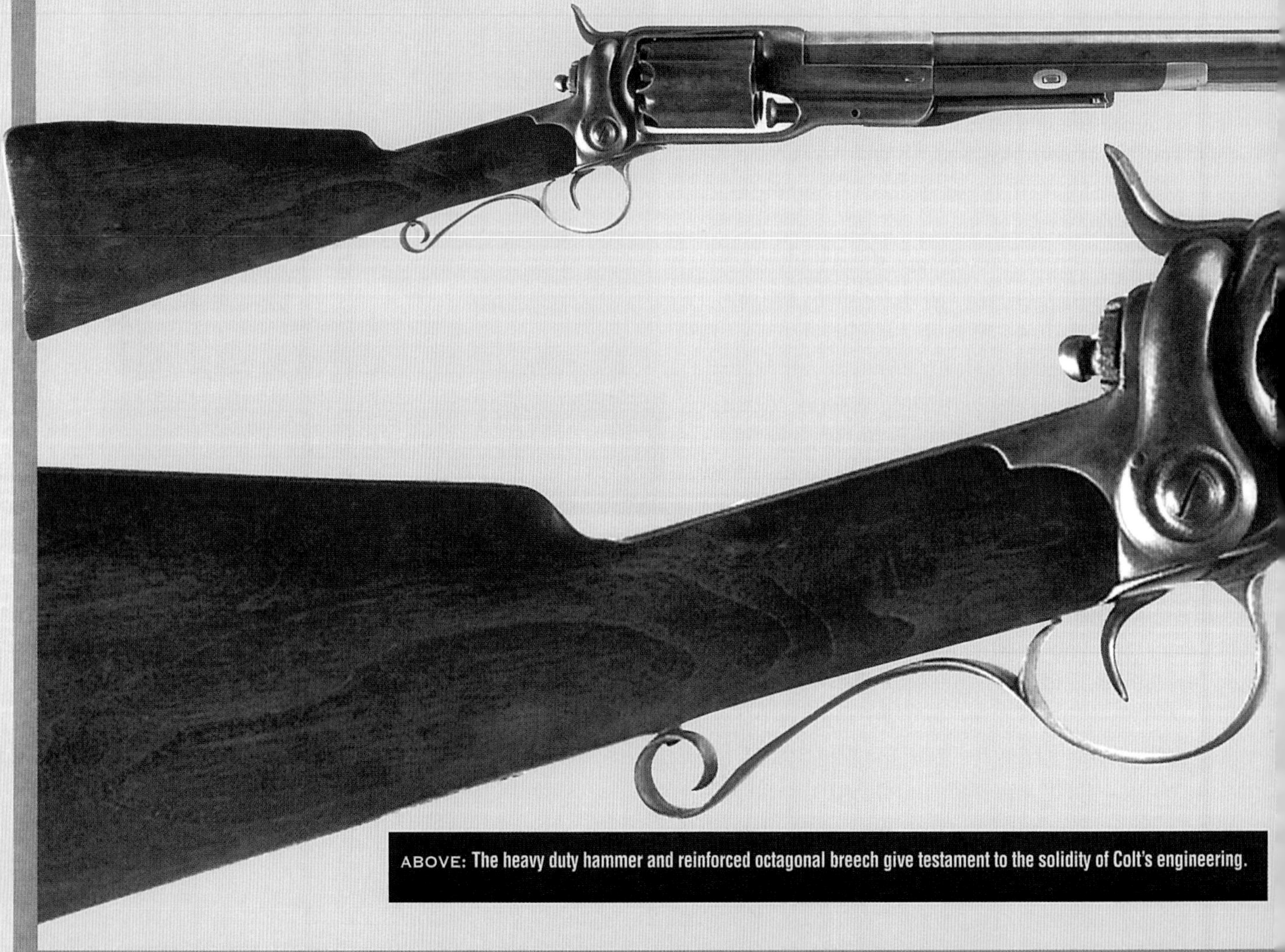

ABOVE: The heavy duty hammer and reinforced octagonal breech give testament to the solidity of Colt's engineering.

reasonable distance when discharged down a 3/4 inch, three foot long barrel! Rather nervous in the dark, Russ Nevers quietly reflects that 'a blast from a shotgun did awful things to a man, and this gun held four shells. And there was the possibility of reloads before they could get to him.' Indeed Colt produced charger flasks to enable all four chambers to be reloaded at once. In terms of rate of fire, this gun was not one to be underestimated.

The weapon owed its existence to the much earlier 1839 Paterson revolving shotgun. In the early days, Samuel Colt believed that rifles, carbines, and shotguns would be the mainstay of his business and set out to apply his revolving mechanism to these types of armaments. The Paterson had a six shot chamber of smaller caliber, .62 of an inch.

The later model was patented on September 10th, 1850 and became the Colt Model 1855. There was a flurry of competition about this time with revolving long arms being introduced by manufacturers such as Roper, Cherington, Porter, and James Warner.

At the time, 'revolving' seemed to be the answer to repeat-shooting firearms, and became so for handguns for the rest of the century. But for rifles and shotguns, the future lay with the Henry and the underlever action of the later Winchesters.

LEFT: The Revolving Shotgun has the appearance of a gun made up from several different weapons.

BELOW: Oval Side nail cover is a detail which harks back to the days of flintlock arms.

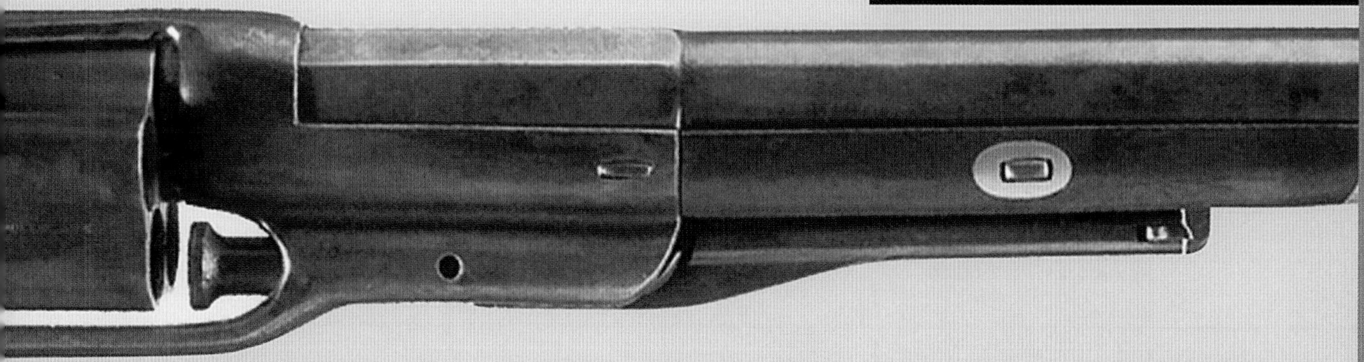

SPECIFICATIONS

CALIBER: 0.75	**ACTION:** Single action four-shot revolver
LENGTH OF BARREL: 36 inches	**YEAR OF MANUFACTURE:** 1855
BARREL SHAPE: Part octagonal	**MANUFACTURER:**
FINISH: Blue, casehardened	Colonel Colt, Hartford, Connecticut
GRIPS: Walnut	

WESTERN TOWNS

Louis L'Amour's towns reflect the preoccupations of the West itself—cattle, gold, the law, and good times. They have a great cinematic quality and are almost characters in their own right. They are also full of colorful Western characters of every description, on both sides of the law. Although the townsfolk may have acquired a thin veneer of domestication, L'Amour points out that, 'In most western towns the butcher, baker and the candlestick-maker were ex-cowhands, Indian-fighters, or Civil War veterans, always aching to get back into the saddle again.' The presentation of his towns is always done in a way that defines them as definitely Western, subtly different than those back East. The scale is different – the landscape is bigger and the towns are smaller. Barney Pike describes Miles City in *Hanging*

A typical western store front, catering to the footwear needs of the local gents.

An interesting line up of stores, catering for life's necessities – liquor, cigars, dry goods, and clothing.

Woman Creek, 'An eastern man looking along that street would think there wasn't much too it, but he would be wrong. In my time I'd been a sight of places, and I'd call Miles City a big town.' When Ruble Noon recovers consciousness in *The Man Called Noon*, he can immediately tell where he is, 'hitching rails along the street, a few cow ponies standing there. Hence it was a western town.'

As in the West itself, the town founders knew that the first thing to establish in any new settlement was the rule of law. This was especially true in the volatile mining communities and cow towns that sprang up without any natural roots. In *The Empty Land*, Dick Felton, one of the founders of gold rush town Confusion says, 'We must have law here.' Indeed the whole town faces obliteration without the imposition of law, and it may already be 'gone too far.' L'Amour rather unflatteringly describes the character of the town and its inhabitants, 'These mining towns aren't like the Kansas cow towns. The men they are up against here aren't like the Texans…most of (these men) are back-shooters, dry-gulchers, murderers. They're thoroughly vicious.' In fact, they include convicts from Australia, ex-inmates of the Yuma prison, and many have even appeared on 'Wanted' posters. Luckily, lawman Matt Coburn is soon on the scene. With his wide experience of

Offices for the mail company, the telegraph office, and more stores supplying dry goods and liquor – a recurrent theme.

A re-creation of a typical general store, with a wonderful interior replete with everything a frontiersperson could need – besom brooms, oven paddles, salt pork (in the barrels), dried meat, grain, flour, molasses, oil lamps, pitchers, pans and some dainty china.

frontier settlements, he 'knew the sound of such towns. Each had its own tone, its own particular hum.' He studies Confusion 'like a chessboard' to enable him to gain control. 'The council want a clean town and I'm going to give it to them.' He announces his intentions with an unambiguous 'Notice.'

To Thieves, Murderers, and Short-Card Artists;
You are no longer welcome in Confusion.
Those listed below can get out or shoot it out,
And start any time they are ready.
(Signed by Matt Coburn)

But perhaps the strongest hint as to the 'tone' of the town is the names of the saloons, and the mines themselves –

The Nugget, The Bucket of Blood, The Main Chance, The Bon-Ton Restaurant, the Discovery, and the Treasure Vault.

Coburn knows that these frontier towns could (and did) evaporate like a puff of smoke, if their water, gold, or luck ran out. 'I like to look at new towns,' he says 'to wonder how long they will last.' At this time, the population of the West was very fluid, with incomers restlessly moving about, searching for land and opportunity. It became scattered with abandoned 'ghost' towns. The coming (or not) of the railroad could also make or break a town. Marshal 'Borden Chantry glanced out the kitchen window toward the train station. When the tracks were built through town they fortunately passed within fifty yards of his home' (*Son of a Wanted Man*), but the train also attracts criminality.

If they developed, the towns went on to cater for the Westerners' every need. One of the first of these was communication, and a feeling of being a part of the civilized world – whether or not this was actually true. Like a Wells Fargo office, a local newspaper gave a flimsy new town a feeling of solidity and permanence.

Most towns needed a sawmill for house-building lumber.

Of course, there were also less usual items on sale on the typical western high street, including gun powder.

APOTHECARY
ESTABLISHED
1852

TOWN MARSHAL

LONE STAR
SALOON

LONESOME DOVE
MINING
CO

WESTERN UNION
Telegraph Office

LIVERY

TEXAS

A panorama of re-created buildings found in a typical frontier town. They reflect the interests of the townsfolk, and the raw nature of western life.

1 The town well
2 The apothecary
3 The Cantina
4 The Town Marshal's office
5 The Lone Star Saloon
6 The office of the Lonesome Dove Mining Company
7 The Western Union Telegraph Office
8 The livery yard
9 The Texas Rangers' office
10 The Gunsmith
11 The town hotel
12 Wells Fargo Office
13 The church meeting house
14 The bank
15 A photographer sets up his tripod in front of the marshal's office

The railroad became hugely important to the cattle industry. Many animals were shipped East on the hoof.

In *Utah Blaine*, Ralston Forbes owns the newspaper at Red Creek, and uses it to see justice done in the town. In Confusion, 'the press' arrives soon after the town gets started: 'Sturdevant Fife is coming up the trail with his printing press. He's a law and order man, and he runs his newspaper with a sawed-off shotgun on his desk.' Fife is shown setting the type for his first front page in Confusion, ' "...Men Killed on the First Day." I'm leaving the number open. The day ain't over yet.' Fife had promised the original owner of his press to 'tell the truth, the whole truth and nothin' but the truth.' Like Ralston Forbes, he ends up wielding a gun rather than a pen, in support of Marshal Coburn.

Red Creek, the town at the centre of the action in *Utah Blaine* is the other archetypal Western settlement, whose economy depends on cattle. 'It was a one-street town with hitching rails before most of the buildings. The bank was conveniently across from the livery stable. Beyond the stable was the blacksmith shop, facing a general store across the street.' The store was at the heart of the town, and was fundamental to its survival, as well as being a social place to visit. Newt Clyde says of Gage, Confusion's understandably nervous storekeeper, 'When he leaves, the town is finished.' 'There was a scattering of other buildings and behind them, rows of residences, some of the yards fenced, most of them bare and untended.' Utah eats in the enticingly named Shoo-Fly Restaurant. L'Amour evokes the town very simply, but we recognize it and the people we meet there. They are both essential Westerners.

Abilene was the first true 'cow town' in the US, and is featured in L'Amour. Illinois businessman J.C. McCoy established the cattle market there in 1867. Over 600,000 heads were driven into the town in a single year, and were then railroaded on the hoof to the Eastern cities. 'Abilene in 1871 was a booming town, but the boom was almost over...(it was) wild and woolly, and it was loud,' full of dusty cowboys and drivers. Abilene's town authorities brought in Wild Bill Hickok as Marshal to try and tame the town. But although he successfully introduced gun control, he failed to establish the kind of peace the townsfolk longed for. They decided to forgo the income from the cattle drives, and the business went to other stops on the line, such as Ellsworth, Newton, and Dodge City itself, the last and most wicked of the Kansas cow towns.

In fact, the 'cow town' tag wasn't considered to be entirely flattering. Towns with other roles liked to point these out, 'Miles City wasn't just a cow town, for Fort Keogh was close by with around a thousand men –

A typical frontier hotel and its guests.

Many towns were abandoned when their gold, silver, water, or luck ran out, and became atmospheric 'ghost' settlements.

soldiers and civilian employees.'

The facilities of a typical Western town reflect the diverse requirements of the townsfolk. The usual range of services included the Assay Office (to register land and stake claims), the livery stables, a hotel, various saloons, a bank, general store, Wells Fargo office, gunsmith, barber, Marshal's office (which might also accommodate the town jail), blacksmith, restaurant, the town well, Western Union Telegraph office, a Texas Rangers office, an apothecary, dentist, school house, newspaper office and printing shop, town photographer, church meeting house and, of course, the town cemetery.

Perhaps the depth of Louis L'Amour's fascination with these frontier towns and settlements is best shown by his intention to recreate a Western town of 1865—Shalako.

'Where the borders of Utah, Arizona, New Mexico, and Colorado meet.' In the very heart of the West, 'Historically authentic from whistle to well, it will be a live, operating town, as well as a movie location and tourist attraction.' Sadly, this ambition was never realized in his lifetime.

REMINGTON DOUBLE BARREL MODEL 1889 SHOTGUN

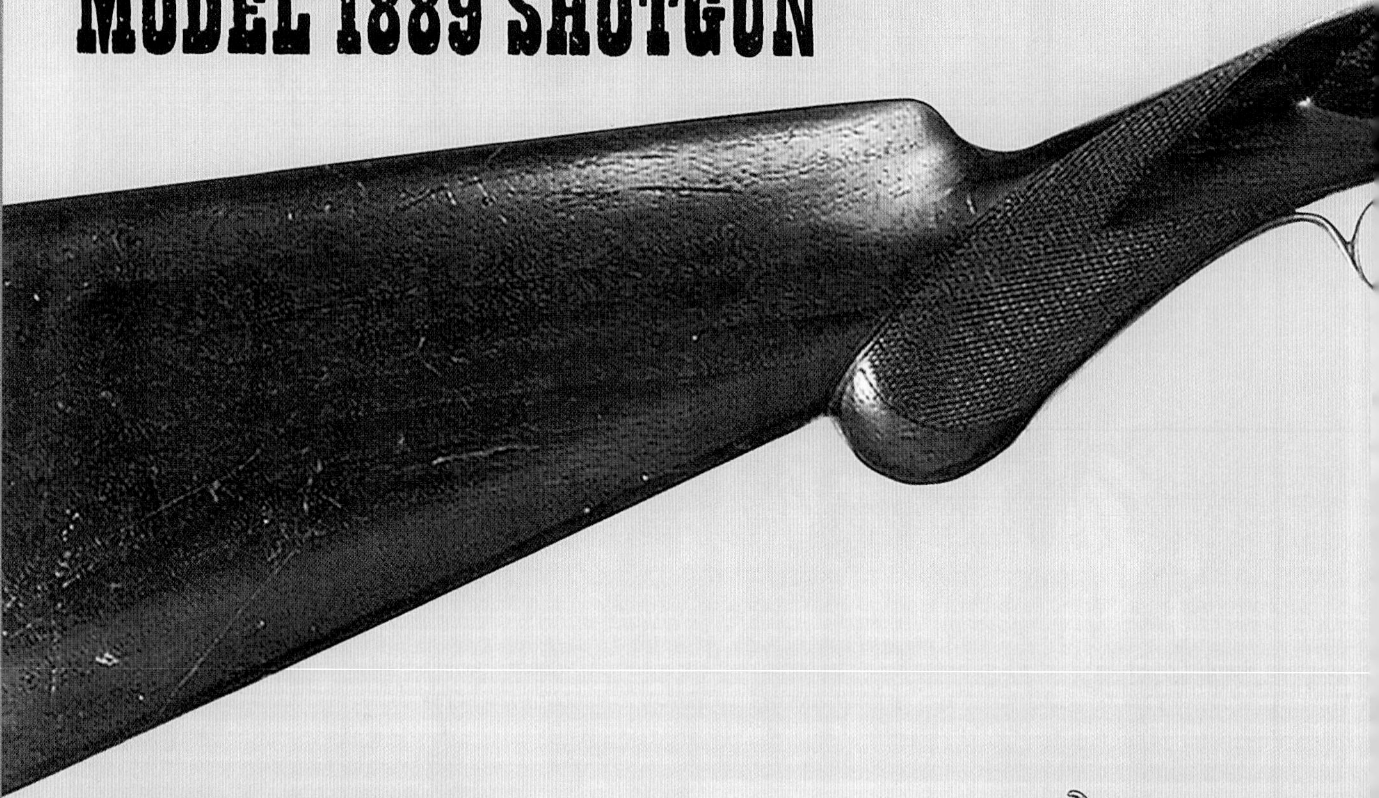

ABOVE: Close up of the checkered pistol grip and double triggers show that the gun has been well used.

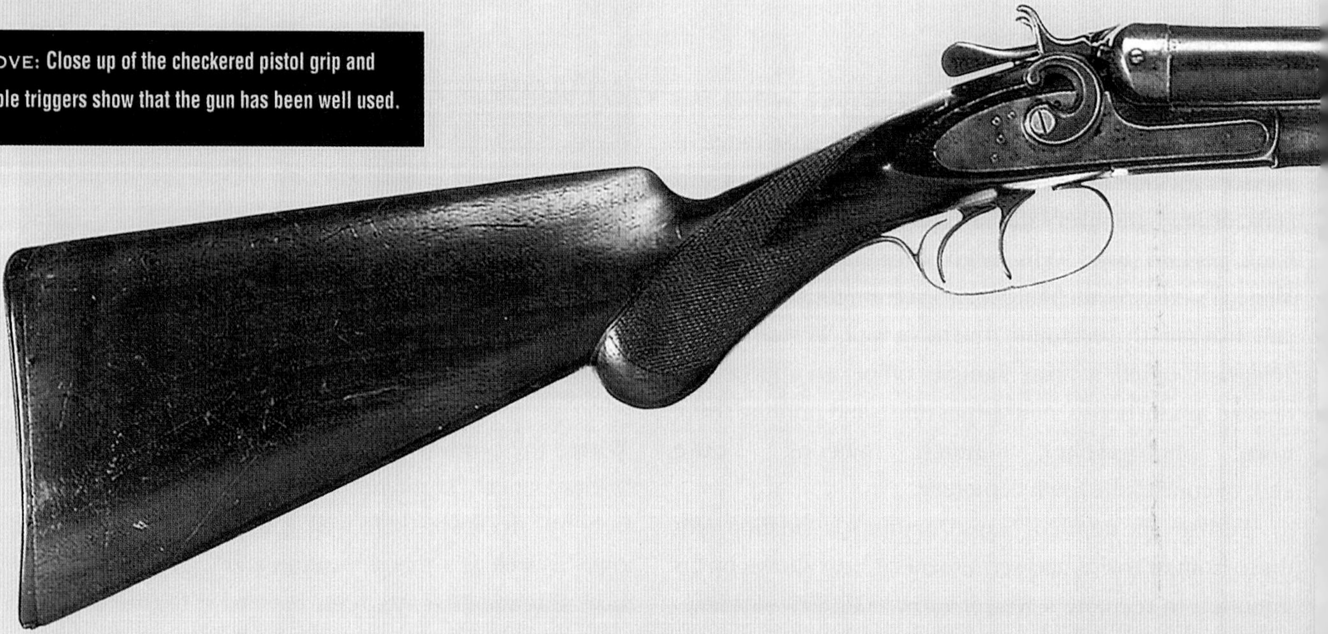

In SON OF A WANTED MAN, we are introduced to Doc Sawyer, a character who is mistaken for a gambler by the sheriff. His respectable dress sets him apart from the cowhands. It is possible that L'Amour based the character – to some extent – on the famous Doc Holliday, who is also mentioned in his work. Holliday was a member of Wyatt Earp's Dodge City Peace Commission. His weapon of choice was usually a shotgun, and Earp described him as 'the nerviest, fastest, deadliest man with a six-gun I ever saw.' He was also a professional gambler and killer. Doc Sawyer is a much nicer man, who although tough is not violent for the sake of it. Mike Bastian, for whom the novel is named, finds the Doc holding four of bad guy Kerb Perrin's men 'backed against the wall,' courtesy of his shotgun.

Western Shotguns were specially designed to create respect in close quarter fights. They had shortened barrels to allow for maneuverability and a widespread shot pattern. To this day, criminals 'saw off' barrels to achieve the same effect. At close quarters Doc Sawyer has the drop on four of Perrin's men simply because a single twitch of his fingers would send them all to hell in pieces.

The guns had a pistol grip stock for firing from the hip and external hammers for quick cocking. They were particularly popular with law enforcement agents and stagecoach guards.

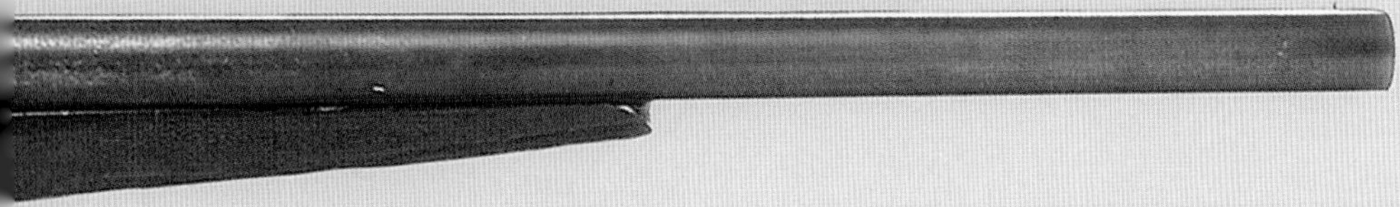

SPECIFICATIONS

CALIBER: 12 gauge	ACTION: Breech loading double barrel
LENGTH OF BARREL: 18 inches	YEAR OF MANUFACTURE: 1889
BARREL SHAPE: Round	MANUFACTURER:
FINISH: Browned steel	Remington Arms Company, Ilion, New York
GRIPS: Walnut, checkered with pistol grip	

THE RAILROAD

'The time is coming, and fast, too, when, in the sense it is now understood, THERE WILL BE NO WEST.'

UNION PACIFIC ENGINEER

At the end of the Civil War, the railroad network ended in Missouri, and there was a general feeling that this was inhibiting the development of the frontier region. In reality, the West was American in name only. As early as 1817, there were calls for a transcontinental railroad, which would be the 'golden vein' of the country. When it finally came, the railroad transformed the life of the West, perhaps even more fundamentally than it had changed that of the East. The transcontinental link was a huge undertaking, which required 1,780 miles of track to be laid. Two companies jointly undertook this massive task, the Central Pacific and Union Pacific Railroad Companies. They were financed by a combination of federal funds and creative accountancy. Their task was to start simultaneously at the east and west extremes of the line, and join the tracks at some initially undetermined point to form a single, transcontinental railroad.

Luggage cart at a station depot.

The dramatic topography of the route demanded stupendous feats of engineering and endurance. The railroad crews used enormous quantities of high explosive to blast tunnels through solid granite, and were beset by devastating extremes of hot and cold climatic conditions. Central Pacific took three years to break out of the High Sierra into the Nevada Desert, while Union Pacific employed over 10,000 men to build their part of the line. The railroad crews came from many different backgrounds, and included many Chinese and Irish workers. The railway also employed ex-Confederate soldiers, Mexicans, Germans, Englishmen, and former slaves. The Chinese workers were given particular dangerous and difficult jobs,

'The great Pacific Railway is commenced.... Immigration will soon pour into these valleys. Ten millions of emigrants will settle in this golden land in twenty years.... This is the grandest enterprise under God!'

GEORGE FRANCIS TRAIN

including handling high explosives. They were also paid at a lower rate than their white co-workers. It is reckoned that 1,200 perished building the Central Pacific section.

'Tent cities' housing the workers were always to be found at the end of the line, replete with prostitutes, pimps, gamblers, saloonkeepers, and gunmen: all eager to relieve the workers of their pay. Unsurprisingly, they were dens of violence, brawling, and disease, colloquially known as 'Hell on Wheels.' L'Amour calls his end-of-line tent town End of the Track, and remarks 'nowhere in so small a space had there ever been concentrated so large a percentage of vice…it was rough, bawdy, brutal.'

In 1869, thc two lines converged in Utah. This marked a hugely significant moment for the entire nation, but came at a tremendous cost. Effectively, the West was changed forever in many different ways—positive and negative.

Many fortunes were built by the railroads, and San Francisco was peppered by the mansions of the rail magnates, like Cleve and Lilith Van Valen's house on Nob Hill. Cleve had risen to the position of President of the San Francisco- Kansas City Railroad. But L'Amour shows how these fortunes were often virtually fictitious, visible only on paper. Lilith is forced to sell up after his death.

The building of the railroad was a major factor in the extinction of the buffalo. Meat hunters like L'Amour's Jethro Stuart depleted the herds to feed the railway workers. Buffalo Bill did this work in real life, and reckoned that he alone shot over 4,000 animals. Buffalo and other game were even shot

The Central Pacific and Union Pacific railroads converged in Utah in 1869. The final spike was made of gold.

The magnificent Union Pacific engine 82, 'Helper' and its crew, between Echo and Evanston in 1872.

from the trains themselves. This became so common that The Kansas Pacific Railroad ran a taxidermy service to mount the trophies of their customers. Even the son of the Russian czar came to hunt buffalo from the train, hiring a luxuriously equipped private train, and Buffalo Bill acted as his guide.

The coming of the railroad was disastrous for the great majority of the indigenous tribes. Many Plains Indians, especially the Cheyenne and Lakota were deeply opposed to the trains forging through their ancestral hunting grounds, and launched attacks on the railroad workers. The Arapahoe also killed many railway employees, including surveyors. Things became so difficult that the US army was forced to protect them, 'for the railroad would not and could not advance even a step without protection from the army.' But this proves to be an almost impossible task, as Lieutenant Zeb Rawlings finds out. The railroad companies consistently broke their word to the Indians, and brought their revenge down on their workers. Zeb tries to arrange a peace deal with Chief Walks-His-Horses, who describes the railroad as the 'blazing and iron trail for the Iron Horse,' but unknown to him, he ends up burying his own uncle, surveyor Sam Prescott, who has been killed in an Indian attack.

The railroad had a huge impact on Western immigration. As Mike King, the railroad contractor in *How the West Was Won* says, 'Anybody should have known people would come West if the railroad gave them a chance.' The railroad companies actively encouraged this immigration. They built stations along the line to encourage settlers to live close to the railroad, and even employed agents to scout for European immigrants.

One of these men alone, C.B. Schmidt, was responsible for the settling of 60,000 German immigrants along the route of the Santa Fe Railroad. These agents also brought many Eastern emigrants out to the West, and carried many men to the later gold rushes. The rail routes out of the West also enabled the cattle industry to export world-wide, particularly after the introduction of refrigerated cars in the 1880s.

Just like every other aspect of Western life, the trains also became of focus for crime. Echoing the real-life crimes of the James gang, there are many train holdups in Louis L'Amour's work. Even though he is wounded, Zeb Rawlings finally shoots down train robber Charlie Gant, and is rewarded with a Winchester '76 engraved with the 'Compliments of the Gold City Mining Company & Citizens.'

Hard on the success of the transcontinental route, many other railway companies began to criss-cross the Plains with their lines: Kansas Pacific, Northern Pacific, Denver Pacific, Texas and Pacific, Burlington and Missouri River, Denver and Rio Grande, Atchison, Topeka, and Santa Fe.

The wilderness was gone forever.

The railroad strode across the West.

PADDY WORKS ON THE RAILROAD

In eighteen hundred and forty-two
I left the old world for the new
Bad cess to the luck that
brought me through
To work upon the railway

Our contractor's name it was Tom King
He kept a store to rob the men
A Yankee clerk with ink and pen
To cheat Pat on the railroad

It's 'Pat do this' and 'Pat do that'
Without a stocking or cravat
And nothing but an old straw hat
While Pat works on the railroad.

WINCHESTER MODEL 1887 LEVER ACTION SHOTGUN

SPECIFICATIONS	
CALIBER: 12-Gauge	**ACTION:** 5 shot lever action
LENGTH OF BARREL: 28 inches	**YEAR OF MANUFACTURE:** 1887
BARREL SHAPE: Round	**MANUFACTURER:** Winchester Repeating Arms Co., New Haven, Connecticut
FINISH: Blue/casehardened	
GRIPS: Walnut	

LEFT: **The 1887 Shotgun was hardly the most elegant of the company's weapons.**

BELOW: **Close-up of the familiar Winchester underlever action and 5 shot magazine tube slung under the barrel.**

In the final years of the Frontier, weapons evolved into more deadly versions of the earlier arms. Gone was the primitive percussion system, which took time to load, and muzzle-loaders that suffered from variable powder charges and poor gas sealing. The center-fire brass cartridge and double action had made the revolver a much more serious weapon. Outlaws like Billy the Kid caught on very quickly to the latest models, such as the Colt Lightning and Frontier types. Rifles were also now available with reliable repeating mechanisms. Similarly, shotgun design had to move with the times.

In Louis L'Amour's Western novels, the plot often calls for a shotgun to pin down opposing forces of overwhelming strength. Shotguns also appear in the role of protecting jails or bullion shipments where their close-range devastation would deter potential hold ups. But to this point they suffered from the serious drawback of having only a two shot capacity in double barrel form. Colt had developed an early version of the revolving shotgun but this never really took off. It was left to Winchester to develop a lever action shotgun to reflect their successful rifles. Designed by John Browning, the 1887 shotgun was chunky and aggressive looking—just right for a weapon designed to intimidate. It had a five-shot magazine in a tube positioned under the barrel, and was available in 10 and 12-gauge. The barrel lengths of the gun ranged from 32 inches to a 'sawn-off' 20 inches for crowd control (or criminal purposes).

The gun was a favorite weapon with the Texas Rangers, and it continued in production until 1920. A weapon of this kind was used by Texan lawman, George W. Scarborough, who killed the assassin of John Wesley Hardin—John Selman—in an alley. The outlaw Kid Curry in turn, murdered Scarborough. Violent times indeed!

WESTERN WOMEN

Despite Barney Pike's assertion (in *Hanging Woman Creek*) that the West is 'hell on horses and women,' Louis L'Amour's heroines often seem more poised and focused than their male equivalents.

From the start of the migration to the West, the position of frontier women was substantially different from that of women in the East. Women in the West represented a highly valued asset in short supply, and this was reflected in the greater status and freedom they enjoyed. Utah was the first territory to enfranchise women, while California was the first state to legislate for married women to retain ownership of their property. This was partly because this was the Mexican tradition, and partly to attract wealthy women to make the move West to get married.

Louis L'Amour describes a very wide spectrum of women in his Western novels, and most of his female characters are very successful in adapting to this new environment. The facts of Western settlement seem to bear this out. Although it is recognized that very few women initiated the trek to the West, once there, the vast majority of the women settlers proved that they were the equals, or even the superiors, of men in trials of bravery and fortitude. For instance, at the end of the appalling winter endured by the Donner party, snowed in the Sierra, the survivors were reduced to cannibalism. But all the women survived while eight out of ten men perished.

Several female L'Amour characters are also credited with out-performing their male counterparts. In *To the Far Blue Mountains*, Barney Sackett describes the redoubtable Lila (his wife Abigail's maid) as being 'worth three men.' She takes a full part in their adventures, and uses her culinary skills to bring an entire pirate ship to heel. As she says of herself 'Wherever a man can go, I can go…I shall be no burden,' and her brother fully endorses this, saying 'As for the savages, if they molest my sister, God have mercy upon them, for she will not!' Cohan similarly describes the hard women of the gold rush towns as being 'tough enough to whip any two men in camp, and ready to do it.'

But we feel that the women L'Amour himself admires the most are his rather more attractive 'love interest' characters. Throughout the canon of his work, his good women, the ones that his heroes fall for, are almost universally described as 'ladies.' According to L'Amour, being a 'lady' has nothing to do with background or upbringing, but is rather a combination of innate qualities: modesty, strength, intelligence, beauty, and self-possession. As Barney Sackett tells Abigail, 'Wherever she grows up…your daughter would be a lady.' Ann Farley, the love interest in *Hanging Woman Creek*, comes all the way from Ireland to assist her brother Philo in his frontier life. Pike's first impression of her is typical in these circumstances, 'She was a lady, every inch of her…and there was something clean and fine about her that made a man look twice.' In *Catlow*, the willful Cordelia Burton is described as having 'courage, and a cool, quiet strength, but above all she was a lady.'

Although many L'Amour women demonstrate their capabilities, their need to do so often results from the illness, incapacity, or death of men. Mary Blake is forced to run her B-Bar ranch following the murder of her father, but she is ultimately dependent on Utah Blaine to retain her property. Fan Davidge becomes beholden to Ruble Noon in similar circumstances. When Barney Sackett falls seriously ill, Abigail takes over his role at the helm of their ship 'She who knew much of men and ships, and in this my illness, took over. When there was doubt, she resolved it, when there was a decision to be made, she made it.' Despite this share of the action, the qualities that the L'Amour women show (such as loyalty and courage) often seem to be a result of their love for men, such as Angie in

Mattie Tom, a beautiful Apache woman photographed in 1899. Indian women were far more knowledgeable about the West than belles coming out from the East.

Utah Blaine who keeps up her lovely home in honor of her dead father, while Abigail submits herself to the danger of a transatlantic voyage to stand by her man. L'Amour is also careful to demonstrate that even very brave, active women do not necessarily become mannish or hardened. Dru Ragan insists on bringing a rifle when she rides with Mike Bastian to save her sister from the clutches of the depraved Ducrow, but he allows her to cry with fear.

L'Amour also shows how a woman can be sexually liberated without losing her feminine charm. Several L'Amour heroines actively choose their own partners, rather than passively waiting to be chosen. In fact, there are several instances where male heroes, courageous in every other way, aren't brave enough to offer themselves to the women of their choice. Eve Prescott chooses Linus Rawlings to be 'her man,' and initiates their courtship, while Madge Healy proposes to Matt Coburn. He is definitely the 'man' of the relationship, but she has the economic power. Neither does L'Amour underestimate the intelligence of women. Ben Cowan is opposed to Diego Recalde's 'Mexican' analysis of Rosita Calderon as being too intelligent. His more 'American viewpoint' can appreciate that a clever wife would be an asset to the politically ambitious officer. Nor do L'Amour's male characters often get an opportunity to deceive their women. Lillith Prescott is immediately aware that Cleve Van Valen is attracted to her, initially at least, by her inherited gold claim.

L'Amour presents his 'good' women, his ladies, as a

A lovely photograph of family life in the West in the early twentieth century, a family swing outside their log cabin.

civilizing influence on their men, and by implication on the frontier itself. His heroines often restore their men to a domestic life they have lost through various unfortunate experiences. Ruble Noon, for example, has a strong sense of home as a higher ideal for a man, and is deeply attracted to the 'love and warmth of (the) quiet house' of the Mexican family who assist him. He had been 'Driven to desperation' but on seeing Fan Davidge, 'he knew how much he wanted to live. She trusted him.... She had placed her faith in him, and he could not fail her.' Love for a good woman can make a man better, and braver. Ironically, Laurie Shannon's comfortable, feminine home and the stability she offers seems to put her out of Matt Coburn's reach—he recognizes that he has more in common with the less 'pure' Madge Healy, 'We've both been drifters,' he says. Madge echoes this, describing them as being 'homeless as a pair of tumbleweeds.'

'She had placed her faith in him, and he could not fail her.' Love for a good woman can make a man better, and braver.

L'Amour also demonstrates that women are often catalysts, helping fundamentally good men to succeed. His work is replete with examples of this phenomenon – Lilith Prescott and Cleve Van Valen, Ann Farley and Barney Pike are just two cases in point. But there is also a sense that this domestication, this 'taming' of men, cannot be achieved without some cost. Linus Rawlings deeply loves his wife Eve, but can't forgo his mountain wanderings.

The refining influence of women is not confined to home and hearth alone. Education is also one of L'Amour's recurring themes, and as in his own background, it is often women who introduce this concept to the male characters. After he meets Ann Farley, Barney Pike takes up a copy of the History of England, which he hadn't considered opening until he spoke to her. 'If a girl like that could learn something...by reading, I might learn something myself by studying. And if I was going to make something of myself, I'd better get down to brass tacks and do something about it.' Barney suddenly seems to discover ambition, realizing that he could achieve more than 'a day's work for a day's pay.' But educational aspirations can also seem incompatible with the rough and ready life of the West. Bess Chantry wants her son Tom to 'go to school back East. I want him to have a fine education.' This harking back to the East is often a reflection of weakness, either malevolent or benign, in his women characters. The appalling Peg Cullane misses the soft (implicitly corrupted) life of the East, while the innocent, but slightly feeble Juliana Ragan is Eastern in her thinking, and needs the protection of her tougher, Western-minded sister.

Mothers are highly valued, almost sanctified in L'Amour. Men who have been raised without a softening maternal influence, like Mike Bastien (in *Son of a Wanted Man*) may well go on to become good men, but their undiluted male upbringing can leave them vulnerable to bad influences. Mike realizes that his adoptive father has led him on a path that could divide him from the woman he loves, and put him beyond a decent life. 'Once he stepped over that boundary that separated the thieves from honest men it would not be the same.' At the other end of the moral spectrum, Charlie the dying outlaw calls on his mother in his hour of death – as though she were a saint – 'ma would find him. She always had, She's know what to do.' This pathetic cry seems to mark him out as fundamentally less depraved than his cohorts Janish and Lang who have led him into this desperate situation. The untimely death of matriarch Prescott seems to affect her youngest son very much for the worse. Zeke goes on to become a brutal outlaw and casual killer.

But not all Louis L'Amour heroines fall into the domestic goddess category. Some of his women, like Madge Healy, are a good deal more ambiguous. She is young, but has 'no wide-eyed innocence about her.' It transpires that, through no fault of her own, experience has tarnished her innocence. She has been brought up in the school of hard knocks and has shot two men who tried to abuse her. L'Amour does not seek to blame her, painting a truly pathetic picture of her motherless childhood—'I never had anybody.... Nobody ever kissed me good-night.... They just worked me.' But he makes it clear that her uncorrupted bloom is gone. Although she is no fallen woman (she 'wore no make-up'), she is deeply world-weary, 'nineteen...going on forty,' and has lost her feminine softness. Matt Coburn describes her as a 'lady, but down inside her she's tough a whipcord.'

Others, like Peg Cullane, are far less ambiguous. A good background and education have not prevented her from complete moral corruption. She is beautiful, but amoral, greedy and selfish. She acts like a 'bad man' in trying to find Fan's treasure, which she has no intention of sharing. Neither does she have any regard for human life. She would be happy to murder her way to wealth. L'Amour describes her as having a hard and unfeminine nature, she is 'not a passionate woman, but one who succeeded in appearing so; one who beneath a passionate façade, was cold and calculating. Peg Cullane was hard as nails...(with no) mercy.' Acting like a man means being treated like one, as Ruble Noon tells her, 'You've chosen to play games with the boys, and when you do that, you accept the penalties.' He proves his own moral superiority by refusing to kill her, even though she is so debased.

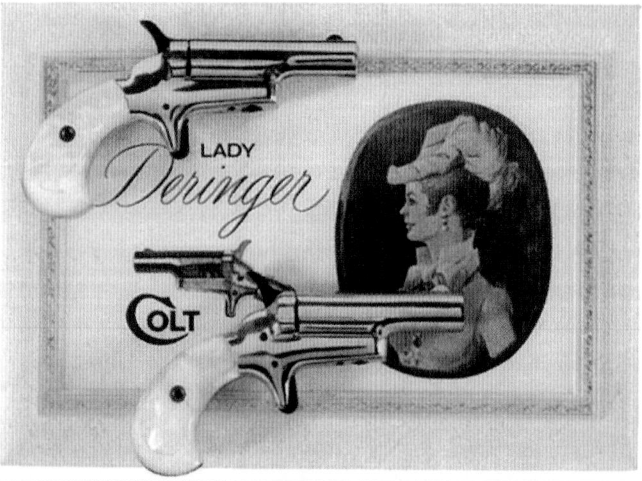

Colt manufactured tiny Deringers, small and elegant enough for a lady to secrete in her purse—the kind of gun Madge Healy would have used.

At the other end of the L'Amour spectrum, and of real Western life itself, are his prostitutes. These vary from the really depraved 'Cheap, tricky women' like the madam Mary Ann who hang out with outlaws 'to make a fast buck the easiest way they can,' to 'soiled doves' that remain essentially 'good' women. Matt Coburn attempts to regulate the tough madams of Confusion, and L'Amour vividly evokes these colourful characters—Kate of the Nugget, Rocking-Chair Emma, and Slanting Annie. But Coburn obviously has some regard for these women, showing respect to Mattie the prostitute, and assuring her that she is still a good woman. In an author's note, Louis L'Amour confirms that these characters were all well known madams in the mining and cow towns of the West. L'Amour obviously sympathizes with these vulnerable women, and uses the fact that the outlaw Perrin had beaten up a prostitute ('and he liked doing it') as proof of the man's vileness.

At the more tawdry end of the spectrum, L'Amour describes the 'large...percentage of vice' available in End of the Track, the tent town of the railway workers. Here, 'You could choose your kind of woman. All nationalities and colors were there, schooled in every sin, and prepared to invent a few new ones at the customer's discretion. It was rough, bawdy, brutal.' This also demonstrates the social phenomenon of single, unprotected women travelling West with the railroad, earning a kind of living in the only way they knew how.

There are also 'burlesque' women characters in L'Amour, which are used to inject humor into the books. One of the funniest moments of male-female interaction is when Barney Pike gives career advice to the simple-minded murderer Lottie Orum. He recommends that she should keep herself clean, and her hair combed to attract a man—while getting employment as a cook. L'Amour also weaves real-life women 'characters,' such as Calamity Jane, into his Western landscape. Barney Pike recalls Calamity Jane as one of the 'least attractive women I ever saw,' and in an author's footnote, L'Amour describes how she was whipped by fellow Western woman Madame Bulldog, in a 'free-for-all fight.'

On the darker side, L'Amour demonstrates how physically vulnerable unprotected women were in the West of this time. Although he makes it clear that only bad, depraved men would consider abusing a 'good woman,' there is a thread of potential and threatened violence in several of his Western novels.

James Bryce wrote that 'Horse-stealing and insults to women (were) the two unpardonable offenses' in the West. In *Utah Blaine*, Ralston Forbes says that 'There are some things this country won't tolerate. Abuse of a good woman and interference with a free press are two of them.' Barney Pike endorses this, 'You could steal cattle or shoot a man and maybe get away with it, but if you bothered a decent woman you stood a good chance of getting lynched…even outlaws had been known to lynch a man for that.' In *Son of a Wanted Man*, Garfield restates this, 'Hell, I never knowed any outlaw to bother women!' Of course, good men are chivalrous, and don't behave in this way. Ben Cowan is embarrassed by the Mexican girl Christina's state of undress during their brawl, despite the fact that she has tried to shoot him, and Ruble Noon declines to kill even the murderous Peg Cullane. But at the other extreme, the would-be rapist, Ducrow, who kidnaps Juliana Ragan tries to dominate her with brute force. 'You're my woman now!' he says, as though he were branding rustled cattle: 'That he would kill her had to be understood, for any attack upon a decent girl was sure to end in hanging.' In *Utah Blaine*, Nevers's threat to kill Angie, and his attempts at rape demonstrate the depths to which he has sunk, 'At no time a good man, he had been on the side of decency by accident only. Now he was over the edge. He would not go back.' Lee Fox goes further, describing him as 'too vile to live.'

Ultimately, L'Amour's women characters are very often used in the Western novels as dramatic devices to define his less open, and more taciturn male characters. But they are by no means two-dimensional ciphers.

Timberline, a noted Dodge City prostitute, still displays some of the good looks she had before dissipation, drink, and disease ruined her and many other such 'soiled doves.'

L'Amour's frontier women are often surprisingly modern in their outlook and behavior, and insist on forging equal partnerships with their male counterparts.

Overall, whatever their type, L'Amour women are given full and dramatic roles to play in the rich pageant of his Wild West.

REMINGTON DOUBLE DERRINGER

RIGHT: A neat piece of the gunsmith's art designed to fit into the daintiest purse.

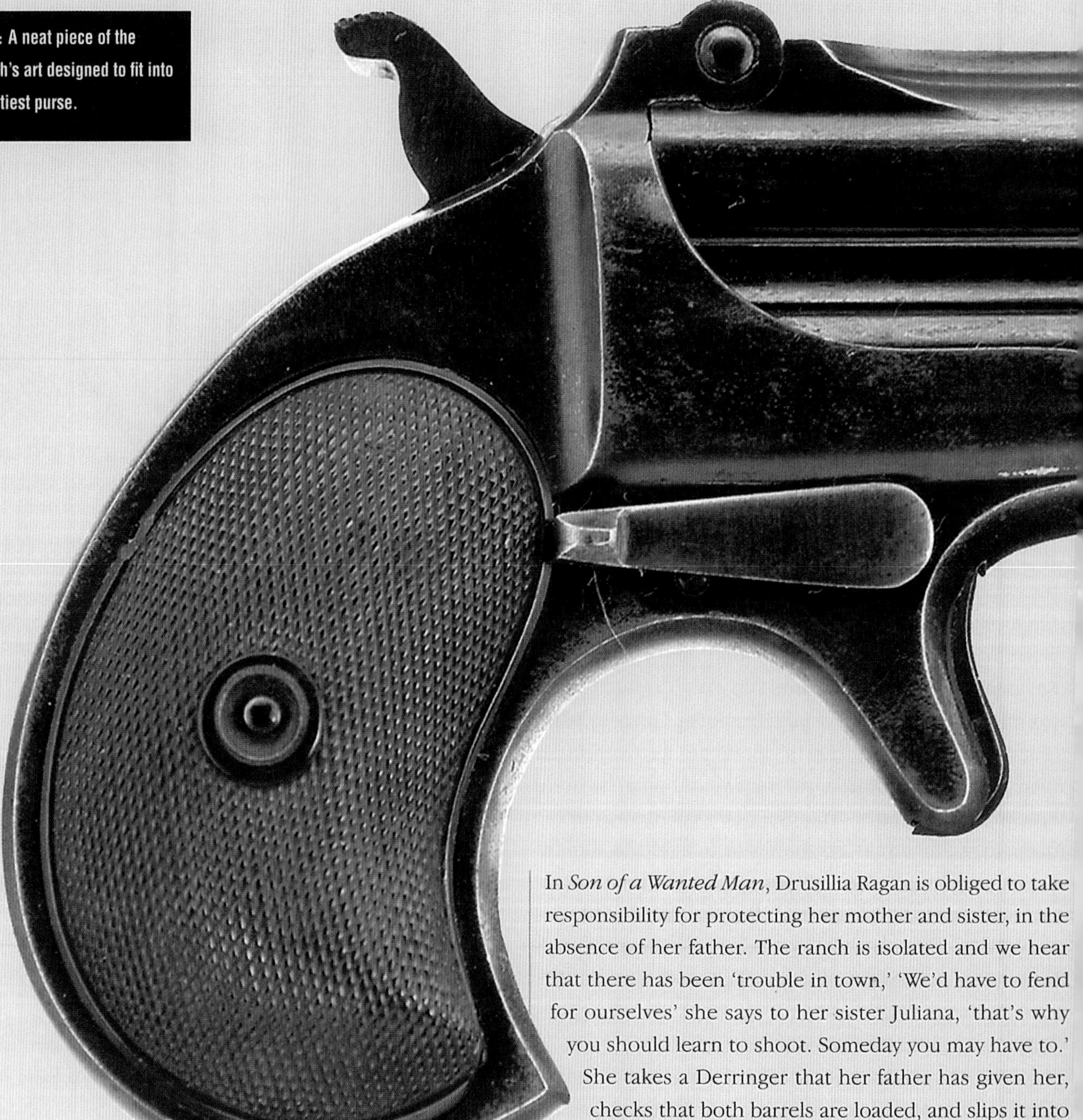

In *Son of a Wanted Man*, Drusillia Ragan is obliged to take responsibility for protecting her mother and sister, in the absence of her father. The ranch is isolated and we hear that there has been 'trouble in town,' 'We'd have to fend for ourselves' she says to her sister Juliana, 'that's why you should learn to shoot. Someday you may have to.'

She takes a Derringer that her father has given her, checks that both barrels are loaded, and slips it into her skirt pocket.

The Derringer was a popular choice as a defensive

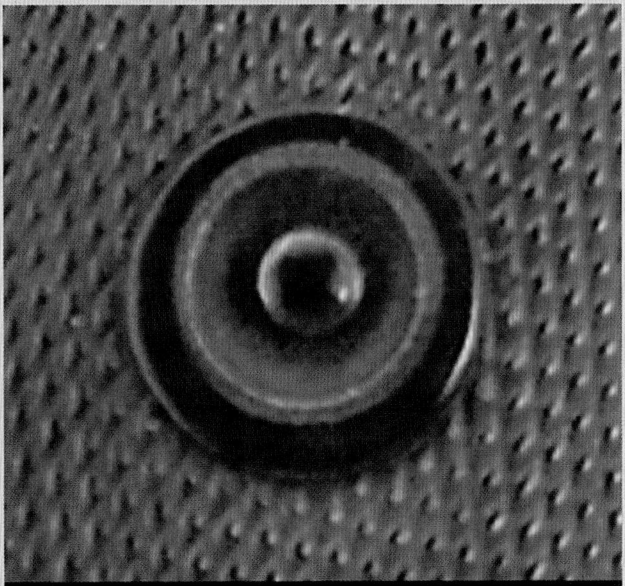

Right: Even the fixing screw for the handgrip was delicately designed.

weapon for frontier women. It was easily concealed in a purse, the pocket of a crinoline dress, or even tucked in a ladies garter. It was named for Henry Deringer, a Philadelphia gunsmith who developed a range of compact, high caliber pocket pistols that, despite their size, had reasonable stopping power. His guns were so successful that his name became synonymous with all weapons of the type. The press report on John Wilkes Booth assassination of Abraham Lincoln wrongly speled the name of the weapon used as a Derringer and this version of the name became common usage.

In the early days, many of these guns were single-shot weapons that relied on a well placed first (and only) shot to stave off an attack – the pressure was on to provide better odds. The two-barreled version that Drusilla carries, the Remington's Double Derringer, would have leveled the stakes considerably, particularly when an assailant was unlikely to expect that a respectable woman would be armed.

SPECIFICATIONS	
CALIBER: .41 Rim fire Cartridge	ACTION: Breech loading double barrel
LENGTH OF BARREL: 3 inches	YEAR OF MANUFACTURE: 1870
BARREL SHAPE: Round/ribbed	MANUFACTURER: Remington Arms Company, Ilion, New York
FINISH: Blue steel	
GRIPS: Hard rubber	

LOUIS L'AMOUR FILMOGRAPHY

It is now over fifty years since the release of the first film based on a Louis L'Amour story, *Hondo*. Not a bad start, with a cast headed up by John Wayne, and directed by John Farrow. From the early '50s, Louis L'Amour's work has been adapted into a major collection of Hollywood films and TV movies. This is hardly surprising – apart from the strong interest in their subject matter and the commercial success of his work, L'Amour's highly visual writing style naturally lends itself to the screen. Not only do his stories have great plots pushing them along with a vital narrative drive, but his characters, locations, and the fantastic sweep of the Western landscape itself are so vivid that they virtually jump from his pages. His writing style is very cinematic, and his scenes and dialogue can be lifted almost directly from the page. L'Amour's use of dramatic irony and coincidence also lend themselves to great cinematic moments.

The quality of the storylines and the complex characters obviously appealed to the cream of contemporary movie actors. John Wayne, Sophia Loren, Sean Connery, Brigitte Bardot, Yul Brynner, Richard Crenna, Leonard Nimoy, Natalie Wood, and Tom Selleck are just some of the glittering stars that grace productions based on L'Amour's work. The first rank of film directors, including John Ford and Sam Wanamaker, were also attracted to movies inspired by his novels.

Here is a listing of the major adaptations of his work, many of which are still available on VHS or DVD. The year of release is shown, and the source of the material is given in parentheses.

HONDO, 1953 (Story: 'The Gift of Cochise')
Hondo stars John Wayne as Hondo Lane, and is generally thought to be one of his seminal films. Geraldine Page is Angie Lowe, Ward Bond stars as Buffalo Baker, and James Arness as Lennie. The film was directed by John Farrow. The film runs for approximately 1 hour 41 minutes.

EAST OF SUMATRA, 1953 (Story)

FOUR GUNS TO THE BORDER,
1954 (aka *Shadow Valley*) (Story)

STRANGER ON HORSEBACK, 1955 (Story)

TREASURE OF RUBY HILLS, 1955 (Story)

BLACKJACK KETCHUM, DESPERADO,
1956 (novel, *Kilkenny*)

THE BURNING HILLS, 1956 (Novel)
The Burning Hills starred Tab Hunter and Natalie Wood as Trace Jordon and Maria Christina Colton, two of the most popular actors of the 1950s. Natalie Wood had starred in *Rebel Without a Cause* in the previous year, while Tab Hunter was most famous for his role in *Battle Cry*. Skip Homeier, Eduard Franz, Earl Holliman, and Claude Atkins also appeared in the movie, which was directed by Stuart Heisler. The film is in color, and runs for 1 hour 32 minutes.

UTAH BLAINE, 1957 (Novel)

THE TALL STRANGER, 1957
(aka *The Rifle* and *Walk Tall*)
(Novel, *Showdown Trail*)

APACHE TERRITORY, 1958
(Novel, *Last Stand at Papago Wells*)

GUNS OF THE TIMBERLAND, 1959 (Novel)

The quintessential landscape of the West, familiar to us from a thousand Western movies.

HELLER IN PINK TIGHTS, 1960
(Novel, *Heller with a Gun*)
Heller in Pink Tights stars Sophia Loren (as Angela Rossini) and Anthony Quinn (as Tom Healy), as members of an itinerant theatrical troupe who perform in rowdy mining camps and cow towns. Interestingly, George Cukor, who was also responsible for *My Fair Lady*, directed this amusing romp, which also stars Margaret O'Brien and Steve Forrest. The movie was scripted by Dudley Nichols (*Bringing Up Baby*) and Walter Bernstein. The film runs for approximately 1 hour 24 minutes.

HOW THE WEST WAS WON, 1962 (Novel)
How the West Was Won is a truly epic film, consisting of five interlocking stories brought to the screen by no less than three directors (Henry Hathaway, George Marshall, and John Ford). It contains some of the most legendary scenes in Western film history and has a fantastic cast of first rank actors including Henry Fonda (Jethro Stuart), Gregory Peck (Cleve Van Valen), Debbie Reynolds (Lilith Prescott), James Stewart (Linus Rawlings), George Peppard (Zeb Rawlings), Spencer Tracy (the voice of the narrator), and John Wayne (General William Tecumseh Sherman). The film was made by Warner Brothers, and runs for 2 hours 42 minutes.

TAGGART, 1965 (Novel)

KID RODELO, 1965 (Novel)

HONDO AND THE APACHES, 1967
(Story, 'The Gift of the Cochise')
This feature was made up from material from the short-lived TV series, 'Hondo,' which was based on the original film, *Hondo*, starring John Wayne. Ralph Teager stars as Hondo Layne, Kathie Browne as Angie Dow, and Noah Beery Jr. as Buffalo Baker. The film runs for approximately 1 hour 13 minutes.

SHALAKO, 1968 (aka Man nennt mich Shalako, West Germany) (Novel).
The cast of *Shalako* is particularly glittering. Sean Connery stars as Shalako, Brigitte Bardot as Countess Irini Lazaar, and the cast also includes Jack Hawkings, Honor Blackman, Peter van Eyck, and Stephen Boyd. The film is in color, was directed by Edward Dmytryk, and runs for approximately 1 hour 53 minutes.

CATLOW, 1971 (aka El Oro de nadie in Spain) (Novel)
Catlow features Yul Brynner and Richard Crenna as friends Catlow and Ben Cowan in this amiable and lighthearted Western caper. Leonard Nimoy is the menacing Miller. This color film was directed by Sam Wanamaker, and runs for 1 hour 43 minutes.

THE MAN CALLED NOON, 1972
(aka Un Hombre llamado Noon in the Spanish version, and Lo chiamavano Mezzogiorno in Italy) (Novel)
This is a classic Western film, with fine performances from Richard Crenna and Stephen Boyd as Noon and Rimes respectively, and Rosanna Schiaffino as Fan Davidge. The film was directed by Peter Collinson and runs for 1 hour 27 minutes.

CANCEL MY RESERVATION, 1972
(Novel, *The Broken Gun*)

THE SACKETTS, 1979 (Two novels)
'The Sacketts' is a made for TV mini series that charts the huge sweep of Louis L'Amour's Sackett family saga, concentrating on the Action of *The Daybreakers* and *Sackett*. These novels seem to cover the entire gamut of the Western experience – cattle, gold, and violence in the untamed territory of New Mexico.

The massive cast of characters is drawn from the first rank of American actors, including Tom Selleck (Orrin Sackett), Sam Elliot (Tell Sackett), Jeff Osterhage (Tyrel Sackett), Glenn Ford (Tom Sunday), Ben Johnson (Cap Roundtree), and Slim Pickens (Jack Bigelow). The action is directed by Robert Totten, and the series ran for a total of 3 hours 18 minutes.

THE SHADOW RIDERS, 1982 (Novel)
The Shadow Riders is an also made for TV movie, but its director, Andrew V. McLaglen, has a great pedigree in Westerns, having also directed *Shennandoah, The Way West, Chisum and Bandolero*. McLaglen also has a great cast to work with, including Tom Selleck (Mac Traven), Sam Elliott (Dal Traven), Ben Johnson (Uncle 'Black Jack' Traven), Geoffrey Lewis (Major Cooper Ashbury), and Jeff Osterhage (Jesse Traven).

DOWN THE LONG HILLS, 1986 (Novel)
A made for TV movie.

THE CHEROKEE TRAIL, 1986 (Novel)
A made for TV movie.

THE QUICK AND THE DEAD, 1987 (Novel)
The Quick and the Dead was a made for TV movie, directed by Robert Day. The feature had a solid cast, including Sam Elliott (Con Vallian), Tom Conti (Duncan McKaskel), and Kenny Morrison (Tom McKaskel). It ran for 1 hour 31 minutes.

CONAGHER, 1991 (Novel)
Conagher was a made for TV movie, directed by Reynaldo Villalobos. The cast includes Sam Elliott (Conn Conagher), Katharine Ross (Evie Teale), Barry Corbin (McCloud), and Billy Green Bush (Jacob Teale). Katharine Ross also starred in *Butch Cassidy and the Sundance Kid*. The movie runs for 1 hour 56 minutes.

SHAUGHNESSY, 1996 (Novel, *The Iron Marshal*) A made for TV movie.

THE CROSSFIRE TRAIL, 2001 (Novel)
The Crossfire Trail was a made for TV movie, directed by Simon Wincer. It rejoices in the tag line 'A Hero is Measured by the Enemies He Makes.' The movie has a strong cast, including Tom Selleck (Rafe Covington), Mark Harmon (Bruce Barkow), Virginia Madsen (Ann Rodney), and Wilford Brimley (Joe Gill). It runs for 1 hour 35 minutes.

THE DIAMOND OF JERU, 2001 (Short story)
The Diamond of Jeru is a made for cable TV movie, written by Beau L'Amour. The cast includes Billy Zane (Mike Kardec), Keith Carradine (John Lacklan), Paris Jefferson (Helen Lacklan), Jackson Raine (Raj), and Piripi Warenti (Jeru). Unusually, the action of the film takes place in Borneo, but has all the usual action. The movie was directed by Ian Barry and Dick Lowry and runs for 1 hour 35 minutes.

Louis L'Amour revived the legend of the American cowboy, and his novels continue to keep this Western icon alive.

ACKNOWLEDGEMENTS

Buffalo Bill Historical Center. Cole at Laredo Western Town. Kansas State Historical Society. The United States Naval Academy Museum (picture page 129). Rock Island Auction Company. L.D.S. Church Archives, Museum of Church History and Art, Salt Lake City. Union Pacific Railroad Museum (picture page 176). The Ian West Collection. Wells Fargo History Museum, with permission from Wells Fargo Bank (pictures page 153, 154). National Cowboy Heritage Museum (pictures page 24, 47, 99 and 105). Mr. Arthur Upham for the Billy The Kid image. The Jefferson Museum of Western Expansion.